WORSHIP IN CONVERSATION

HWARANG MOON

WORSHIP IN CONVERSATION

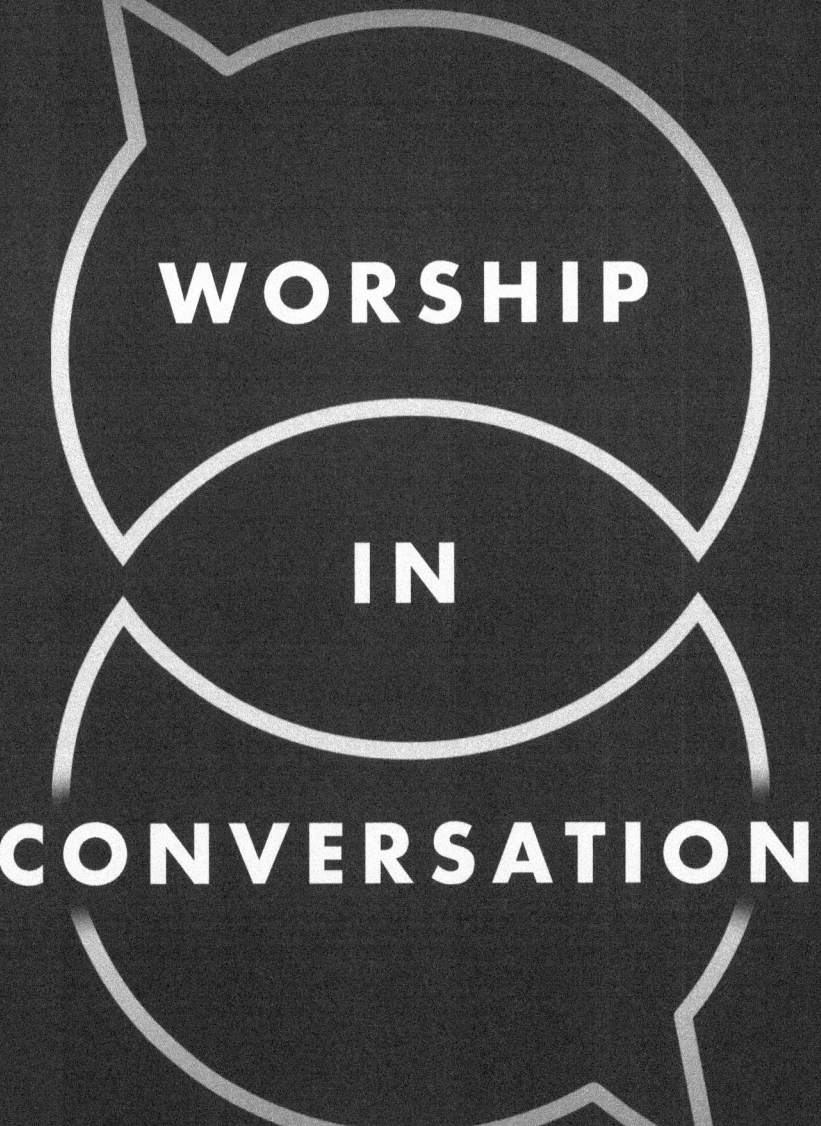

DIALOGUES WITH LEADING LITURGICAL THEOLOGIANS

1845BOOKS

© 2025 by 1845 Books, an imprint of Baylor University Press
Waco, Texas 76798

All Rights Reserved. No part of this publication may be reproduced, stored in a retrieval system, or transmitted, in any form or by any means, electronic, mechanical, photocopying, recording, or otherwise, without the prior permission in writing of Baylor University Press.

Cover and book design by Elyxandra Encarnación

Library of Congress Cataloging-in-Publication Data

Names: Moon, Hwarang, author

Title: Worship in conversation: dialogues with leading liturgical theologians / Hwarang Moon.

Description: Waco, Texas: 1845 Books, an imprint of Baylor University Press, [2025] | Includes bibliographical references. | Summary: "Dialogues with leading liturgical theologians which offer a fresh understanding of the promises and challenges of contemporary worship"—Provided by publisher.

Identifiers: LCCN 2025007658 (print) | LCCN 2025007659 (ebook) | ISBN 9781481323406 paperback | ISBN 9781481323420 adobe pdf | ISBN 9781481323413 epub

Subjects: LCSH: Worship | Liturgics | Theologians—Interviews

Classification: LCC BV10.3 .W677 2026 (print) | LCC BV10.3 (ebook)

LC record available at https://lccn.loc.gov/2025007658

LC ebook record available at https://lccn.loc.gov/2025007659

CONTENTS

Preface and Acknowledgments		vii

INTRODUCTION
Get Yourself Out of the Box:
Allowing Abundance of Worship Through Diversity   1

1	John D. Witvliet	11
2	Don E. Saliers	19
3	Edward Foley	35
4	Frank Senn	49
5	Lester Ruth	61
6	Melanie Ross	77
7	Gordon Lathrop	93
8	E. Byron Anderson	105
9	David Hogue	121

10	William Willimon	143
11	Paul Westermeyer	153
12	Ruth Meyers	165
13	Stefanos Alexopoulos	177
14	David Gambrell	189

CONCLUSION
Enriching Worship: Illuminating the Perspective of Worship through its Deeper Understanding — 203

PREFACE AND ACKNOWLEDGMENTS

This volume emerges as the fruit of a two-year journey of dialogue with leading liturgical theologians representing diverse denominations across North America. The interviews were conducted primarily between 2022 and 2023, most often through extended email correspondence. In several instances I was also able to meet the scholars in person at academic conferences or during visits to the United States, and those encounters led naturally to further exchanges through follow-up emails.

Every question posed in these conversations was crafted with care, arising from sustained engagement with the interviewees' published works. To preserve the integrity and cadence of each scholar's voice, I have presented the interviews in their original format, making only minimal stylistic and grammatical adjustments. These questions were not casually formulated; they reflect years of reading, reflection, and scholarly curiosity. They are the kinds of questions one might ask not only as a fellow academic but also as a devoted reader, colleague, and admirer of the interviewees' contributions to the field of liturgical theology.

Portions of a few interviews have appeared previously in abbreviated form in Korean theological publications. Between July 2022 and June 2023, twelve interviews were serialized in the journal *Ministry and Theology* (목회와신학). One appeared in the July 2023 issue of *Monthly Ministry* (월간 목회), and another was published in the January 2024 issue of *Theological Thought* (신학사상). These, however, were partial extracts. This book now brings together, for the first time, the complete and unabridged versions of all interviews in English.

The scholars featured here are not only distinguished authors and researchers but also respected leaders in their respective denominations—pastors, educators, musicians, and liturgical reformers. I am deeply grateful for their generosity in accepting my invitation to dialogue and for their openness in sharing their stories, perspectives, and hopes for the future of Christian worship.

This project would not have been possible without the encouragement and support of many individuals. I owe heartfelt gratitude to Dean Edgardo Colón-Emeric of Duke Divinity School, who welcomed me as a visiting scholar during the spring semester of 2023 and provided a space for concentrated research. I am likewise thankful to Dr. Lester Ruth, who accompanied me on many walks around the Duke campus as a friend and conversation partner, and to Dr. William Willimon, whose warm counsel and wit rekindled my academic energy. I am especially indebted to Dr. Mark Skeen and his wife, Sherbie Skeen, who not only provided housing and transportation but welcomed me into their lives as family, embodying for me the warmth of American hospitality. My sincere thanks also extend to Tammy Wiens and her husband, Dr. Sheldon Sorge, who graciously connected me with the Skeens.

I am equally grateful to the pastors who generously supported this work—Rev. Sangho Kim of Youngshin Presbyterian Church in Seoul and Rev. Daesik Yoo of Eunseong Church, whose encouragement and assistance sustained my research. I am especially indebted to Rev. Byungwook Oh of Hana Church, whose generous support made the publication of this book possible.

At the heart of this journey lies the love, prayer, and sacrifice of my family. I am forever grateful to my father, Jongkyu Moon; my mother, Sangyoung Chang; my father-in-law, Seogu Cho; and my mother-in-law, Soonduk Han—each of whom has faithfully sustained me with prayer and with pride in my ministry for the Lord. Without their love and intercession, I would not be who I am today.

Above all, I dedicate this book to my beloved wife, Kyungmok Cho, who has stood beside me with quiet strength for more than two decades. I am equally thankful for my two precious daughters, Sujung and Susie, who have shown their father constant care and affection.

I am deeply indebted as well to Dr. R. David Nelson of Baylor University Press, who believed in this project and supported it with thoughtful editorial guidance and encouragement from beginning to end. Without his trust and insight, this book would not have come to fruition.

I am also grateful to Liturgical Press for granting permission to include excerpts from the work of Dr. Ed Foley. Their generosity has meaningfully enriched this volume.

Finally, I extend my deepest gratitude to my mentor, Dr. E. Byron Anderson, who has shaped my academic journey with wisdom, care, and unwavering support. His guidance and trust have left an imprint upon this work more profound than any footnote ever could.

INTRODUCTION
GET YOURSELF OUT OF THE BOX
Allowing Abundance of Worship Through Diversity

A young worship leader who was attending seminary was assigned to a church with a long tradition. Full of motivation, he selected the newest gospel songs that are most popular with young people and practiced hard for a week with performers and singers. The service finally started, and the leader felt full of joy. The congregation seemed to like it too. Finishing the service with a sense of pride, he was about to leave the main hall after tidying up, but then the elder of the church called out to him, "Kim Jeondosanim!!"* The worship leader was feeling lighthearted and anticipating praise. He thought, "What compliment are you going to pay me?" but his expression remained humble. "Yes? What would you like to tell me?" he replied.

The elder wondered if it was okay to sing so many "gospel songs" instead of singing hymns at the Sunday public services, and inquired why the worship team lightly raised their hands and encouraged the congregation to clap. Pastor Kim felt frustration stirring inside him, but his mind went blank and only these words came out of his mouth, "I also arranged and sang several hymns . . ." But the elder interrupted to add a point, "Why did you arrange the hymn carelessly like that, when the original author had his intentions?"

---

   * In Korea, congregations call a seminarian Jeondosa. Jeondosanim is generally an honorific title for a Jeondosa in the church.

This is a scenario that is experienced too frequently in Korean churches. There are many stereotypes contained in the elder's words. The fixed idea that Sunday public worship must include hymns is common. There are many Christians, like the elder in the story, who strongly express the opinion that not only the music used during worship, but also the elements of worship, the structure of worship, and the arrangement of worship should align to a traditional worship structure. If we question their reasons for thinking this way, we see many cases where the historical and theological basis is poor. At the same time, we often see people who make extreme claims that except for this form and content of worship, everything else is wrong or close to heresy, while citing very peripheral grounds.

Even though we have been attending church and living a life of faith for decades, how much do we really know about worship in other churches or other denominations? Through my liturgical studies, I have sought to learn the meaning and theological considerations in practice while participating in the worship of other denominations instead of just learning the worship of other denominations through books. At first, it came as a shock, and sometimes I found my initial reaction to be a resistance or rejection. However, after reserving judgment and participating with respect for the other church's practice itself, I tried to approach the conversation from the perspective of the tradition I experienced, and my heart resonated strongly.

"God did not make us uniform but allowed us to be diverse." "God did not ignore the characteristics of each era and each culture and has allowed us abundant grace." So then, why have many different traditions of worship come down through history? In fact, different worship practices themselves are not wrong in the realm of liturgical studies. Each tradition of worship has sought, in its own way, to worship faithfully to the Bible. Biblical and hermeneutical efforts have structured their worship practices. However, there are some differences in the cultural and historical situations and perspectives of these practices.

Put aside the tempting, one-sided notion that only one tradition is "biblical" and others are "unbiblical" until you've finished reading this book. The more you understand worship, the more deeply you can experience its richness. In fact, can I be sure that I know all of my traditions? Not necessarily. In order to know my tradition better, I need to compare it with other traditions. In the process of comparing different traditions, the characteristics of my own liturgical tradition become clearer. You can discover the strengths and weaknesses of both your tradition and others.

Therefore, I am sure that your horizon of understanding will expand through the insights provided by my conversations with worship scholars across various denominations throughout this book.

(1) Stereotypes About Worship Make Believers Militant and Hinder Them from Enjoying Grace

It was such a great blessing to be able to enter the world of theology at the age of twenty-one, when I had enough physical strength and was overflowing with intellectual desire. The subjects of the Bible, systematic theology, church history, and various practical theologies taught by great professors opened my eyes to theology.

However, there was one problem—me. I was full of youthful folly, and I had very critical views while studying theology. When I encountered theological opinions that crossed the boundaries of a specific Bible interpretation, methodology, or theology taught by respected professors or pastors, the idea, "This is a wrong theology" was established in my mind. Sometimes there were even feelings of anger beyond criticism.

Attending worship services with this kind of mindset cannot be grace. When I listened to some pastors' sermons, I felt a resistance and found myself thinking, "This is a different interpretation from what I learned in class at school," and "That's a view that deviates from our theological tradition so why are you doing that?" In addition, I was able to discover myself not enjoying worship as a true worshiper, but as a judge of worship, judging and scoring the elements and order of worship, as well as the leaders and performers.

I could feel my soul drying up during these years. Instead of judging the theology and practice of others, I started thinking I should become a true worshiper. However, this story does not seem to be merely my own "dark history." While teaching students at a seminary or traveling across the country giving lectures on worship, I often come across people who have the same attitude that I had during those years.

In my seminary, I enthusiastically teach the history and theology of worship, the liturgy and ceremonies of worship, and how to evaluate them from a Reformed perspective and apply them to our church. The majority of students respond very favorably to me and leave good course evaluations that they have experienced "breaking stereotypes and sinking into a richer world of worship." However, every semester, two or three students speak to me in a very cynical tone that only the narrow boundary of worship they think is true is claimed by our denomination and Reformed tradition.

Someone once said, "Even if 99 percent of the congregation likes you, it is the ministry of losing sleep at night because of one saint who opposes you." Since I am not a senior pastor, I am sleeping well, but I desperately feel the lifelong task of connecting the conservative theology of the Reformed theological tradition to which I belong with the wider world for mutual benefit.

(2) Journeys That Broadened My Thoughts on Worship: Chaplain Ministry, Calvin and Garrett Seminary, North American Academy of Liturgy and Societas Liturgica

Like everyone else, what I learned as a child and the atmosphere of the church and denomination I belong to serve as the basis for theological judgment even as an adult. If there are 100 people in a church, 100 people may have different thoughts about worship because their past experiences and backgrounds of faith formation are different. Why would a worship war occur among believers? For some believers, "the worship that the esteemed pastor taught" and "the worship held at the mother church as a child" are established as the norms for proper worship. From that fixed point of view, we are judging the current state of the church.

The firmer one's theological beliefs, the more one is confident in one's knowledge of theology. It is common to observe those with a confident and rigid attitude toward their own tradition of worship criticize those that do not align with their traditions and characterize practices they are unfamiliar with as worship that God does not accept.

My thoughts, which were insufficient and narrow, have been corrected and refined through various experiences prepared by God. First, through the experience of being chaplain to the 15th Regiment of the 1st Division of the Korean Army, I was able to directly witness how various kinds of praises can shape the faith of believers. In other words, it was a direct experience of the faith-forming power of praise. In church history, the old adage, "He who sings, prays twice" has been passed down for a long time. As this expression shows, I was able to experience that praise has a great effect on not only the formation of individual faith, but also the formation of community faith. I came to understand that worship is not only centered on preaching, but that praise is also a vital means of worship and a gracious gift given to us by God.

After being honorably discharged from chaplaincy, I was able to enter the worship studies program at Calvin Theological Seminary in the United States through John Witvliet, a master of Reformed worship studies. During this time, I was able to break my stereotypes at Calvin Theological Seminary.

I wanted to hear a firm axiomatic explanation that "Reformed worship should be like this," but John Witvliet made me realize how narrow and militant the Reformed theology I had been learning and my way of thinking had become. A question from an American colleague who was listening to my presentation of an article on Reformed worship is still fresh in my ears. "Reformed Theology? What kind of Reformed theology? Sixteenth century? Seventeenth century? Or Protestant Orthodoxy? What are you talking about regionally? Dutch Reformed? South Africa? Or Europe? Reformed Worship? Whose thoughts are you talking about? Calvin? Zwingli? Martin Bucer?" The more I learned about the history of worship, the more I could feel how many different forms of worship exist in the world and how diverse the ideas and styles of worship are, even among Reformed theologians.

Later, at Garrett-Evangelical Theological Seminary, I was able to learn about the formative power of "liturgy" by meeting the masters of liturgical studies, such as E. Byron Anderson, Ruth Duck, and Frank Senn. I learned that liturgy was not simply in the Roman Catholic Church but was present in the worship of all denominations. Through the coursework, I was able to learn that our worship forms our faith, and that liturgies and rituals have formative power. I came to realize that liturgical theology is not a simple, practical theology, but a special area at the intersection of systematic theology, historical theology, and practical theology. This realization later led to fellowship with worship scholars around the world.

By the recommendation of my doctoral advisor, Dr. E. Byron Anderson, in 2012, while writing my doctoral dissertation, I first participated in the North American Liturgical Society held in Albuquerque, New Mexico. I was surprised that all the authors of the books I read during my master's and doctoral courses were there. It was an event like the Olympics or a festival of the liturgical studies department in which stars from the worship studies world, regardless of denomination, participated, such as Don Saliers, Gordon Lathrop, Frank Senn, and Ed Foley. Of course, among the members, there were many Roman Catholic theologians, Lutherans, United Methodists, Anglicans, and a few Reformed theologians (Jewish and Orthodox also attend). My professor, John Witvliet, a well-known and respected representative of the Reformed group, also attended that year.

The masters of the academic world of worship were always kind and free-spirited. A lot of the attendees were over seventy years old and were full of passion for the subject matter. In contrast to the atmosphere in Korea, where it is sometimes difficult to come up with anything new over the age of fifty, their thinking was flexible. Even when sharp opinions were at odds with each other, they behaved as gentlemen toward each other. As iron sharpens iron, the attitude of learning from each other was stronger. People tend to confront each other because of small differences, but I felt the attitude of the heart that there are more things in common.

This tendency could be felt in the Societas Liturgica as well. European scholars participate in the North American Academy of Liturgy, but more European scholars participate in the Societas Liturgica, which is held every two years. In 2015, I participated in a conference held in Quebec, Canada. Although the official language is English, the subgroups are divided into German and French. I came to realize that there are many books and articles, like unknown gems, in the European-speaking world. Afterwards, I was convinced that participating in their gatherings every year, even if I have no research funds, was the way to help Korean academia and churches. I have been participating in these societies every year to refine my skills as a scholar, and this has become a decisive opportunity to build friendships and exchanges with the characters in this book.

(3) Why These Scholars? Criteria for Selecting Fourteen Interviewees

The scholars that were chosen for interviews have been influential in the field of liturgical studies not only in North America but also around the world over the past few decades. They not only made great contributions to the development of liturgical studies through significant writings, but also greatly influenced the development of worship in various denominations, including the promotion of mutual understanding among denominations. In particular, they played a role as a driving force in writing books of worship and hymns of each denomination and had a great influence on the restoration of worship and spiritual growth of each church. The criteria for choosing them are as follows:

First, I tried to select worship scholars representing various denominations.

Each denomination has advantages, disadvantages, and uniqueness of worship. No one can objectively deem one form of worship or denomination superior to another, and that is not our purpose in this exploration.

It is necessary for each of us to widen the scope of understanding with an open mind by diachronically examining worship in the historical flow, and by seeing the worship offered by various denominations synchronically. The very narrow and shallow knowledge I have obtained is not all about worship. God did not create us uniformly, but He allowed each of us to be unique and diverse. Therefore, our various forms of worship should not be the object of criticism but taken rather as God's gift of abundance.

From this point of view, I invited worship scholars from various denominations, regardless of each denomination's power or size. Think of World Cup soccer for a moment. Countries such as Brazil and Argentina, which have a wide soccer base and are always considered favorites for the championship, have numerous star players on their national teams. However, there are few players known to the world other than Son Heung-min and Gareth Bale in countries that are not football powerhouses such as Korea and Wales. Nonetheless, the charm of the World Cup lies in the fact that the soccer teams, which represent countries around the world, have various colors, tactics, and national characteristics, making the period a richer festival. Such is the object of this book. It is not simply to respect the worship forms and rites of denominations that have many prominent liturgical theologians, but also denominations whose following is small or are not liturgical in worship. I selected figures who can add richness to the understanding of theology and the practice of worship. The list of scholars by denomination is as follows:

- Anglican (Ruth Meyers)
- Christian Reformed Church (John Witvliet)
- Evangelical Lutheran Church in America (Frank Senn, Gordon Lathrop, and Paul Westermeyer)
- Nondenominational Evangelical (Melanie Ross)
- Orthodox (Stefanos Alexopoulos)
- Presbyterian Church (U.S.A.) (David Gambrell and David Hogue)
- Roman Catholic (Ed Foley)
- United Methodist Church (Don Saliers, E. Byron Anderson, Lester Ruth, and William Willimon)

Second, I selected people who had a great influence on theology and the practice of worship for a long time through their books and articles.

There is a close relationship between the theology of worship and the practice of worship. Worship scholars who appear in this book not only have outstanding theological abilities, but also have been active as preachers and presiders in the field of ministry, as researchers in charge of the worship theology and practice of the church, or as musicians of the church. Because they know the praxis of the church, the history of worship, the characteristics of other denominations' worship, and the thoughts of the congregation of the church overall, they have the ability to easily and deeply unravel their specific practice and the meaning contained in it, while looking at the synchronic and diachronic landscape of worship.

Frank Senn, Gordon Lathrop, Paul Westermeyer, Ed Foley, Don Saliers, and William Willimon are in their 70s and 80s. Nevertheless, even now, through books and articles, they are showing their skills and passion with energy that surpasses that of young scholars. These scholars have made a mark in the academic world of worship with their books, behind-the-scenes stories, and honest academic journeys. I have asked these scholars questions about their writings in order to help their readers better grasp an understanding of each one's point of view.

Third, there are various specialties in worship studies. Examples include worship history, liturgical theology, ritual studies, hermeneutics, music theology, sacramental theology, and so on. I considered areas of specialization when selecting which experts in this field to interview.

The history of Christian worship is an essential field for the study of worship. Only by dealing with special events in worship history that are not covered in general church history, and the contents and background of major books and worship documents, can we discuss how the theology and practices of various denominations have arisen and developed to the present age, and how they can move forward. Given his extensive background on this subject matter, I would like to discuss the historical perspective through Frank Senn, who has written many books on the history of worship. Let's think about the discussion of contemporary worship since the 1960s with Lester Ruth, who teaches at Duke University, and about the history, strengths, and weaknesses of evangelical worship with Melanie Ross at Yale University.

Worship is closely related to hermeneutics. The hermeneutic perspective not only provides the power to look at books on worship, but also provides the power to analyze what theological and logical grounds are flowing in the practice of worship in the church field. So, in the case of the United States, a philosophical hermeneutics course is always included in the curriculum in the first semester of the liturgical studies major. For this part, I would like to proceed through interviews with Garrett-Evangelical Theological Seminary's E. Byron Anderson and Lutheran theologian

Gordon Lathrop. In particular, Gordon Lathrop provides a perspective on why biblical theology is important in liturgical studies through discussions on biblical interpretation as well as philosophical hermeneutics.

The flower of worship studies is liturgical theology. In the early twentieth century, there were debates between Geoffrey Wainwright (Methodist), Alexander Schmemann (Orthodox), and Aidan Kavanagh (Benedictine Roman Catholic) about the relationship between systematic and liturgical theology. Liturgical theology is not simply practical theology, but has an academic priority as a primary theology that enables systematic theology. Systematic theology emerged from the practice of liturgy in the public worship. Establishing such a liturgy academically is liturgical theology. Conversations between Ed Foley, Don Saliers, Gordon Lathrop, and Stefanos Alexopoulos will open up a new horizon of understanding for readers.

In addition, worship is closely related to ritual studies. In every worship service there are the rituals of the community, and ritual provides knowledge that is engraved on the body and heart to the participants through repeated actions. For in-depth discussion on this subject matter, I will talk with David Hogue, an expert in brain research, neuroscience, and ritual studies. Also, William Willimon's insights on ritual will widen the understanding about the necessity of ritual in Christian worship.

Another subject that has recently gained the spotlight in worship studies is church music, that is, the area of music theology. It is essential to establish theological criteria for the hymns to be sung in church. In particular, at this point where music is as much emphasized as sacraments, I would like to discuss the relationship between music and theology through Paul Westermeyer and Don Saliers.

In addition, this book will look at Orthodox worship, which has left an important footprint in the history of world worship. Through Stefanos Alexopoulos, one of the most prominent Orthodox liturgical theologians today, we will deepen our understanding of Orthodox worship, which is still relatively unknown in much of the Western ecclesial world. In addition, we will look at the tradition of the Anglican Church, which is an important branch of Protestantism and currently has the most liturgical worship among Protestants. I will interview Ruth Meyers, who is a representative scholar of the Episcopal Church and wrote an important book on missional worship that has recently received worldwide attention in the missional church movement. Lastly, although there are various sorts of books of worship in North America, many congregations have come to lose concern about the book of worship. Regarding this matter, I will talk with David Gambrell of the Presbyterian Church (U.S.A.) about why denominations that have not had a book of worship around the world need one and advice on how to make a book of worship.

Lastly, rather than simply meeting indirectly through their writings, I directly selected scholars with whom I was able to meet and listen to their lectures in the field, have direct conversations at meetings such as the North American Liturgical Society, and whose academic reputation I have confirmed in person.

Though part of a growing number of Korean and other Asian liturgical scholars, I am on the periphery of North American liturgical studies circles. I am racially Asian, and theologically influenced by the Presbyterian Church and the Reformed Church, which are far from the liturgical denominations. I am nothing more than a scholar on the fringes (although I have published several articles in major journals in liturgical theology circles).

However, I think this kind of background will be an advantage in selecting great scholars more objectively. I am uniquely suited to this work—I have no personal interests, academic connections, or psychological burden of selecting scholars from mainstream denominations, and since I have been a person who lived on the periphery of liturgical studies all my life, I can see those who are active in the center of the liturgical studies more objectively. In addition, the experience of studying for master's and doctoral degrees in the United States, and later as an active member of the North American Liturgical Society, makes me aware of top scholars in this area, leading scholars in the subdisciplines of liturgical studies, whom I can interview on the issue of liturgical studies.

Now, let's meet the world's best worship scholars in our times one by one. In the world of humanities, it would be very foolish and disrespectful to rank them. However, these people are recognized as top scholars in the subdivision of liturgical studies. Even if they are members of different denominations than yours, I hope you will suspend judgment, listen to their stories, and then try to have a dialogue between your theology and your newly acquired perspective. Obviously, the horizon of understanding about worship and liturgy will be broadened. And the advantages and disadvantages of worship that are familiar to you will come to mind. Remember the fact that, in matters of worship, we have more in common than not!

1
JOHN D. WITVLIET

John Witvliet majored in music at Calvin University. Afterward, he earned a Master of Theology (MTS) from Calvin Theological Seminary and a Master of Music (MMus) from the University of Illinois. He later earned his MA and PhD in liturgical studies from the University of Notre Dame. He serves as the director of the Calvin Institute of Christian Worship and teaches worship at Calvin University and Calvin Theological Seminary. He is known all over the world as a liturgical theologian representing the Reformed churches. He is also well-known in the North American Academy of Liturgy, where liturgical denominations, such as Catholic and Lutheran, occupy the majority. He has written numerous articles and works, including *Worship Seeking Understanding* (Grand Rapids: Baker Academic, 2003).

Interview with John Witvliet

Welcome, Professor Witvliet. It is our pleasure to have you join us today. On behalf of myself and the future readers of this interview, thank you for agreeing to answer these questions. As a liturgical theologian representing the Reformed churches, you are well known not only in North America but also in Asia, not to mention that your book has been translated into Korean. Professor, I understand that you are one of the best scholars not only in the Reformed churches but also in North America, so I thank you for sparing your valuable time.

1. I find your background interesting. You majored in music before majoring in worship studies. After that, you went to Notre Dame to obtain your master's and PhD. From what I understand, Notre Dame has the best program for liturgical studies. Is there any particular reason why you studied worship and music? And what was your reason for choosing to study at Notre Dame despite your involvement with the Reformed churches?

I sensed a call to study different, intersecting dimensions of public worship. Theology is essential. But it is also essential to see how a theological vision is embodied, how it comes to life in various practices. Studying both theology and music, and learning from both social and intellectual historians, both musicologists and composers, both systematic and practical theologians was always energizing. Notre Dame offered a robustly ecumenical program, welcoming Catholic, Orthodox, and Protestant students to learn together in community. We learned not only about each other's traditions but also to explain our own traditions—which is not always easy to do well!

2. I'm aware that the Reformed theological schools in the United States do not offer a doctorate in worship studies, whereas Catholic and Methodist schools do. Is there any special reason for this? What are the characteristics of liturgical studies that differentiate them from systematic theology and historical theology?

Historically, Reformed seminaries and divinity schools have not always insisted that liturgy and worship should be a required area of study. I think this is a mistake that historically has led us into practices that at times undermine the very theological vision at the center of the Reformed confessions. Liturgical studies at its best integrates insights from biblical, systematic, historical, and practical theology, while also drawing freely from academic studies in the arts and social sciences.

Every single worship service can be studied from the perspective of the theological vision it conveys and the theological rationale behind decisions that pastoral leaders make, as well as from the perspective of the social context and cultures represented. Since pastoral leadership of worship is best done by perceptive leaders that integrate insights from such a wide range of disciplines, liturgical studies should mirror that as faculty do the same.

3. I remember that your doctoral thesis is about the holy Trinity. Richard Mouw said that we tend to worship only one of the three persons in worship. How can our worship be Trinitarian?

Richard Mouw did make a quip that most traditions tend to favor one person of the Trinity, and there is certainly some truth in that! It's a compelling way to begin a conversation. Indeed, in worship, we address our prayer and praise "to the Father, to the Son, and to the Holy Spirit." We also rightly pray "to the Father, through the Son, in the Holy Spirit." Both kinds of prayers are compelling! Both kinds of prayers can be found in the early church. And both kinds of prayers call attention to essential aspects of a full-orbed Trinitarian vision. Learning to pray in both ways—and to explain why each is valuable—is an essential pastoral task. Beyond that, I think it is essential to consider how each and every element of worship can be understood in Trinitarian terms—even though this will, at times, be implicit rather than explicit.

4. The theology of worship in the Christian Reformed Church seems to be somewhat different from the Reformed Church in Europe or other Reformed denominations in the United States. Rather than being theologically stubborn or exclusive, they kept a neutral attitude and inclusive approach. Do you agree with this? Is there any reason or motive for this?

This is a complex question. The Christian Reformed Church in North America is one of several small denominations that emerged out of immigration from the Netherlands. Most CRC members originally came from groups that had left the state church in the Netherlands. Historically, the CRCNA has been committed to doctrinal orthodoxy, to fostering a warm, Christ-centered piety, and to engaging culture in the name of Jesus, confident that the Holy Spirit is at work redemptively not just in the church but also through God's common grace in the world. At its best, this means that the CRC is open to learning and growth, while cherishing historic doctrine and affirming a high view of the Bible. Like every denomination, the CRC is not always consistent on this. We need each other!

5. **What kind of effort is the Christian Reformed Church putting together for the development of worship? Are there any special institutions within the denomination? When I was researching the issue of infant communion, I was surprised to see that it became an issue in the Christian Reformed Church in the 1960s and that they held meetings about it until 2006. Usually, when such theological issues are at stake, it is common for denominations to fight over the issue and end up falling apart. Were there any such instances?**

The major university of the CRCNA (Calvin University) has partnered with Calvin Theological Seminary to host the Calvin Institute of Christian Worship, the research and ministry center I lead. The CRCNA also sponsors an office of worship—which, in turn, sponsors *Reformed Worship* magazine. The CRCNA Synod has also commissioned two major studies of worship, affirmed in 1968 and then again in 1998. Paedocommunion has been robustly studied by synodical committees. At our best, the CRCNA commissions special committees to pay deep attention to an issue and to write a denominational position paper, which the Synod can affirm. Over the years, that approach has often helped us avoid falling apart on several divisive issues. But it does take time. Sometimes, an issue requires more than one committee or report.

6. **What should the relationship between worship and culture be? There seem to be various positions as to how far cultural factors should be allowed in worship. It requires proper inculturation, but sometimes there seems to be a fear of syncretism as well. How can we best approach this issue? Furthermore, what should we keep in mind when teaching worship in a mission field and helping to establish worship?**

All worship reflects a local culture—often in ways that we don't even realize. Cultural approaches to time, leadership, emotional expression, and communal practices are vastly influential. The first step is simply for us to become aware of how our worship practices reflect culture. But it is also the case that our worship practices should intentionally resist or challenge some cultural assumptions. If we live in a materialistic culture, we should resist that in worship. I find the Nairobi Statement on Worship and Culture to be helpful. It insists that Christian worship always involves *transcultural* practices done in *contextual* ways, often through *cross-cultural* sharing and with a *countercultural* stance. All four of these considerations matter. This perspective also helps us missionally. We may well travel into another culture aiming to practice the Lord's Supper or preaching or singing (transcultural practices), but we will always pause to ask how we can do that in a contextually fitting way.

7. Most of the churches in Korea are small churches with a small number of members, but they seem to be greatly influenced by the worship of megachurches. How has megachurch worship influenced general worship since the twentieth century?

I do believe that congregations can flourish whether they have 50, 500, or 5000 members. I also think that very large churches can, at times, call too much attention to the celebrity status of their pastoral leaders or market their churches as if they are businesses. They can be too consumerist. That doesn't mean they always are. Every church should honestly assess the temptations they must struggle against. Here, too, we need each other. We need honest conversations with pastoral leaders from different kinds of congregations.

8. Looking at the hymnals of the North American Reformed Church, it seems that they have used various types: the *Psalter Hymnal* with gray cover, the *Sing! A New Creation* with green cover, and the latest version called *Lift Up Your Heart*, published in 2013. What are the characteristics of each hymnal? It takes a lot of human and financial resources when creating a hymnal. How do you deal with these things? And since there were many different books of hymns, was there any confusion during worship?

A hymnal is a large project. It is also very exciting. There is so much to learn in compiling a balanced diet of songs, including both historic and newer compositions. I warmly encourage every denomination to have a dedicated group of people who review and recommend songs that convey a balanced diet of biblical themes—even if that material is not published in a hymnal. At one time, all CRCNA churches used the same hymnal (including for most of the twentieth century). In recent years, churches have changed and there is a tremendous diversity of practices across churches, including many congregations that do not use hymnals at all. This diversity is a big challenge. While it often leads to vital worship in individual congregations, it leaves us without a common group of songs that everyone knows.

9. The Christian Reformed Church has been working on modernizing the traditional Psalms. I am curious about how it's working out and what difficulties there are. Please tell us what kind of benefits there are from using the Psalms in public worship.

Every generation should re-engage the Psalms. And in our generation, with so many new forms of music, this is especially important. The Psalms challenge us to pray more intentionally and biblically—provided we take time to study them well and to think deeply about how they are used in the New Testament and how their meaning is further clarified by New Testament teaching. We are learning a lot about this. The publication *Psalms for All Seasons* features settings of all 150 psalms, some with multiple musical settings. While not every church is equally committed to psalm singing, we are grateful for many who are.

10. Choosing the right kind of hymn for public worship seems to be a hot topic not only for scholars and pastors but also for lay people. I'm curious what your thoughts are on this matter. Depending on the theological orientation, there are those who take extreme views on the use of hymns. For example, some argue that only psalms should be used and that contemporary Christian music should not be sung during Sunday public worship. How should we approach the concerns about using hymns and other Christian music during public worship?

I agree that Psalms are compelling and essential. I also think that there are many New Testament texts we should sing—including many poetic expressions of praise and prayer to God. With this in place, I also believe that other texts can be sung, particularly when they are written with the clear intent of conveying deep biblical content. Over the centuries, believers have written thousands of theologically faithful texts. The key is that people who choose music for each worship service do so in ways that are deeply theological and pastoral, leading people into deep and rich practices of singing that can sustain faith over a lifetime.

11. Some Reformed churches are open to a modern style of worship, but there are others who argue that only a specific type of worship is the right kind. Could you please comment on this view?

I do believe that theologically rooted, pastorally sound worship is possible in many styles. I also believe that every style has some potential concerns and challenges. Some traditional worship can be too cerebral.

Some contemporary worship is theologically shallow. To me the question is whether worship, regardless of style, is theologically robust, consistent with Reformed confessions, and pastorally formative—leading people to grow in faith, prayer, love, joy, and deep engagement.

12. Among Presbyterian churches, there seems to be a debate on whether it's possible to use a play or a liturgical dance during a public service. What is your personal opinion on this, professor?

I do believe that each art form can potentially contribute to worship—but also that each art form must first deeply consider the purposes of worship. Each art form needs to be transformed in some ways for it to contribute to worship. A drama could be used to convey a Bible reading, especially of a narrative portion of scripture. Movement and gesture have long contributed to worship—both on the part of all of us and on the part of those with particular gifts for dance. The challenge is discerning culturally appropriate ways for those art forms to contribute in ways that deepen prayer and proclamation of God's word.

13. The Worship Symposium at Calvin Theological Seminary is held annually, inviting famous instructors who draw numerous attendees. Recently, it has become popular in many nations that do not speak English as well. If you could tell us some benefits of the Worship Symposium for non-English readers, what would they be?

This annual conference gathers people from many cultures, traditions, generations, and areas of expertise to discern together the shape of faithful worship. We have sessions that explore Bible reading, preaching, public prayer, baptism and Lord's Supper practices, music, art, architecture, and more. We have much to learn from each other! We warmly welcome guests to join us in Grand Rapids, Michigan or to participate via livestream when available.

14. How did the Christian Reformed Church mainly worship in the midst of the COVID-19 pandemic? Online worship and sacrament debates drew attention in Korea. Is there any denominational position of the Christian Reformed Church? If there is none, I would like to hear your position, professor.

The CRCNA does not have any official position on this. Congregations have experimented with a variety of practices. Some initially tried something—but then changed their approach over time. I want to affirm how valuable in-person worship is. What a gift to be together whenever we can! I also am deeply aware of some people who simply can't come to church for health reasons. What a gift it is for them to be able to participate via livestream.

15. The decreased participation of the next generation seems to be a hardship for all churches around the world. What solutions (or good ideas) does the Christian Reformed Church have for this matter?

It is essential both that we remain faithful, continuing to practice a robust Christian faith, and that we are very intentional about ways of inviting people to join us, including young people.

I am distressed both when churches make no effort to invite others to join and also when other churches invite people but then water down key aspects of the Christian faith in order to make worship seem more appealing. Those are two opposite mistakes to avoid.

The better path is to continually seek ways of practicing a robust and welcoming form of Christianity that values both hospitality and continual learning and growth in Christ.

Selected Bibliography

Brink, Emily, and John D. Witvliet, eds. *The Worship Sourcebook*. Grand Rapids: Baker, 2013.

Maag, Karin, and John D. Witvliet, eds. *Worship in Medieval and Early Modern Europe: Change and Continuity in Religious Practice*. Notre Dame, IN: University of Notre Dame Press, 2004.

Ruth, Lester, Carrie Steenwyk, and John D. Witvliet. *Walking Where Jesus Walked: Worship in Fourth-Century Jerusalem*. Grand Rapids: Eerdmans, 2010.

Witvliet, John D. *The Biblical Psalms in Christian Worship: A Brief Introduction and Guide to Resources*. Grand Rapids: Eerdmans, 2007.

Witvliet, John D. *A Child Shall Lead: Children in Worship*. Dallas, TX: Choristers Guild, 2003.

Witvliet, John D. *Worship Seeking Understanding: Windows into Christian Practice*. Grand Rapids: Baker Academic, 2003.

Witvliet, John D., and David Vroege, eds. *Proclaiming the Christmas Gospel: Ancient Sermons and Hymns for Contemporary Christian Inspiration*. Grand Rapids: Baker, 2004.

2
DON E. SALIERS

Don Saliers is an internationally renowned liturgical theologian to the extent that further explanation is hardly necessary. He taught for many years at Emory University in the United States and mentored numerous liturgical theologians. His numerous publications and articles have made significant contributions to the research and development of liturgical theology. Throughout the world, translations of his works including *Worship as Theology*, *Worship and Spirituality*, *The Soul in Paraphrase*, *Music and Theology*, and *The Lord Be with You: A Visual Handbook for Presiding in Christian Worship* have sparked deep interest in worship among many readers. He is acclaimed for advancing liturgical theology more academically with profound organizational and theological depth. In 1992, he received the prestigious Berakah Award for the top worship scholar and continues to serve as theologian-in-residence at Emory to this day, well into his eighties. He is still actively engaged in various scholarly lectures, passionately researching and serving as a great mentor to liturgical theologians.

Interview with Don E. Saliers

Thank you, Dr. Saliers, for accepting this interview for our readers. I first met you back in 2008, when you visited Calvin Theological Seminary for a lecture. I requested a photo with you, and I remember that you gladly agreed. In 2009, I had Professor Ron Anderson as my advisor for my doctorate, so I believe that makes you my teacher's teacher. I guess that's why I read your works with particular interest. I think many people will be very interested in the contents of this interview.

1. Are there any liturgical theologians or books that have greatly influenced you?

I gleaned a lot from the Orthodox theologian, Alexander Schmemann's *Introduction to Liturgical Theology*. While reading the books of Robert Taft, I entered a deeper world of liturgical studies by seeing the difference between Eastern and Western liturgies, and while reading *Doxology* by Geoffrey Wainwright, I thought of how to integrate liturgical theology and the systematic theological perspective. The books of Gordon Lathrop also helped me to add depth to my knowledge of liturgical theology, and the book of Roman Catholic theologians, Teresa Berger and David N. Power, *Unsearchable Riches: Symbolic Nature of Liturgy* had a great influence on me.

2. I am curious about the process of your formation as a liturgical scholar. How did you come to study liturgical studies, and how did you develop your academic capabilities?

I was active in a local congregation as a young person. My musical training allowed me to participate in ecumenical sharing throughout my teenage years, in Methodist, Presbyterian, Lutheran, Holiness, and Roman Catholic parish life. In college I majored in philosophy and music (piano and organ) while serving as a pastor of a small country church. My religious and academic interests converged on the study of worship—its history, theology, and practice. I began to develop my interest in Jewish sources of Christian worship. In seminary at Yale Divinity School, I began serious study of liturgical history.

My doctoral studies at Yale and at Cambridge University allowed me to pursue both liturgical studies as a discipline and questions of aesthetics and theology. Consequently, I was the first to offer systematic and constructive courses on history, theology, and practice of worship at Yale Divinity School.

Of profound influence was the North American Academy of Liturgy (I eventually served as president) and the international liturgy organization, Societas Liturgica. In these academies I had direct conversation with the major figures and developments stemming from Vatican II and its significance for Protestant forms of liturgy and worship. In addition, the Monastery of Saint Benedict in Collegeville, Minnesota shaped my experience and reflection on modes of prayer and forms of Christian community. I taught there for eight summers.

My philosophical background has played an important role in my writing and teaching, while focusing also on the pastoral contexts of actual church communities. Being a church musician has been immensely helpful and formative.

3. Your students seem to be actively working in North American liturgical studies. For example, Bruce Morrill of Vanderbilt, E. Byron Anderson of Garrett-Evangelical Seminary, and other top scholars are your students. Personally, I would like to call it the Saliers School. What I felt as I read their works was that they had a solid background in systematic theology and liturgical studies. What was your main focus while studying worship studies? Could you tell me what distinguishes you from other scholars, if there is any difference?

I am very glad to claim friendship with those students and a large number of pastors and priests with whom I maintain dialogue. I'm not sure about calling my influence a "school," but I consider my work on the dynamics and the analysis of human emotion to be distinctive. This is found in a number of essays, and especially in the book, *The Soul in Paraphrase*. Questions about belief are also questions about formation in religious affections. My conviction is that our fundamental beliefs are discovered in the form of dispositions and affective appraisals of the world. To believe in God is to be vulnerable to suffering, but especially to the depth of love.

In addition, all of my students have had a strong concern for actual worshiping assemblies across a wide ecumenical and cultural spectrum. In that sense there is a strong element of *integrating* theological, ethical, and aesthetic aspects of Christian liturgy in my work and my student's development. This is evident in *Liturgy and the Moral Self* (Pueblo, 1988).

4. You emphasize that the law of prayer (*lex orandi*) should go beyond the law of faith (*lex credendi*) and ultimately get to the law of action (*lex agendi*). This seems to be an important message for the Korean church.

Korean churches experienced global growth in the past, but since the 2000s have been on a downward slope. The reasons may vary, but it seems to be closely related to churches' failure to deliver prophetic messages on social issues, while fulfilling the role of salt and light. What could restore the public trust in Korean churches moving forward?

This is a central question for the Christian churches. To pray is to love and to take courage in the midst of the turmoil of life. This means that we must speak words of prophetic critique of untruth, injustice, and human malice and misunderstanding of the Gospel, but our "speaking" must also be a way of life.

Authentic prayer requires works of mercy and living out what we proclaim as truth. This is the way the law of prayer and of believing is best lived out in intentions to act. The nonverbal depth of prayer is found in the qualities of human intention and actions. Thus, to lament and to praise are actual ways of life, and not only words we offer to God. Prayer that leads to compassion and a pattern of redemptive action in the world is an extension of the being and action of Jesus Christ in the midst of the complexities of the world.

One of the contributing factors to the decline you mention is "cultural distraction"—and the subsequent weakening of sustained education (catechesis) in the sources and theology of worship. This is true of both Korea and the United States. Public trust requires a consistent speaking of truth to power, and to continually offer the riches of the Christian tradition for life and thought. Social media does not immediately find this profitable.

5. Continuing from the previous question, what elements and order of worship should be considered if we want our weekly worship to lead to a law of conduct (*lex agendi*) in people's minds?

At the heart of Christian worship is doxology, lament, and especially intercession for the whole world as well as the local community. The church is to be a community of intercession, connecting weekly worship to commitments to act in Christ's name. We can always begin by placing the Beatitudes of Jesus Christ together with Matthew 25. These must be sounded in our singing, praying and the music of our sanctuaries.

The observance of Christian time—from Advent to Pentecost—is a series of images we must preach and "live into" over time. This is a never-ending process of formation, action, and communal expression. The liturgy of the sanctuary and the liturgy of the church's life in the world of service and risk are one and the same: as Merton said, "Contemplation in a world of action."

6. I heard that you majored in music for your undergraduate degree, and I've seen videos of you teaching while playing the piano in classes. You also wrote a book about church music. How is music important for worship?

Music is the language of the heart and soul made audible. Therefore, the words we sing and the music we make to praise God must have strength and durability. There is a "music" in the sound of prayer, even when no explicit music is made. The most important thing is to sing texts that have biblical depth and existential import for the assembly. We must seek poetry that can bear the weight of all the modes of worship: praise, lament, consolation, prophecy, and "sense making" in our social worlds. Depth of memory, not nostalgia is required.

The singing congregation is a blessing to the world, especially when we draw on the depth of Christian theology and Scripture, and when music making continually inspires awe and wonder! Encouraging musical experience and good training among young people is a crucial ministry of the church, but music also carries cultural force—for good or for ill. In a recent book, *Music and Imagination: Themes and Variations*, I develop the relationship between music and the role of imagination in the moral life of communities.

7. Looking at worship in the twenty-first century, it seems that the old and new generations have many different ideas about worship. Disagreements about worship music and congregational praise are sharp. There are various opinions from denominations and scholars, but I would appreciate it if you could tell me your opinion about what worship music and congregational hymns are desirable.

First, we must respect the musical traditions that are already part of a congregation's (or denomination's) gifts. But then we must embrace the long history of musical forms. In my opinion, every congregation should practice some form of chant—especially simple chant forms for praying the psalms. New composers across cultures are providing excellent resources.

Every congregation should keep learning new hymnic forms: from Ambrosian hymns translated from Latin to Lutheran choral tunes to the wonderful hymnody of Watts and Wesley. We should be a bit cautious about using too many texts and tunes that sound just like popular culture. Some are quite powerful and appropriate, but we should always ask about their theological content and the capacity of hymnody (and sung anthems) to carry the depth of biblical images and the real struggles of faith.

I recommend periodic hymn festivals that can expose our congregations to both the riches of the past and the high quality of new music. But I also recommend that we have many occasions simply to have a "hymn sing" in which many can sing their favorites alongside new or more challenging texts and musical settings.

We should encourage preaching on some of the great hymns, and on the Psalms. Every congregation should explore the profound relationship between lament and praise. Encouraging cross-cultural music for worship is a challenging but necessary ecumenical work in our world.

8. I think the most important part of a hymn is the lyrics. It is critical to examine how the lyrics express biblical and theological messages. However, with the variety of music genres, deciding which tune or rhythm is suitable for public worship seems to be a very complex matter. What should the standard for selecting congregational hymns be?

Careful consideration must be given to how a particular hymn connects in a particular worship service with Scripture readings, the forms of congregation and pastoral prayer, and, of course, the sermon. The context of the congregation's life as well as its ability to sing should be considered in any hymn selection. (This could lead to developing musical education for a local congregation in the history of hymns as well as in improving singing practices.) We should explore how many "classical" hymn texts (e.g., "Love Divine, All Loves Excelling," "Amazing Grace," etc.) may be set to new musical melodies and harmonies, thus refreshing our understanding of the texts in new ways. We must always strive to balance scriptural, theological, cultural, and contextual aspects of the musical repertoire of our local churches.

A vibrant congregation will continue to grow musically over time, with attention also to cross-generational participation. At the same time, there is so much life-giving theology and spirituality in many of the hymns in our hymnals we have never explored! Hymn texts must have theological integrity, poetic beauty and power, the ability to open up the Scriptures richly, pastoral relevance, and be singable by most of the congregation.

9. **During the COVID-19 crisis, there were fierce debates about on-site and online worship among the churches. Topics such as an online communion service and an online baptism service were also major issues for the theologians and believers. I'd appreciate it if you could share your personal views on this matter.**

Christian faith and public worship require human embodiment. Thus, it is important that the church gathers together physically to sing, pray, preach, and celebrate the sacraments. But during COVID-19, many churches turned to online services. This created various issues, but it is now obvious that many churches will continue to both meet physically and virtually for worship. This is especially true in the United States. Three things are problematic: the practice of a "virtual" sacrament, the habit of convenience (simply staying at home and watching), and the disconnection between worship and the shared works of mercy that connect actual ministries with embodied prayer. Yet, I see the pastoral value of giving persons who are shut in or prevented by health or other circumstances access to participation in the congregation's life of worship. So, the first priority is the gathered assembly if at all possible. I fear the loss of sacramentality when churches come to *rely* on online worship. It also prompts church shopping. This can become a form of spiritual deception, or of church attendance by virtue of attraction to the "best" worship experiences.

Sacramentality requires an embodied community *over time*, with the whole range of energies and committed relationships in worship and ministry.

10. **How can we educate believers about worship? Seminary students will learn many things through worship studies at school, but how can the public be taught?**

Our local churches should become schools for musical training, scriptural dialogue, and places of public discussion of the relevance of Christian faith for the pressing issues of the world. The churches must provide occasions for learning, but also occasions for awe and wonder! Sessions open to the general public are crucial: hymn festivals, artistic festivals that feature major Christian images and teachings. The church can be a place of "public dialogue and discussion about issues that concern the society (without being dogmatic or defensive!)."

11. I think the book *The Lord Be with You*, which you coauthored with Charles D. Hackett, is a slim but great book. Before, there was no book to which one could refer on how to use gestures in conducting ceremonies. However, the pictures and explanations in this book give confidence to perform various ceremonies and rites. Why are symbols and gestures important in worship or when performing liturgies? Could you introduce other books regarding the method of presiding over sacraments and ceremonies?

Gestures in leading and celebrating worship must be inviting, generous, and grounded in images from the larger tradition, just as the primary symbols should be. Gordon Lathrop's work on keeping the primary symbols at the center is important: these will be both scriptural and sacramental. Robert Hovda's book on presiding and Virginia Sloyan's book on qualities of liturgical celebration (yes, even for free church Protestants) are great resources. Perhaps the Korean churches could develop visual resources for teaching films that demonstrate how an ordinary church can deepen the quality of presiding and especially on the role of the worship congregation. Artists are required: dancers, potters, musicians. . . .

12. Your book *Worship Come to Its Senses* is considered one of your best. For unfamiliar readers, could you explain the purpose and message of this book?

Christian worship both shapes and gives expression to deep emotions. These are not so much "feelings" as they are dispositions to be and act in the world. So, the "affections" I mention are central to living the faith: gratitude, hope, delight, joy, courage. We sometimes do not distinguish between intense feelings and emotional capacities that endure over time. We must continually ask: are we growing in the depth of our gratitude, compassion, and hope over time? This means practicing the relationships between sorrow and joy, between suffering and hope, between lament and praise. The Christian year—well practiced—can offer us access to this continual deepening of faith in experience and in thought and action. But we must explore the richness that we sometimes take for granted.

13. If you look at the worship services of some churches, especially those that overemphasize doctrine and suppress the sensory elements of worship, it seems that worship is often approached as a study session for

Scripture and doctrine rather than as a joyful festival. In such cases, the pastors and members frequently criticize other churches. How can we prevent such conflicts and preserve the spirit of harmony in worship?

We must restore the notion that Sunday worship is primarily a resurrection feast, but this means more study of the larger history—beginning especially with the earliest sources. (Do we know the wondrous variety of prayers from the early church?) Doctrine and living praise go together. While there will always be different emphases and accents between churches, the fundamental reality is that we are "all one in Christ." As in John 17, Jesus Christ continually prays for our unity (without diversity).

Are the riches of practice and experience we need to share across churches and local cultures, as well as denominations? Worshiping together on special days may be part of our learning across our divisions.

14. In your book, you mentioned that modern worship lacks lament, and that restoration of lament is necessary in aspects of worship spirituality. How can we restore this? How can human lamentation lead to trust in God in the ordo (or elements) of worship?

Can we take a clue from the Psalms? There we see that the rhythms of lament and praise are also the rhythm of life for God's people over the ages.

15. I learned a lot from reading your book *Worship as Theology*. I would appreciate it if you could explain the key ideas of this book and elaborate a little more on the statement, "Christian Worship has an eschatological character."

Worship as Theology proposes that the public worship of the Church is itself a form of "performed theology." We might compare this to the relationship between a musical score (notation) and the actual musical performance of a musical composition. Worship is active engagement of communal relationship to God. The order of service is not the music. Worship therefore sounds and enacts the theology of the texts in a living community. Active participation in worship is thus a theological action, not merely the recital of what we believe. Of course, some churches do involve the recitation of creeds and set prayers as well. The act of worship is far more than words—it is the life of faith in the presence of God "at full stretch."

Christian worship exists between the promises of God and the actuality of our human lives. This is the tension between the "already" of the incarnation of Jesus Christ and the "not yet" of the fullness of God's kingdom. This is the basis for my claim that Christian worship is always eschatological. So, we preach, pray, sing, and celebrate the sacraments as acts of hope and trust that what God has promised in the Scriptures and in the history of God's people is true. The witness of the prophets and all the saints is to a new creation—the fulfillment of God's kingdom "on earth as in heaven." Christian worship is thus always in time and place while anticipating the fulfillment of what has been promised in Christ. So, what we sing, preach, and pray is always in anticipation of "thy kingdom come." In this way Christian worship stands in tension with all ideologies and against the present principalities and powers of the world.

The Christian year helps us remember the whole story of creation and redemption, so we move through time remembering what God has done and promised through feasts and seasons of the Christian year. I emphasized Advent in the book as the season of expectation that marks our Christian lives. Our hope is in God's future for us and for the whole of creation. This is why we can bring our honest "hopes and fears through all the years" to God every Sunday and every day in our worship.

16. In this book, you explained Christian worship as the encounter of human pathos and divine ethos. You developed a theological argument on the relationship while explaining the priority of God's self-giving in worship. How can the dynamic relationship between the two, God and human, flow smoothly? How can God's glory be revealed in the ordo and elements of worship, as well as lead to human transformation (or sanctification)?

God continually offers the grace and hope of the divine life to the world in faithful worship. Obviously, we must think of both God's initiating power and the quality of human reception and response. This is the eternal divine-human encounter at the heart of true Christian worship. The glory of God, we claim, is found in creation, in the prophets, and in the ongoing "holy history" of God's acts in human life. This means that the sacraments themselves engage our real humanity in time and space. So, the most profound intimacy with God is found in meals and common works of mercy as well as in baptismal washing, anointing of the Spirit in healing and witness, and all the myriad ways that God works through the created order. This binds sacraments and justice forever. Thus, worship works through our human pathos (suffering and seeking) to sanctify time, place, and people. The work of sanctification occurs at the deepest intersection of God's continual self-giving in word and sacrament and human transformative response. Holiness is thus a profound reciprocity between God and humanity—initiated and sustained by God through the honesty and beauty of worship. God has chosen to work in, with, and through us. We see this supremely in the teachings, actions, suffering, death, and resurrection of Christ.

It is possible, of course, to substitute idolatry for true worship, but we trust that God knows our human weaknesses and is ever-ready to forgive and empower us toward fidelity with him and with our fellow creatures. What we say in the Apostles' Creed must be lived in our lives of worship and service. This is the dynamism of divine grace.

17. You said that one problem faced by the worship tradition of the Roman Catholic Church is that the symbols used in worship are too limited and fossilized, whereas the Protestant worship tradition today has little or no awareness of symbols or serious doubts about the realm of symbols. How can Protestant churches overcome their doubts about symbols? What are the advantages and roles of symbols?

As Paul Tillich observed, theologians have often opposed "Catholic substance" and "Protestant principle." Protestantism was born in "protest" of church practices and beliefs that seemed unfaithful and opposed to God's will for the church, but prior to the sixteenth century there had always been "reforming" and prophetically critical movements. Furthermore, Protestantism continues the tendency to protest by subdividing denominations and splintering into more sectarian groups. Often this is over questions of symbols (What is true holiness? Can women symbolically represent Christ? Who can claim to interpret Scripture faithfully?). Both Protestants and Catholics, as well as Orthodox, employ many biblical symbols in teaching and practice. The question is not whether we will use symbols, but what are the primary symbols required by Christian faith and life? We need a more adequate understanding of the nature of symbolic thinking in faith and thought. It is difficult, if not impossible, to conceive of God without thinking in analogies and symbols drawn from human experience.

A central symbol for all Christians is the cross. Is this a symbol of torture and death, or a symbol of resurrection and new life? Is it to be thought of as a blood sacrifice or as God's act of solidarity with humanity's suffering? These are theological questions that divide traditions. Careful conversation and sustained dialogue are required in order to understand the full range of meaning of this primary symbol. But the symbol itself cannot be dismissed as "merely" or "only" a symbol. Mature theology requires us to understand how the cross is to be interpreted.

This requires us to understand how this primary symbol is used in worship and in devotional life. Religious symbols take us to the mystery they signify. Symbols such as the Body of Christ open up for the church the question of how we can both participate and come to understand the depth of our worship experiences—hence of our enacted theology.

Local congregations need more adequate teaching and learning about symbolic imagination and its role in shaping our lives and theologies. This is necessary to understand much of how the Bible works, and to receive how the Scripture enters public worship and liturgy. Symbols both point to and participate in the reality and power of that which they reveal to us. Without symbolic imagination, Christianity falls into fundamentalisms of various sorts—psychological, spiritual, and biblical.

18. You stated in your book that worship and art have a close relationship. You also said that human beings are formed religiously, liturgically, and aesthetically. What is proper worship art? Between high culture and pop culture, which one should a church choose?

There is no single worship aesthetic that applies to all of Christianity. Art serves the liturgy and forms of religious faith. Art is always embedded in specific cultural forms. Think of the differences in music between the German Lutheran chorales, the Genevan psalm tunes, the ancient Greek and Roman chant forms, evangelical hymns of recent centuries, Latin American and African melodies and rhythms, and the emergence of popular entertainment forms. These shape the sound of words and prayers in distinctive ways. We begin with what our own culture offers us. We then ask questions about the adequacy of the musical settings to the texts, biblical and otherwise, that we offer in worship. But the same is true of language and forms of speech, of gesture and movement, of cultural styles of expression or of the role of silence in worship. It is crucial to ask: how can faith find honest ways of expressing itself in particular cultural (even "subcultural") contexts. The rise of commercial music and speech idioms present Christian worship with important issues to be faced. When does Christian worship become captive to the latest popular idiom? When is it important to preserve aspects of a larger Christian tradition in music, gesture, patterns of order, central symbols?

Churches in Korea are increasingly exposed to worship patterns and forms that may or may not be adequate to the Gospel. This calls for discernment and learning. Asking aesthetic questions about language, music, movement, design, and what forms faith deeply are required of us all.

We can learn from differing traditions, but we must also ask how the artistic forms we use can keep us open to God while remaining faithful. This means looking for how Christian faith both uses cultural means and offers a critique of what the culture becomes captivated by.

Can the arts we use in our worship lead us to more maturity, to be more capable of joy, sorrow, gratitude, and hope? We need more poetic depth, not less; we need deeper sharing of lament and praise, not conformity to what we take to be "standard" or "expected." The hearing and sharing of the Gospel in our lives requires a deepening aesthetic of how God works through creation and through human experience. Here Scripture, prayer, and worship meet with our real lives. This means that both so-called "high culture" (Bach, Mozart, etc.) and more popular or folk cultures (Negro Spirituals, folk instrumentation) have something to contribute. But the trends in popular commercialized art usually prove too shallow to carry the depth of faith over time—the lamentable and the praiseworthy in the presence of God.

19. What do you think about the use of drama or liturgical dance during Sunday public service?

There are certainly ways in which drama, dance, and dialogues can enhance public worship. At the same time, care must be taken in using these elements. Such elements can illustrate and intensify the use of Scripture if carefully thought through. During the Medieval period in European Christianity, many sequences in the local vernacular gave worshipers access to the biblical stories, parables, and images. In fact, much of what we now know of the great Easter Vigil was born in the uses of drama (both in and outside the sanctuary of cathedrals).

But simply putting a skit or a play in the service to entertain may not be an effective communication of the central message of Christian faith. Wisdom, biblical imagination, and coherence with the aim of public worship is required to do these things well.

20. Among the influential worship scholars in North America, there seem to be many scholars from Emory University as well as the University of Notre Dame. In your view, what are the strengths and academic characteristics of Emory and Notre Dame in the field of liturgical studies?

Both Emory and Notre Dame have rich resources to offer the field of liturgical studies. Generally speaking, Notre Dame focuses well on the history and development of Christian liturgy, with a distinctive Roman Catholic theological ethos. Some of the most important ecumenical voices continue to teach there. Emory has a distinctive cultural and pastoral interest in the history and the present status of liturgical studies. At Emory, there is a clear multidisciplinary ethos with attention to liturgy and ethics, pastoral care, and with attention to contemporary theological developments. The emergence there of a distinctive Catholic studies program, with special accent on Latin American and Latinx developments is noteworthy.

Both of these graduate programs in theology and liturgical studies are among the best places for current study and for the development of strong, focused scholarly studies of Christian worship. Both offer ample resources in Jewish and related religious traditions as a helpful comparative context for the present situation of Christian liturgy in a larger world. Emory has especially strong interest in Christian ethics flowing to and from the worship life of churches in a multireligious context.

21. Throughout your life, you have had many achievements while studying worship. If you could go back in time, what kind of research would you have liked to do more of in the field of worship?

If I had to improve on my early training and research, I would focus on two things more intensively: language training, especially biblical languages, and iconography—and a more extensive knowledge of the early development of various forms of Orthodoxy and the emerging Western Church. I came into liturgical studies with strong theological and pastoral training, as well as musical experience. At the same time, I now wish that I had paid earlier attention to the poetic cultural background in both the Roman and Eastern churches.

Selected Bibliography

Saliers, Don E. *Music and Theology*. Nashville: Abingdon, 2007.

Saliers, Don E. *The Soul in Paraphrase: Prayer and the Religious Affections*. New York: Seabury, 1980.

Saliers, Don E. *Themes and Variations: Music and Imagination*. Chicago: GIA, 2020.

Saliers, Don E. *Worship Come to Its Senses*. Nashville: Abingdon, 1996.

Saliers, Don E. *Worship as Theology: Foretaste of Glory Divine*. Nashville: Abingdon, 1994.

Saliers, Don E. *Worship and Spirituality*. Franklinville, NJ: OSL Publications, 1984.

Saliers, Don E., Louis Dupré, and John Meyendorff, eds. *Christian Spirituality: Post-Reformation and Modern*. Chestnut Ridge, NY: Crossroad, 1989.

Saliers, Don E., and Nancy Eiesland. *Human Disability and the Service of God: Reassessing Religious Practice*. Nashville: Abingdon, 1998.

Saliers, Don E., Hoyt Hickman, Laurence Hull Stookey, and James F. White. *Handbook for the Christian Year, Second Edition*. Nashville: Abingdon, 1992.

Saliers, Don E., and Emily Saliers. *A Song to Sing, A Life to Live: Reflections on Music as Spiritual Practice*. New York: Wiley, 2006.

3
EDWARD FOLEY

Edward Bernard Foley is a Roman Catholic priest and educator, widely recognized as a gifted practical theologian and liturgist. As an undergraduate, he majored in music education and philosophy at St. Joseph's College and earned a master's degree in conducting from the University of Wisconsin. Afterward, he studied liturgy and theology at the University of Notre Dame, earning his master's and doctoral degrees. For a long time (1984–2020), he taught liturgy and practical theology at the Catholic Theological Union in Chicago, Illinois and was a visiting professor at various schools, including the University of Chicago. He served as president of the North American Academy of Liturgy and was awarded the 2013 Berakah Award for a lifetime of outstanding scholarship. As a key figure in the world of practical theology, he is deeply committed to research and writing even after retirement.

Interview with Edward Foley

Thank you, Fr. Foley, for agreeing to be interviewed. It is a great honor to discuss liturgical studies with one of the top liturgical scholars in North America who also happens to be the recipient of the Berakah Award, which is the highest North American honor in worship. When I was studying liturgical studies at Garrett-Evangelical Theological Seminary in Chicago, I came across your book *Mighty Stories, Dangerous Rituals: Weaving Together the Human and the Divine* (San Francisco: Jossey Bass, 1997), coauthored with Herbert Anderson. It helped me a lot to understand the relationship between ritual and theology.

In 2013, I finally met you in person at the North American Academy of Liturgy held in Orlando. I was also very happy to see that your books were recently introduced in Korea. *From Age to Age: How Christians Have Celebrated the Eucharist* (Minneapolis: Liturgical Press, 2016) is a masterpiece that has been translated into Korean and has inspired many Korean readers.

1. Looking at your body of work—from your book *From Age to Age* on the history of worship to your book *Mighty Stories, Dangerous Rituals* on ritual—it seems that you are interested in various fields. Not only that, you have also written articles on practical theology, postcolonialism, and church music. What is your educational background, and what brought you to pursue these various fields?

I began my studies with a degree in music education and philosophy. I had studied music as an adolescent and continued to pursue that study first with an undergraduate degree and then a graduate degree in conducting (MMus, University of Wisconsin-Milwaukee). After my MDiv, required for ordination, I began to study liturgy, first with an MA in Liturgical Research from Notre Dame, and then another MA and a PhD in theology from Notre Dame with a concentration in liturgical history.

When I began teaching at Catholic Theological Union in the 1984 academic year, my colleagues but especially my many international students expanded my academic horizons. I began to read about mission, ritual studies, postcolonial theory, and practical theology. Developing our professional doctoral program in practical theology led me to friendships with luminaries such as Don Browning at the University of Chicago, who mentored me in practical theology and led the way for my membership in the International Academy of Practical Theology. More recently, because of my ongoing ministry of preaching—I have consistently preached in two parishes in Chicago over the past thirty years—I have been doing more research into the nature of liturgical preaching. More specifically, I have begun a project on the contribution of the sciences to preaching, and in 2019 I was awarded a major grant in preaching and the sciences from the John Templeton Foundation and another from the Lilly Endowment in 2023. My current research concerns not only the value of employing the sciences in preaching but trying to determine if certain sciences—especially neuroscience—can help preachers understand what makes their preaching effective and transformative.

2. What was your motivation for writing the book *From Age to Age: How Christians Have Celebrated the Eucharist*?

That book, like much of my writing, developed out of my teaching and parish work. Since I was hired at Catholic Theological Union, I have taught a required course on eucharistic theology. In the process of teaching that course, I found many of the resources too theoretical and text-centered. As I was learning, especially through practical theology, liturgy is not a text but an event that occurs in a specific place and time, employing powerful symbols like music and art. Thus, I decided to craft my lectures employing slides and music. I employed this technique when giving various presentations outside of the school. Eventually I was asked by a publisher to gather these into a book. It was an exciting project, especially working with the visual artists who were hired to punctuate the book with many drawings and illustrations.

Because the book has been adopted as a textbook in so many places, and because of valuable critiques from reviews and colleagues, I decided to revise and expand the book in 2008. It has been translated into Spanish, Japanese, Korean, and soon Portuguese.

3. How long did it take you to write, and how did you prepare for it?

The original writing was connected to my early years of teaching the Eucharist course. It took a few years to get my lectures for that course in shape. After the basic course lectures were in place, it took another two years to craft the text and develop the illustrations and all of the side panel quotations. The design was an attempt to make the book more dynamic.

4. What changes were made in sacramental theology between the sixteenth century Roman Catholic Church and the twenty-first? Some Protestant scholars and church members have a tendency to judge the sacramental theology of the Roman Catholic Church from a sixteenth century perspective, but the Catholic Church's sacramental thoughts were developing around the Second Vatican Council. For example, if we

read Edward Schillebeeckx's or Karl Rahner's books, there is definitely a change. What is your explanation for this change?

There are innumerable changes that have occurred in sacramental theology over the centuries in the Christian churches including the Roman Catholic Church. While it is not possible to document all of them here, one dynamic turn for many Roman Catholic theologians was the turn to relationality and the experience of "encounter" as a fundamental starting point for theologizing.

Roman Catholic sacramental theology after the Council of Trent (1545–63) was firmly rooted in a philosophy of nature, particularly as articulated by the Greek philosopher Aristotle (d. 322 BCE). For a variety of reasons, that foundation was challenged. Part of it was clearly the emergence of more vibrant philosophical frames in the West that valued individual cognition and experience and explored the subjective nature of knowing.

Besides philosophy, there were political and scientific developments that took human experience seriously and newly valued the perceptions and feelings of ordinary folk. Many of these various developments converged around issues of relationality, dialogue, and encounter. The Jewish philosopher-theologian Martin Buber (d. 1965) exemplified this in his understanding of human existence itself as essentially dialogical and rooted in the experience of encounter.

Multiple Roman Catholic theologians of the early and mid-twentieth century, all essentially trained in the traditional forms of sacramental theology grounded in the work of Aristotle, began to reimagine sacramental theology in these terms. A classic summary of this work is that of the Belgian theologian Edward Schillebeeckx's (d. 2009) *Christ the Sacrament of the Encounter with God*. Schillebeeckx and Karl Rahner (d. 1984), both of whom served as theological experts at the Second Vatican Council (1962–65) along with multiple others pushed Roman Catholics to think outside of categories such as matter and form, or substance and accidents—all nouns—to frameworks of encountering, conversing, and dialoguing—all verbs. Sacrament from this broadened perspective is not a thing or a noun or an object—like water or bread or oil—but a verb.

This kind of thinking also changed Roman Catholic perception of the nature of God's grace. Often grace has been treated as a kind of thing or holy quantity that people receive, for example, when they go to communion. Rahner and others, however, have helped us understand that grace is

God's self-communication. It is God's own life that is shared, encountered, often received but also sometimes refused.

This frame of encounter was adopted by the Catechism of the Catholic Church. When discussing the sacraments, it notes that each liturgical action—especially the Eucharist and other sacraments—"is an encounter between Christ and the Church" (no. 1097).

Pope Francis deeply embraces this framework, especially in his *The Joy of the Gospel*. Not only does the word appear dozens of times in that exhortation—starting with its opening sentence—but, more importantly, it is central to the Pope's understanding of discipleship and evangelization. Besides inviting all Christians "to a renewed personal encounter with Jesus Christ" (no. 3) that blossoms into friendship (no. 8), Francis repeatedly defines our shared Christian vocation as missionary disciples by our willingness to encounter others.

5. Our understanding of the traditional theme of transubstantiation has evolved over time. Please explain the difference between transubstantiation, transfiguration, and transignification for the readers.

Transfiguration and transignification are terms that were developed by Edward Schillebeeckx in trying to penetrate but not explain the mystery of Christ's presence. All language that theologians use here is analogous language, that is, holding together both similarity and difference. This is a way to respect the mystery. These new terms are grounded in his and other theologians' concern not to place the presence of Christ outside the context of relationship. Classical medieval frameworks for understanding sacramentality distinguished between:

- *sacramentum* [sign] and *res* [essence]
- *sacramentum tantum* [sign itself] and *res tantum* [underlying reality]
- *res et sacramentum* [body of Christ] and *res sacramenti* [effect in grace]

The Council of Trent emphasized the *res et sacramentum*, that is the Body of Christ in and of itself. Schillebeeckx and theologians like him want to emphasize *res sacramenti*, that is, the purpose of the sacrament and the purpose of Christ's real presence in his Body and Blood.

This led Schillebeeckx to a new progression of thought in considering eucharistic presence, and thus his new terms. He goes back to the biblical faith and discerns three stages that are important to thinking about Eucharist. First, the scriptures indicate that through their shared table ministry and time together, the disciples' relationship to Jesus changed over time. Because of this relationship change, second, one could reason that the disciples' relationship to the bread changed. Third, because of these two changed relationships—first to Jesus and then to the bread—one could assert that the bread changed.

Schillebeeckx argues that you cannot simply start with three: the bread changing. That change has to be embedded in the relational development between Jesus and his disciples. It is in this context that he can offer an analogous understanding of real presence in a parallel set of three moves. He begins by asserting that in the eucharistic action the significance of the bread has changed, no longer signifying physical nourishment but spiritual nourishment. He calls this change transignification.

Next, he argues that the purpose of the bread has changed, no longer simply to sustain human life but to sustain eternal life. He calls this change transfinalization. It is because of these two changes that one can, thirdly, state that, in the eucharistic action, the reality of the bread itself has changed. This change is called transubstantiation. As in addressing the biblical faith, here again one cannot start with number three (transubstantiation) for that imperfect explanation of the mystery of the Eucharist is reliant in Schillebeeckx's view on the changes in the bread's significance and purpose.

6. From the Protestant point of view, the liturgy of the Catholic Church seems to have weight and numerous rites. In Protestant seminaries there are preaching courses with an emphasis on the word, but there are no courses to practice the ceremony itself. What kind of curriculum is there in Catholic seminaries for learning and practicing liturgical ceremonies?

Actually, in many Protestant seminaries there are courses that teach ministry candidates what Roman Catholics sometimes call presiding. I taught for a number of years in the divinity school at the University of Chicago, and team-taught a course that included mostly Protestants, but also Jews and Muslims, Sikhs and Buddhists who were pursuing their MDiv Degree. We called the course "Ritual Speaking and Ritual Leadership."

We employed the same basic skill building process that I would employ when teaching Roman Catholic ordination candidates the various presiding and preaching skills for the various sacraments. This includes having a strong theological foundation for understanding the sacraments. Thus, we have various "theory" courses on the history and theology of Eucharist, Reconciliation, Marriage, Anointing, etc. In these courses we look at the theological and dogmatic teachings about them, but we also look at the ritual books themselves, which are an important and official source of sacramental theology, since these rites reveal in a unique way how sacraments are actions and the way you enact these rites generates different theologies.

Finally, we have distinctive practicum courses in sacramental presiding, the same way as we have practicum courses in preaching. In those courses students practice leading all the various sacramental rites, are often videotaped when doing so, and join in peer evaluations of their performance. Such evaluations start with commendations, that is, what was strong and well done, and recommendations, that is, where improvement is possible and necessary.

7. It seems like younger generations are leaving the church (this situation is worldwide). I wonder what the current situation of the Catholic churches in the United States is like. Do you have any ideas or plans to address this problem? Are there any good solutions for recovering the number from the younger generations?

My goal is not, first of all, to bring back young people to the church. There have been many movements in the US Catholic Church directed at young people to "come home." As one specialist in young adult ministry has noted, for many young people the church was never their home but only the home of their parents and grandparents. Over decades we have failed to listen to young people and failed to address their needs. In the lead up to the 2018 Synod on Young People with Pope Francis, many young adults were interviewed and asked what they wanted from the synod. What they wanted most was to be heard.

While young people are leaving major religious institutions all over the Western world, evidence demonstrates that they still believe that religious institutions like the Catholic Church are credible dialogue partners in the struggle for justice and upholding human dignity. This gives me direction for ministry, especially for preaching. There is an ancient maxim that grace builds on nature. The nature we share is human nature. Thus, I take a Christian humanist approach to my ministry and especially my preaching. My goal is to demonstrate that the Church is a credible dialogue partner here that listens to the "cry of the poor."

Another strategy in my preaching and ministry is to engage the sciences. Most young people in the United States today are not studying humanities but rather science, technology, engineering, and math (STEM). Few preachers, however, engage these resources. Employing examples and insights from STEM sources is another way to demonstrate that the church is a listening and not just an instructing church.

8. During the COVID-19 situation, it seems that the issue of church worship became a topic of debate not only in theological circles but also among lay members. Issues such as online worship, online communion, and online baptism swept across North America and the world. I'm curious about your personal opinion on this matter. What is the policy or the stance of the Catholic Church (in the USA) on worship during a pandemic? In Korea, some churches preferred online worship, but many conservative churches adhered to onsite worship. If another pandemic happens in the future, how will you respond?

I preside and preach in a community that was doing livestreaming before COVID, though that number was relatively small. On an average Sunday this community had about three thousand face-to-face worshipers. The first Sunday the community went to full livestream for its only Sunday Mass there were over thirty thousand hits. Even today, when we are returning to face-to-face worship, we are getting over four thousand hits for Sunday livestream . . . and if there is more than one person on the same device, that is easily twice as many online worshipers for one Mass than we had for a whole weekend pre-COVID.

Some think that eventually we will all get over this pandemic and the challenges it has posed to education and business and worship, but I am not so sure. I wonder if the tectonic shift from face-to-face to digital in liturgy and life is here to stay. Over a decade ago as I was acquiring certification as an online instructor, I kept hearing from educators of every stripe that online learning was the very future of higher education across the globe. How quickly that has come to pass. Analogously, I think the unanticipated transition from physical proximity to altar, ambo, and assembly to the digital interconnectedness of congregation and communion via computer is here to stay.

Some argue that digital engagement is not true participation. Theorists in media studies, however, disagree. Online engagement can be true engagement. The challenge that lies before churches in the twenty-first century is to wed our face-to-face presence with new forms of digital and online ministries, so that we can reach the homebound, the elderly, the disaffiliated, and seekers, as well as committed believers.

9. What is liturgical preaching? What is its character, and how is it different from a Protestant sermon?

I and many other Roman Catholics distinguish between a sermon and a "homily," which is the central form of liturgical preaching for us. I would not distinguish between Catholic and Protestant preaching, because many Protestants do preach a "homily," while some deliver sermons.

As I have written in other places, my definition of a homily is: a ritual conversation between God and the liturgical assembly that announces God's reign as revealed in Jesus Christ through the mediation of a preacher, who offers a credible and imaginative interpretation for Christian living, in dialogue with the lives of the faithful, that draws upon the whole of the liturgy—especially the lectionary texts—in the context of a particular community at a prescribed moment of their shared life. From my perspective, the homily has a few distinctive characteristics:

The homily is a liturgical act. The homily is not only in but essentially of the liturgy, which means that such preaching itself is a liturgical event. There are multiple practical and theological consequences of this assertion. From a practical perspective, an authentic homily needs to be in dialogue with the whole of the liturgical context. Besides the lectionary, which we will consider below, that includes the primary texts, ritual actions, and theologies of a given liturgy. Thus, homilizing is inherently mystagogical. Homilizing at weddings, for example, needs to take into account not only the chosen readings for the day but the exchange of vows and rings and the underlying theology of those actions that recognize that the couple are the ministers of the sacrament to each other.

The homily affirms the assembly as active participants in the preaching. Recognizing the homily as an integral liturgical element also theologically underscores that it is not simply a communication between the preacher and an audience. Vatican II clearly teaches that liturgy is an action of Christ, head and members (*Sacrosanctum Concilium*, no. 7). Thus, the homily as well must be an encounter between Christ and the faithful. Members of the assembly are not the objects of such preaching, but subjects of the homiletic event with Christ, just as they are subjects of the whole of the liturgy with Christ. Pope Francis underscores this point in *Evangelii Gaudium* when he speaks about the dialogue between God and God's people and recognizes that the homily requires an "intermediary" (*EG*, no. 143) to enable this dialogue.

The homily is rooted in the lectionary. The homily is a particular genre of liturgical preaching that is not simply biblical or scriptural but rooted in the lectionary. The lectionary is a unique genre of ecclesial literature. It is not identical to the Bible but drawn from its contents by selecting passages from the biblical material (decontextualizing) and then placing these readings within a new literary and liturgical context (recontextualizing), thus creating a new ecclesial genre. This recontextualization of former biblical material calls for a new way of interpretation, one that takes into consideration the liturgical character and setting of the lectionary readings (see Dianne Bergant and Richard Fragomeni, *Preaching the New Lectionary*, 2001, vii). It is the juxtaposition of the three readings along with the psalm in the liturgical context that gives the homily its particular dynamic.

The homily is a rhetorical event. Just as the liturgy is not a book or text but an experience, so the homily is not merely words on a page but an event. While a prepared text is ordinarily helpful in this form of preaching, properly speaking the homily is not the text but a rhetorical performance. Since liturgy, as noted above, is an action that Christ does (head and members) then the rhetorical task here is not primarily to persuade the assembly to agree with the preacher, but to persuade them to encounter Christ in both the liturgy of the church and, as importantly, in what Karl Rahner (d. 1984) called the liturgy of the world.

While a homily can be instructional, it is not fundamentally a catechetical act, biblical exegesis, nor a way to supply the assembly with a set of injunctions that they should observe in their lives. Rather, like the New Testament parables, it is intended to be an engaging conversation requiring the active participation of the hearers so that they might experience the surprising revelation of God's reign in their own lives. Because the homily is persuading people into encountering Christ—into loving God, others, and self as Jesus modeled in his earthly ministry—there is a clear place for poetic, lyrical, and nondiscursive language in the homily. Reminiscent of ancient preaching from the East that wed poetry together with theology, today's reimagined homily is more about moving hearts than informing intellects. Jesus consistently achieved this through his parables, and storytelling in parabolic mode is a particularly apt mode for homilizing. While employing the idioms and speech of the local community, the homily is yet an art form that is to reflect the very beauty of God.

The homily is an act of public theology. While clearly an ecclesial event, intended to help enable a life-giving encounter between Jesus Christ and the baptized, in this digital age of growing religious pluriformity and disaffection, it seems appropriate to consider the homily in a more centrifugal mode as also an act of public theology. Public theology as envisioned by Christian theologians at the end of the twentieth century is not designed to win converts to a particular church or bolster the public standing of some denomination. Rather, public theology is a kind of theological speech which claims to point to publicly accessible truth and to contribute to public discussion by witnessing to a truth that is relevant to what is going on in the world and to the pressing issues facing peoples and societies today.

10. Even though there are several books on methods of preaching, it is hard to find a book that explains, "How can we prepare lectionary preaching?"

This is something I have explored in past publications. The excerpt and image below are reprinted from "The Lectionary and Holy Billiards," chapter 3 in *Preaching as Paying Attention*.[*]

> The Lectionary and Holy Billiards
>
> In the classic musical *The Music Man*, recently enjoying a celebrated revival on Broadway, the loveable huckster Harold Hill begins his public swindle of the folk of River City, Iowa with a romping tirade against the game of pool. "Ya got trouble" is widely recognized as one of the preeminent show stoppers in the history of the Great White Way and helped Robert Preston—the original Harold Hill—garner multiple awards for his performances on both stage and screen. While neither a pool prohibitionist nor advocate, when it comes to lectionary preaching I prefer billiards and the corresponding wisdom it offers.
>
> The object of the game of pool—also known as pocket billiards—is to sink the balls in one of the six pockets around the table's circumference. The game of eight-ball specifically requires players to

[*] Edward Foley, *Preaching as Paying Attention* (Chicago: Liturgical Training Publications, 2021), Edward Foley, © 2021. All rights reserved. Used with permission. Archdiocese of Chicago: Liturgy Training Publications. www.LTP.org.

call the shots they intend to make and then pocket either the solids (numbered 1 through 7) or the stripes (9 through 15), then finally the black 8-ball in order to win. Carom or French billiards, on the other hand, is played on a table with no pockets and only three balls: ordinarily two white and one red. One scores points in this game not by pocketing any balls, but by driving one of the white balls into both of the others in a single stroke. Thus, this table game requires a nuanced ability to calculate vectors in order to achieve the hoped-for ricochet. This task is rendered even more complex in three-cushion billiards. In this variation, the cue ball strikes one other ball and then three or more cushions before striking the second object ball. One wonders whether you need an advanced degree in Euclidean geometry or even calculus in order to be successful in this sport.

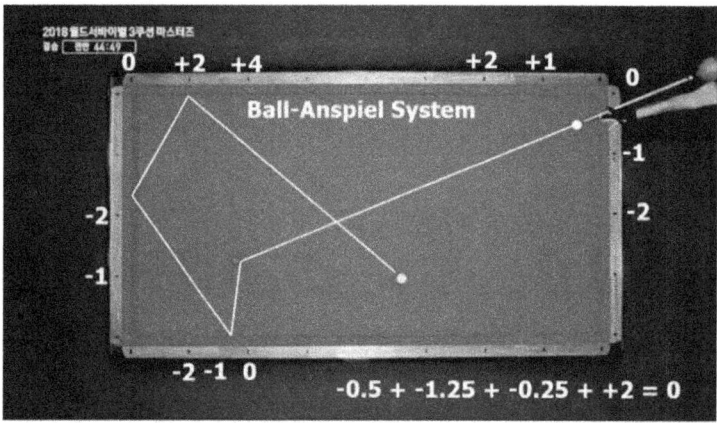

While crafting a homily rooted in the lectionary is not exactly playing billiards with God, it does require some homiletic calculus that can position the readings of the day so that they can metaphorically ricochet off one other for a more fulsome unfolding of God's word. Roman Catholics have had over a half century to become familiar with the structure of the reformed lectionary mandated by Vatican II. On a typical Sunday we are given a gospel from the designated synoptic writer for that liturgical year (e.g., Matthew for Cycle A), a first reading ordinarily chosen to somehow harmonize with that gospel, and a semi-continuous second reading that often has little to do with the narratives or themes of the other two readings. Then, of course, there is the Psalm. While the responsorial Psalm is most often considered to be a "response" to God's word, this somewhat misleading title does not diminish the fact that the Psalm is also God's word and thus an integral part of the scriptural assets that equip us for preaching.

One of the unusual aspects of the current lectionary that sometimes complicates our engagement in this holy billiards is the way that the scriptural texts have been edited for use at Mass. With some regularity our lectionary texts have been trimmed and cropped with particular verses and even large sections of a chapter either listed as optional or removed altogether. This is almost always the case with the responsorial Psalm and frequently occurs with the first reading in order to align it more closely with the Gospel. Not surprisingly, this approach has received much criticism. Some have simply rejected this form of scriptural surgery and crafted their own lectionaries as a corrective.

Our task as preachers in the Roman Catholic tradition is not to craft our own lectionary or redesign the Roman Missal. These are remarkable gifts to the universal Church that have largely achieved one key reforming goal of Vatican II: to open up more lavishly the treasures of the bible and provide God's people a "richer fare . . . at the table of God's Word" (*Constitution on the Sacred Liturgy*, no. 51). In the process, these newly configured resources call preachers to develop interpretative approaches to the lectionary that are related but not identical to the skills of biblical exegesis we may have learned in school.

Selected Bibliography

Foley, Edward, ed. *A Commentary on the Order of Mass of The Roman Missal: A New English Translation*. Minneapolis: Liturgical Press, 2011.

Foley, Edward. *Developmental Disabilities and Sacramental Access*. Eugene, OR: Wipf and Stock, 2020.

Foley, Edward. *Foundations of Christian Music*. Eugene, OR: Wipf and Stock, 2020.

Foley, Edward. *From Age to Age: How Christians Have Celebrated the Eucharist*. Minneapolis: Liturgical Press, 2016.

Foley, Edward. *Preaching as Paying Attention: Theological Reflection in the Pulpit*. Chicago: Liturgy Training Publications, 2021.

Foley, Edward, and Herbert Anderson. *Mighty Stories, Dangerous Rituals: Weaving Together the Human and the Divine*. San Francisco: Jossey-Bass, 2001.

4
FRANK SENN

Frank C. Senn was ordained as a minister of word and sacraments in the Evangelical Lutheran Church in America in 1969. He has served five congregations, including Immanuel Lutheran Church in Evanston, Illinois for twenty-three years. He earned a PhD in liturgical studies at the University of Notre Dame and has taught liturgy and sacraments at the Lutheran School of Theology at Chicago and Garrett-Evangelical Theological Seminary. As a global teacher, he has also offered courses in Singapore and Indonesia. Dr. Senn has served as president of the National Liturgical Conference and the North American Academy of Liturgy. He has contributed to the development of liturgical theology through many books and articles. Among his influential writings are *Christian Liturgy: Catholic and Evangelical* (1997), *New Creation: A Liturgical Worldview* (2000), and *Embodied Liturgy: Lessons in Christian Ritual* (2016).

Interview with Frank Senn

Hello, Professor Senn. Thank you for agreeing to this interview on behalf of myself and your readers. You contributed to the international study of Christian liturgy through numerous books, including *Christian Liturgy: Catholic and Evangelical* (Fortress Press, 1997). Moreover, you are known for your expertise in the history of worship. When I was at Calvin Seminary to do my master's program, Professor David Diephouse, who taught me history of worship, said that he was a secular historian. And I remember him saying, "If you want to learn the history of worship, look for Frank Senn in Chicago."

1. Are there any unique characteristics or methodologies for studying the history of worship that are different from general historical studies or church history studies?

Thank you for your introduction, Professor Moon. Liturgists who study the history of Christian liturgy need to know general church history and historical theology. When we study historical texts, we need to bring the same historical-critical methods to those texts as a historian would bring to any other historical text. But liturgists also need to know the social history of the churches and people who used those texts, because liturgy is more than texts. It is also actions and interactions that take place when the church gathers for worship. Moreover, liturgical documents are what Paul Bradshaw calls "living documents." They are always evolving through use. For example, look at the history of hymnals. Every new hymnal contains old and new hymns, and some of the old hymns get modified in texts and music. Worship books are the same: new prayers are added in the new book even as old prayers are retained. And the old prayers are amended for current use since language changes over time.

2. You wrote a social history of the liturgy, *The People's Work* (Fortress Press, 2006). How should we study the history of worship? It appears to be too broad.

You must base a general history of worship on the findings of research into local liturgies and then inquire whether there are general patterns between them. Sometimes liturgists in the past have painted the picture of worship in a particular historical period with too broad a brush. This was especially true in the study of ancient liturgy. The tendency today is to acknowledge local variations in liturgical rites.

3. In your opinion, what are some turning points in the history of worship?

There have been some major turning points. The legalization of Christian worship by Constantine the Great in 313 resulted in the relocation of the venue of liturgy from house churches into basilicas during the fourth century. The invention of printing with Gutenberg's moveable type press in the fifteenth century was another turning point because it made standardization of liturgical books possible. The Reformation in the sixteenth century created a profusion of different rites reflecting different confessional commitments (both Catholic and Protestant). Liturgical renewal in the mid-twentieth century led to an emphasis on the conscious participation of the people in their "public work" (as *leitourgia* came to be understood). This introduced the concept of "being culturally relevant." At the same time, what the late Methodist scholar James White called the American "frontier camp meeting ordo" became the basis of revival worship and contemporary worship that has spread around the world through evangelicalism, sometimes replacing historic orders of worship in many Protestant traditions.

4. Among conservative Christians, there seems to be a tendency to overemphasize the legacy of the past, saying, "Let's go back to the early church" and "let's imitate the Reformation." From a liturgical point of view, what do you think of these propositions?

I have seen this also in the Reformed church in Indonesia. There is a concern to recover the theologically solid roots of Christian worship that is thought to be lacking in the contemporary worship that is offered in many churches. Going back to the past, however, whether to the ancient church or the Reformation churches, is impossible, because the social settings of worship are different today from what they were in the past.

5. It seems that there are difficulties in studying the worship of the early church. For example, there are almost no worship documents from the first and second centuries, and it seems that there are not that many worship documents until the sixth century. Besides this, what other difficulties are there?

Well, we are not totally lacking worship documents from the first and second centuries. There is the *Didache* at the end of the first century and the *Apology* of Justin Martyr around 150, which provide texts as well as orders of baptism and Sunday liturgies of word and sacrament. Tertullian around 200 wrote detailed treatises on baptism, penance, and prayer. By the fourth century we have church orders, catechetical sermons by the bishops of the churches (examples: Cyril of Jerusalem, John Chrysostom,

Theodore of Mopsuestia, Ambrose of Milan) that explain the sacramental liturgies to the newly baptized, as well as the *Travel Diary* of the Spanish nun Egeria from her pilgrimage to the Holy Land in the 380s, and many references to liturgical practices from other sermons of the church fathers such as Augustine of Hippo. In terms of worship practices in the first two centuries, we know the pattern of the Greco-Roman symposium banquet that provides the cultural setting of the Christian eucharist as well as the Jewish Passover Seder. Also, the rituals of the Roman public bath are clearly replicated in the rituals of Christian initiation. It's true, however, that liturgical books with full texts of prayers are not found until later (I'd say the seventh and eighth centuries in both the East and the West). But what we do have provides a pretty full picture of Christian liturgies in different regional churches and in many languages. We tend to think of Greek and Latin as classical languages of Christian liturgy. But church orders are also found in Syriac (many!), Coptic, Ethiopic, Arabic, Armenian, Georgian, etc., and we see borrowings between churches.

6. If you study the worship service of the Reformation, you can see that the form of worship differs greatly among Reformers. For example, Luther, Zwingli, Calvin, and Bucer all had their own characteristics of worship. However, there seem to be cases where they strongly criticize other forms of worship, saying, "Reformed churches should worship like this." As you have studied the history of worship throughout your life, what do you think of this position?

Saying that "Reformed churches should worship like this" is a product of the post-Reformation period, the age of confessionalism when churches defined themselves over against one another. The liturgical orders of the great Reformers like Luther and Calvin carried great weight because of the theological stature of these Reformers, but as Lutheran and Calvinist orders were implemented in various territories and nations, they reflected the sensitivities of the local political situations. For example, John Knox did not just implement Calvin's liturgy in Scotland without paying attention to "conditions on the ground," as we say. For that matter, Calvin was far more influential outside of Geneva than within it. The Swedish Church pursued its liturgical development independent of the Lutheran church orders in Germany. Bucer was consulting with everyone, including the Anglicans.

7. **According to James White's chart of the evolution of worship in each denomination, it seems that Lutherans were the closest denomination to Roman Catholicism in the sixteenth century, but in the twenty-first century, Anglicans were closest to Catholicism, followed by Lutherans. Could you explain why there was such change?**

The simple answer is that the Lutheran Reformation wasn't interested in starting over but in purifying the tradition they had received. But in the eighteenth and nineteenth centuries Lutherans were influenced by rationalism and pietism, which reacted against ritualism, and many older practices were lost or changed. In the sixteenth century, Anglicans were influenced by Reformed practices, but in the nineteenth century the Oxford Movement helped some Anglicans to reclaim the Catholic tradition. Even so, there are many evangelical Anglicans in the world today and many catholic Lutherans. In North America, Anglicans/Episcopalians and Lutherans have very similar liturgical practices and sacramental practices.

8. **One of the characteristics of contemporary worship seems to be "consumer-centered worship." The traditional liturgy appears to have been streamlined and shifted towards a music-centric and culture-centric worship. As a liturgical scholar, what is your view on contemporary worship?**

Contemporary worship is no longer so "contemporary" since it's been around since the 1960s. Contemporary worship developed as an outreach to modern Western culture, especially the youth culture, and in the interest of church growth. It used the popular music styles the youth favored. Popular music styles changed over the decades from folk to rock and roll to heavy metal to whatever is popular now. The problem with contemporary worship is not so much the use of popular music, but that it diminishes proclamation of the word and the administration of the sacraments. Word and sacrament must be central in Christian worship. Worship that is a concert with a message is inadequate for Christian worship. That's why many young people, raised in evangelical churches with contemporary services, are looking for more substantial forms of worship. Some are even converting to Eastern Orthodoxy.

9. **In the twenty-first century, it seems that music plays a larger role in worship. I feel like music is valued more than the word or the sacrament in many churches. What do you think about this? What kind of music**

is suitable for worship? What are the requirements for a good hymn (or worship music)?

Protestants may be unaware that music has always had a big role in worship. In ancient times, texts were chanted, not spoken. That's how they were heard and memorized. In Eastern Byzantine and Oriental traditions, the entire liturgy is sung, including the scripture readings, as well as psalms, hymns, spiritual songs, and all prayers. The same was true in the Western Church until the Roman Mass was split between "high" (sung, public) mass and "low" (spoken, often private) mass. In historic Lutheranism, congregation and choir sang psalms and hymns; clergy chanted the scripture readings, prayers, and the Nicene Creed in Latin (unless the congregation sang the Creed in Luther's German metrical form); and the choir and organ added concerted church music. The prayer offices (liturgy of the hours), consisting primarily of psalms, were always sung throughout. In Anglicanism, choral Evensong is very popular. In the Reformed churches, the congregation sang metrical psalms. Isaac Watts got the English people singing hymns beyond the psalms. In Methodism and the revival meetings "gospel songs" became very popular. Charles Wesley wrote thousands of hymns.

In recent times contemporary worship introduced the idea of a song medley as "worship and praise" before the "message," although this pattern had already been established in the frontier revival "preliminaries" before the sermon. The difference between the historic liturgies and contemporary worship is that in liturgical worship music serves the word. It takes its place within and throughout the order of worship. Music is inseparable from the whole order of worship. In contemporary worship the song medley *is* the "worship." The term *worship* is being used in different ways between traditional and contemporary worship. In contemporary worship, only the songs are "worship." In liturgical worship everything in the order is worship, even the sermon.

A good hymn or worship music serves the word, even proclaims the word. Hymns are chosen to fit the liturgical day or season and relate to the assigned scripture readings in the lectionary. Hymns are also chosen according to their use in the order of worship: for example, entrance, response to the readings, during communion, closing. Hymns and worship music should reflect the corporate ("we") character of public worship rather than the individualistic ("I") character. Hymns and worship music should facilitate the singing of the congregation, supported by choir and instruments as needed.

10. Don't take this too seriously, but if you compare the chants of the early church and medieval church with contemporary rap, don't they have something in common in that they focus on the delivery of lyrics? Yet, chant is used in modern liturgical denominations while rap seems to be rejected. What difference is there between the two?

Yes, there is a chant-like character to rap. But the traditional chants were ways of singing biblical texts, such as psalms and canticles. Rap has stories to tell that come out of contemporary life experiences. All texted music is concerned with delivering lyrics, no matter the style. The issue is: what lyrics are being delivered? Maybe rap could be used for preaching.

11. Due to the COVID-19 pandemic, there were many difficulties with worship for believers around the world. From a historical point of view, what response did churches have during the plagues and pandemics of the past?

In the face of any pandemic, ancient, medieval, or modern, it is impossible for the church to carry on as usual. In the COVID-19 pandemic, modern technologies such as Zoom and livestream enabled the people of the church to stay connected in a way that was impossible in earlier times. But earlier Christians had a sense that natural disasters and diseases were the result of God's wrath, which means God's withholding of grace. Their response was to sing and pray psalms of lament and litanies, often in procession. Penitential processions through the streets of the town brought the words of Scripture to the people in their houses. They lamented their situation and prayed for God's intervention with his grace. These Christians were theologically more sophisticated than we have been during our plague. For example, even knowing that recent pandemics have resulted from the migration of viruses from animals to humans, we have had no discussion of this as a sign of our human alienation from nature and our poor stewardship of the creation. In the coronavirus pandemic and global warming, we are reaping what we have sown. We ought to have liturgies of lament and repentance.

12. After COVID-19, online worship became a hot topic in many churches. In the United States, I understand that there were many discussions in 2020. There may be different opinions, but what do you think of the claims of Theresa Berger, a worship scholar at Yale, who argues, "Online worship should be considered positively in temporal simultaneity instead of spatial simultaneity"?

There has been an advantage in online worship in terms of temporal simultaneity in that we could join others in prayer anywhere around the world. Zoom and livestream have been a boost in opportunities to pray the daily prayer offices of the church (Morning Prayer, Evening Prayer/ Vespers, Compline) with others in your congregation or in other congregations. Sunday services of the word and preaching have continued during the pandemic. But it has been a disaster for sacramental worship.

13. I would also like to discuss the debate about online communion. What are the problems with online communion from a liturgical point of view? If technology improved, would online communion be possible with wearable machines that allow virtual and augmented reality?

No, because Holy Communion involves sharing the same bread and cup and receiving these elements into our bodies. Without eating and drinking there is no Communion as our Lord instituted it in his Supper. Elements from the congregation's celebration can be shared by extended distribution, that is, taking the bread and wine to the absent (for example, the homebound and hospitalized). Roman Catholics have taught the value of spiritual Communion, that is, receiving the blessings of Communion by watching the celebration and desiring to receive. But this is not the fullness of the sacrament. Moreover, people cannot just use their own bread and wine at home and believe that it is consecrated by hearing or speaking the words of institution. As St. Paul wrote in 1 Corinthians 11:21, they are celebrating "their own supper," not the Lord's Supper. They are not "discerning the body," that is, the church assembled and eating and drinking together.

14. Another pandemic could happen again in the future. Considering this, how should churches prepare?

We have learned a lot from this experience. Science and governments will be better on top of the situation from the beginning. We will also understand the limits of human cooperation with the governing authorities and perhaps develop better ways of communicating what is happening and what needs to be done. Churches will be better prepared to follow mitigations that help to prevent rapid contagion. Many congregations and Christians have "put the Lord to the test" by ignoring masks and physical distancing and resisting vaccination.

15. What are the characteristics of Lutheran worship that set it apart from other denominations? There seem to be many Lutherans in worship studies. For example, Mark Johnson, who teaches at Notre Dame, and Gordon Lathrop, now retired. Is there any particular reason for this?

Lutherans have a rich liturgical and musical heritage that needs to be studied and taught. I mentioned above that rationalism and pietism had a negative effect on the liturgy in Lutheran churches. A number of Lutheran scholars have studied Lutheran liturgy and liturgy generally beginning in the late nineteenth century in an effort to restore and renew it. These pioneer liturgical scholars came to the study of liturgy from systematic theology, church history, music and the arts, and other related areas. The academic field of liturgical studies opened up only after the Second Vatican Council (1962–1965). The first school in the United States to offer a PhD in liturgical studies was the University of Notre Dame. I was the first Lutheran to earn a PhD in the liturgical studies program in the theology department, which had an ecumenical faculty. Other Lutherans followed me in the program. Like in Roman Catholic seminaries, professorships in liturgy and worship were established in Lutheran seminaries. Seminary positions in liturgy and worship were filled by Lutheran liturgists, several of whom received their PhD at Notre Dame. Lutherans have been very interested in the complex relationship between liturgy and culture, and several Lutheran liturgists contributed to the important Nairobi Statement on Worship and Culture adopted by the Lutheran World Federation in 1996 and the study books that led up to it.

16. I've seen statistics showing that there are about 3–7 million Lutherans in the United States now. That's a large number. Yet I've never seen or heard about a Lutheran megachurch. This tells me that the local churches have a small number of members, but the Lutheran churches collectively have many members. Is there a reason for this?

The current number of Lutherans in the United States in various Lutheran church bodies is probably around 6 million. You are correct that there are not many Lutheran megachurches—less than a dozen. Our most famous one was the Community of Joy in Scottsdale, Arizona, which had a congregation of 12,000. It has recently developed more of an interest in making disciples and left the ELCA and merged with Dream Church, which was formerly a Pentecostal Assemblies of God church. The concept of the megachurch comes out of the evangelical and Pentecostal revival movements that operate with what is called a "decision theology." (For example, making a "decision for Christ" as in the Billy Graham crusades.) This doesn't relate to the Lutheran emphasis that God made a decision for us in the death and resurrection of Christ, and we are initiated into Christ's death and resurrection in holy baptism. Lutheran congregations have focused on the means of grace, the word and the sacraments. We have some congregations with thousands of members, especially in Minnesota (Mount Olivet in Minneapolis has 14,000 members but isn't considered a megachurch, just a big congregation). These are traditional congregations that use some version of the Lutheran liturgy, even if some also have contemporary music. Most of our congregations are small, with only 50–100 people at worship. Our people value congregations in which people know and care for one another. We should also remember that most of these congregations were founded by immigrants from Germany and the Scandinavian countries. (Mount Olivet, for example, was founded by Swedish immigrants.) Ethnic culture may have limited Lutheran outreach, but it also provided a strong social bond that helped to keep people together.

17. It seemed like there were few young people and children when I visited the Lutheran Church. At this point when the next generation is disappearing in church, are there any alternatives being discussed at the denominational level?

When I arrived at Immanuel in 1990 the only young children belonged to our family and the organist's. But my pastoral predecessor had told the baby boomers that if they want to grow the congregation, they had better start having babies. They did. We had a number of children born into the congregation in my early years at Immanuel and even had an active youth group. By the time you visited twenty years later many of those kids had gone off to college. As a downtown church surrounded by high rise condos, we weren't in a community in which there would be a lot of families with young children moving in.

The reality is that the United States, like countries in Europe as well as several East Asian countries, is not replacing its population. The members of the millennial generation are marrying later in life and don't seem interested in procreation. Sheltering at home during COVID-19 didn't cause births to spike but actually depressed birth rates even further. Perhaps COVID anxieties were depressing libidos. The influx of new immigrants in the United States is not offsetting long term trends in fertility. This affects school populations and the workforce, as well as churches. For example, in spite of immigration into Chicago, the population of Chicago public schools plunged from 434,000 students in 2003 to 330,400 students in 2020. The whole state of Illinois has lost population over the last ten years.

As my predecessor said, if you want to grow the church, start having babies. I have no idea whether these demographic trends are being discussed in my denomination or any denomination. I'm a retired pastor. But I'm sure congregations will not flourish if they have more funerals than baptisms. Even the megachurches stand to lose members over the long haul if they don't convince their young members to get married and produce more children. This is the biggest issue. Young adults have usually drifted away from the church when they go off to the universities, but they returned to church to get married and raise their families. If young adults aren't getting married and having children, they're also not returning to church. Our congregations will continue to age. The one area where we see church growth is in the start-up of new immigrant congregations, mostly Hispanic, Asian, and African. We should become more welcoming of immigrants, employ the worship and culture principles of the Nairobi Statement, and learn more global music.

Selected Bibliography

Senn, Frank C. *Christian Liturgy: Catholic and Evangelical*. Minneapolis: Fortress, 1997.

Senn, Frank C. *Christian Worship and Its Cultural Setting*. Philadelphia: Fortress, 1983.

Senn, Frank C. *Embodied Liturgy: Lessons in Christian Ritual*. Minneapolis: Fortress, 2016.

Senn, Frank C. *Eucharistic Body*. Minneapolis: Fortress, 2017.

Senn, Frank C. *Introduction to Christian Liturgy*. Minneapolis: Fortress, 2012.

Senn, Frank C. *New Creation: A Liturgical Worldview*. Minneapolis: Fortress, 2000.

Senn, Frank C. *The People's Work: A Social History of the Liturgy*. Minneapolis: Fortress, 2006.

Senn, Frank C. *A Stewardship of the Mysteries*. New York: Paulist, 1999.

Senn, Frank C. *The Witness of the Worshiping Community: Liturgy and the Practice of Evangelism*. New York: Paulist, 1993.

5
LESTER RUTH

Lester Ruth is currently teaching worship at Duke University in Durham, North Carolina. He received an MDiv from Asbury Theological Seminary, a ThM from Candler School at Emory University, and later earned a doctorate from the University of Notre Dame with his work *A Little Heaven Below: Worship at Early Methodist Quarterly Meetings*. He has solid capabilities in research on the history of worship, has combined well his interest in contemporary culture, worship, and praise, and has published many theological and practical works necessary for the church of this era. Major works include *Early Methodist Life and Spirituality*, *A History of Contemporary Worship and Praise*, and *Lovin' On Jesus*.

Interview with Lester Ruth

Hello, Professor Ruth. It is a pleasure to meet you. I would like to express my sincere gratitude and respect to you for making a great contribution to academia while devoting yourself to the study of worship despite your busy schedule as a professor at Duke University. I believe that this interview about "contemporary worship" will be of great interest and help to today's churches.

1. Could you briefly introduce which fields of study you were in before becoming a liturgical theologian, please?

My college degree is in accounting. Before I was called into ministry, my intent was to go to law school and become a lawyer specializing in taxation. After college, I attended Asbury Theological Seminary and received a general Master of Divinity to prepare me for pastoral ministry. After seminary and before becoming a full-time worship professor, I was the pastor for several churches in Texas. I started working on specialized degrees in liturgical studies in 1987, receiving a Master of Theology on that topic from Candler School of Theology (Emory University) in 1988. I next attended the University of Notre Dame, receiving a Master of Arts and a PhD in liturgical studies in 1994 and 1996 respectively.

2. Was there any reason that led you to major in liturgical studies? Could you introduce some scholars or books that influenced your research, if there were any?

One reason was that I have always found liturgical studies such a personally satisfying topic with respect to my own spirituality. Although I grew up in a Methodist church and attended occasionally with my family, I was never attracted to its worship. It was more of a duty than a joy. At Asbury Seminary I was introduced to worship-related materials from the early church that had a vitality and spiritual richness that intrigued me. These materials were deeply biblical, strongly communal, deeply sacramental, and boldly proclaimed the Gospel of Jesus Christ and the wonder of God the Father's saving work. I found that combination fascinating and life-giving. One example of that sort of material would be the so-called *Apostolic Tradition* of Hippolytus from the third century. Later on, I discovered authors on worship that spoke of worship in such robust terms related to God's original created order and to the restoration of that order in the second coming of Jesus Christ. Such a vision has worship not simply as some peripheral thing that churches happen to do but places it as a critical part of what God is bringing about in his Son, Jesus Christ. To learn to worship in spirit and truth is thus part of God restoring our destiny, dignity, and vocation to us as humans. Along this line is the Eastern Orthodox theologian, Alexander Schmemann, and his work entitled *For the Life of the World*.

Another reason I have been drawn to liturgical studies is that my call to ministry from God has always had a strong element of assisting local congregations to be strong and faithful. Since worship is the lifeblood of every Christian congregation, any work that I do with respect to worship fulfills my original calling. I like to say I first was a pastor with an interest in worship history and later I became a worship historian who has maintained his pastoral concerns. The authors who have influenced me here would be almost all of my own professors, including James White, as well as innumerable scholars who were part of the twentieth century Liturgical Movement, especially a European theologian named Romano Guardini.

Finally, I have been drawn to liturgical studies because it has allowed me to reaffirm and deepen my sense of being part of my own tradition, which is Methodism or Wesleyanism. My doctoral dissertation was on the worship of early Methodists. Working on it, I read every diary and writing I could find from eighteenth-century Methodists. I was amazed by how much they struggled to find the words to talk about how gracious God had been to them when they worshiped. That deepened my commitment as a Wesleyan. If I wanted to point to one source, I think it would be Charles Wesley's *Hymns on the Lord's Supper*.

3. When we think about worship historians from Notre Dame, we tend to imagine studying ancient manuscripts in a Hogwarts-looking building from the Harry Potter movies—like your work on fourth-century worship in Jerusalem. Yet your main research is on contemporary worship. What motivated you to become interested in this field?

Part of my motivation comes from how impactful these new ways of contemporary worship were in my own journey as a disciple of Jesus Christ. I would say that I came to a living faith as part of a campus ministry when I was studying at my first university. It was the first time I had ever seen worship led by a guitar and the congregation singing simple Scripture choruses. Because of that positive experience, being able to work on contemporary worship as a scholar has never seemed like a foreign experience for me. From my own start as a Christian I know this world, feel comfortable within it, and am indebted to it.

Part of my attraction to contemporary worship grows out of my prior work in earlier forms of evangelical worship like the early Methodists I worked on in my dissertation. Since then, I have been interested in the worship of communities who tend to pray extemporaneously, who do not rely upon written worship resources, and who make worship decisions at the congregational level.

Finally, there was one event at Notre Dame that sparked my interest. A classmate, John Witvliet, brought a book to campus one day by a Pentecostal author. The book was entitled *God's Presence Through Music* and the author was Ruth Ann Ashton. It was a discussion of how the tabernacle of Moses provided a template for how to put together a worship service through congregational singing. I remember wondering this question: "Where does this approach come from?" For over twenty years I have pondered that question until my recent research with Dr. Lim Swee Hong has answered it.

4. What are the differences and commonalities between ancient worship and contemporary worship?

One of the biggest commonalities between ancient ways of worship and modern (or contemporary) worship is that the praise of God is such an important part of the services. If you look at all classic forms of Christian worship, what they include over and over again is praising and honoring God. Contemporary worship, especially in its early forms and in its best examples, has done the same. Indeed, common names for this form of worship highlights this significance either in the phrase "Praise and Worship" or "Worship and Praise."

Another big commonality is that both ancient worship and contemporary worship have highlighted the significance of the full participation of the whole people of God. If you take a look at descriptions of ancient worship, you will see that it was loud, boisterous, and with deep vocal engagement of the people. Contemporary worship at its best has done the same. (I am a little concerned when the operation of the sound system drowns out the congregation's voice while singing.)

I see three big points of difference between ancient and contemporary worship. The first is the breadth and fullness of what is remembered about God's activity. Ancient services on the whole had more content about God's activity with Israel before the coming of Jesus, more content about the events in the life of Jesus, and much more content about expecting the return of Jesus Christ. Ancient services also followed the apostolic pattern seen in the New Testament of making God the Father the primary recipient of worship and prayer. In many modern congregations I visit, Jesus Christ has become the primary recipient of praise and worship and the main divine figure to whom prayer is addressed. If there was more time, I could go into some of the historical reasons for this shift. Finally, ancient services placed more emphasis on baptism and the Lord's Supper as critical for both the individual disciple as well as the church community.

5. Your book *Worshiping with the Anaheim Vineyard: The Emergence of Contemporary Worship* has been translated into Korean. Personally, I enjoyed reading this book very much. Could you provide a brief introduction to this book for the reader?

I am happy to provide this introduction. This book is a case study of one congregation in California. Through interviews, unpublished materials, and materials that were once published but are now hard to find, we tell the history of what worship in this congregation was like, starting with its first days as a home Bible study and ending when the congregation was beginning to achieve megachurch status of several thousand worshipers. The congregation is important because it and its pastor, John Wimber, became the leaders in a new denomination, the Vineyard Fellowships. They also helped spread some ideas through teaching and songs that are now widespread in contemporary worship. Perhaps one of the most commonplace is the notion of worship as intimacy with God.

6. I think the book *A History of Contemporary Praise and Worship* that you wrote two years ago should be translated and introduced in Korea. Please introduce this book for readers.

This book, which I worked on with Dr. Lim Swee Hong who is originally from Singapore, is our attempt to tell the broad historical foundations of this new way of band-based worship. We do so not by emphasizing and focusing on the music as the way to tell the history. That approach has already been done. Instead, we focus on the wrestling with Scripture that the originators and promoters were doing. Thus, a new question comes to the center of how contemporary praise and worship emerged and spread. That new question is, "What guidance does the Bible provide about how we should worship?" Half of the book is about the people who emphasized Psalm 22:3, which speaks of God inhabiting the praises of his people, and how this notion more fully developed as a theology of worship that connects praising God and experiencing God's presence. This became the driving force in the development of contemporary praise and worship. The other half of the book is about another driving force. It is about those historical figures who became concerned that older forms of worship were out of touch with modern, contemporary people. Their scriptural touchstone was 1 Corinthians 9:22, in which the apostle Paul talks about adapting himself and his ministry in order to be able to reach a range of people well. And so, this other half of the history is about the impulse toward creativity and adaptation so that worship was appealing to people who otherwise cared little about worship and about hearing the Gospel.

7. I would like to share a few words about the book *Worshiping with the Anaheim Vineyard: The Emergence of Contemporary Worship*. Most traditional churches with conservative theology have a negative evaluation of the Vineyard Movement. The issue is mainly related to their doctrine of pneumatology. However, the book clearly depicts how their worship started and developed as a way of expressing intimacy and love with God. They expected to work in the presence and power of the Holy Spirit. Could you tell us some pros and cons of their worship, please?

Thank you for asking me this question. As a worship historian, I think there is always something to be learned from every historical example of worship even if we disagree with that historical church in significant other ways. With respect to this congregation, I think one of the biggest pros to how they worship is their early teaching on worship that stressed worship as involving love for God. In a fundamental way, it is hard to argue with that emphasis, since loving God is one of the two key commandments that Jesus emphasized in his teaching. I especially think of the emphasis on love for God as a motivation to want to worship. They thought that a love for God had to be cultivated in someone first before expecting them to want to worship and to be able to participate fully in worship. I think there is a perceptive insight here.

I also applaud the quality of the congregational singing. When the congregation sang, the sound was strong, loud, and appealing. Strong worship by a congregation can be its own form of evangelism (see 1 Corinthians 14) and it was in this congregation. Part of the background to this strength was in how they provided members opportunities for small group worship outside of Sunday morning. It was in the small groups that members learned the song repertoire and thus enabled them to sing it robustly when assembled on Sunday (even without being provided with the lyrics). These small groups also enhanced the quality of the fellowship of the people as a backdrop to worship. The people actually knew and loved each other.

When teaching, I often suggest that a congregation's strength in worship is often connected to a weakness in its worship, too. I think that is the case here. While I celebrate their emphasis on love, I think it is a weakness that the teaching was too dependent upon images and metaphors from cultural ways of speaking about romantic love. In the United States, those sorts of images can be too dependent upon feelings and thus miss a fuller biblical way of speaking about love for God.

8. The style of Vineyard's worship and music has had a huge impact on the whole world and across denominations. In other words, regardless of the denomination, band-style worship music seems to dominate the first half of worship. The same goes for the worship services of the Presbyterian Church in Korea. How can we evaluate this current situation? Looking back on the history of worship, has there ever been a time when the importance of music was as great as it is now?

This question is a difficult one since music in one form or another has almost always been important in Christian worship. There are only a few exceptions where it has not. I can think of several instances in which music was as important. One is the first centuries of the church in which robust unison singing without harmony and without instruments was an important way in which congregations expressed their unity in Jesus Christ. Another instance is the golden period of chanting Psalms in monasteries during the Middle Ages. For the monks and nuns involved in the multiple times of prayer services during the days, this musical expression of the Psalms was a key way in which this part of the Bible began to dwell deeply in their souls. Another instance is in the sixteenth-century Reformation, especially among Reformed congregations following John Calvin. In these congregations the singing of new settings of the Psalms restored strong congregational singing for the first time in many centuries. And I could point to my own Methodist tradition. Active, lively singing of hymns (not scriptural texts like the Psalms) was a means by which God was active in touching those people.

That does not mean that there are no differences to what is happening today. For one thing, very long times of congregational singing in which the songs go from one to another is a novelty. In some early instances of contemporary praise and worship, these periods could last for an hour. That length of time is unusual in the history of Christian worship.

So is associating so strongly the making of music with experiencing God's presence. In some lines of contemporary praise and worship, music has almost become the primary sacrament or means of grace. By that I mean that it is in the singing that people most regularly expect to experience God's presence. One of your questions later comes back to this point and so I won't say more here.

Finally, the equation that some people make between the words *music* and *worship* is also novel in the history of worship. I really do not know of another time in Christian worship history when people would say "worship" and all that they meant was the time of making music.

9. Under the influence of Vineyard, it seems the interest in the work of the Holy Spirit, the gifts of the Spirit, and healing ministry have increased. While I stayed in the United States, I visited churches of various denominations and several of them offered "healing worship." Those churches were not Pentecostal. I wonder what kind of position many major denominations in the United States take on "healing," Vineyard, and New Apostolic worship.

I think what you are seeing is the impact of an earlier movement in the United States called the Charismatic Renewal movement. Starting in the 1950s and picking up energy in the 1960s and 1970s, this movement allowed several traditional Pentecostal emphases like healing to enter into more traditional denominations like Methodist, Anglican, Roman Catholic, and Presbyterian. Nearly all non-Pentecostal denominations in the United States had some influence from the Charismatic Renewal movement, although the level of impact was different depending upon the specific denomination and the specific congregation.

10. I would like to ask you a question about your coauthored book, *Flow*. Why is "flow" so important in worship? Looking at the history of worship, what have our parents and ancestors in the faith contributed to this "flow"? How can we facilitate flow in worship?

Flow in worship is important for several reasons. The foremost reason is that having good flow in a service puts the emphasis upon the *activity* or *actions* of worship. Without good flow, an order of worship can seem too much like a business meeting where every item of business is an independent thing. Individual acts of worship are not independent things like items on a business meeting agenda. Acts of worship are opportunities for God's people to interact with God and with each other.

Another reason why flow is important is that unnecessary breaks in the flow in terms of a waste of time dull the spiritual senses to discern the deeper spiritual realities of worship. I know of one church, for example, that uses lay readers to read the Bible passages every Sunday. The readers are not conveniently placed to the microphone. Time is wasted while they walk the length of the space from their seat to the microphone. The congregation's attention is thus diverted unnecessarily from seeing these readings as a word from God to a time of paying attention to the human readers.

Another reason why flow is important is the way our cultures have shaped our perception of group events. For better or worse, most Christians today live in cultures heavily saturated with easily viewed types of entertainment. In entertainment that is well done, the presentation is usually done so that one thing leads to another quickly and seamlessly and one activity leads to the next in the same way. When there are unnecessary or unintentional breaks, people think something is wrong or become bored. The same can happen in worship.

In the history of worship, having good flow has come and gone. In the earliest centuries of the church, the culture of worship was an oral culture and there was little dependence upon having anything written down except for the Scriptures, of course. In oral cultures transitions between activities can seem natural and spontaneous. Early descriptions of Christian worship seem to show that. A big change occurred in the last one hundred years as individual congregations got machines that allowed them to mass produce worship bulletins containing the order of worship for that Sunday and place them in the hands of each worshiper. Seeing the order of worship look like a list on a piece of paper can lead worshipers to think of each act of worship as a separate item.

On the one hand, good flow can come about by being well planned, especially in terms of transitions (both physical and spoken) between acts of worship. On the other hand, good flow also requires sensitivity to what is happening in the service between God and the people, a sensitivity that sometimes requires improvising or speaking spontaneously at that moment.

11. You mentioned that when we study ancient Christian worship, we can find more similarities to contemporary worship than traditional worship. I think many readers might strongly disagree with this. Could you explain a bit more about what you mean?

Allow me to begin with your last question first. The point we are trying to make in saying that there are similarities between contemporary worship and ancient worship is to undercut the notion that the ancient church, which contributed so many fundamental things to Christian liturgy like orders of worship, the Christian calendar, and an emphasis on sacraments, had the same style or feel to worship as we presume from recent "traditional worship" churches. In other words, we often presume that the style of ancient worship was like the style of traditional churches: reverence was shown by being quiet, being physically passive, doing only one thing at a time, using well-written worship texts, and having everything done in a nice, clear sequence in which there are clear starts and stops to each act of worship.

But these are wrong presumptions. This style or way of worship only developed later. The worship of churches through the first several centuries in the history of Christian worship was loud, boisterous, and physically expressive. And, in the earliest centuries, it showed three characteristics that are central to contemporary worship: (1) There was a timelessness in that the end of acts of worship was not predetermined. Thus, worship leaders in the ancient church (as worship leaders in contemporary services now do today) had to be attentive to when it seemed fitting to bring something to a close. (2) The spoken prayers were done extemporaneously without having any written prayer texts. Thus, worship leaders in the ancient church (as with contemporary worship leaders) were expected to be able to pray well, doing spontaneous creation of the prayers. And (3), the emphasis in leading worship was on important worship activities that flowed naturally and quickly from one to the next. The stop-and-go nature of many worship bulletins for traditional worship and the jerky nature in which some of those services are led would have seemed foreign to the ancient church. It is in contemporary services where I see this ancient concern for a good flow between acts of worship.

12. Some people would say that "contemporary worship" is no longer contemporary in the year 2022. What style of worship is in the spotlight now? Although there are many different denominations in North America, is there a general trend in today's worship?

These are very difficult questions. I find these questions difficult partly because I do not think there has been a major shift in worship like we saw in the period between the mid-1960s and the mid-1990s. Much of what I see today is just a continuation of that prior shift at a core level even if it might look a little different today than it did several decades ago. Having said that, I do think one thing that has developed is that there is a centralization and industrialization of songwriting today unlike what we had prior to the mid-1990s. Most of the top songs in contemporary or modern worship tend to come from a small group of songwriters, who are often associated with certain really large churches.

Another reason that I find these questions difficult is that I have not been able to travel as much and visit as many churches since the COVID-19 pandemic started. My level of awareness is not as great as it was three years ago.

Having acknowledged the difficulties, I can point to two things that I think are continuing to develop. Both are related to technology. Just like in general culture, technology continues to advance and become more sophisticated even as its relative cost decreases. And so, the technology used in worship is becoming more widespread in terms of the numbers of congregations using electronic technology like projection and is becoming more sophisticated even as churches explore what it can do. The second technologically related development is that the pandemic has brought a huge increase to the number of churches that are now providing access to their worship services in some kind of online format. Even small churches like my home church are concerned about making sure people who cannot come or who want to visit online first have the opportunity to see our services streamed on Facebook.

12. In the case of the United Methodist Church, to which you belong, there is a deep understanding of the liturgy and broad familiarity with liturgical worship among Protestant churches. When looking at the United Methodist Church as a whole, what do you think the ratio of Sunday morning worship services is among traditional, contemporary, and blended worship?

That ratio is hard to tell because in many places and with many people "contemporary" worship has become their new tradition. They just expect certain things from the "contemporary worship" world to be found more broadly. And so, I think United Methodist worship is getting more blended even if that term *blended* is not used.

But there are still quite a few United Methodist churches that have separate traditional and contemporary services. To have both is very common, whereas thirty years ago contemporary services were still novel. Generally, what I see in the United Methodist Church is that congregations that have been in existence for thirty years or more tend to have at least a traditional service and perhaps both a traditional and contemporary service. New congregations that have started within the last thirty years tend to have contemporary worship only. Of course, there are exceptions to those tendencies.

13. I learned a lot from your article "A Rose by Any Other Name," published in *The Conviction of Things Not Seen*. In this article, you present a theological reflection on how to classify the worship services of various modern churches. In addition to the common classifications of "traditional, modern, and blended worship," you also suggest a unique taxonomy based on James White's historical taxonomy. I'd appreciate it if you could explain your style of classification for the readers.

I am glad to provide this explanation for the readers. James White's taxonomy uses a political metaphor to provide the categories for developing his taxonomy. By more "conservative" Protestant liturgical traditions, he means whether the tradition is closer to Roman Catholic ways of worship and by more "liberal" Protestant worship traditions he means traditions that are farther from Roman Catholic worship. (He does not mean at all that Protestants who are liturgically "conservative" are also conservative with respect to politics.)

By these labels he creates a taxonomy that is very useful for understanding the differences in Protestant ways of worship, especially with respect to the origins and first years of a particular Protestant way of worship. In his full taxonomy, he has nine different Protestant liturgical traditions, starting with the more conservative and going to the more liberal: Lutheran, Anglican, Reformed, Methodist, Puritan, Anabaptists, Frontier, Pentecostal, and Quaker.

For me the problem with White's taxonomy is its limited usefulness in describing different ways of Protestant worship now. For one thing, there are no more Puritans by that name. For another thing, it does not account for several important commonalities and points of difference in Protestant ways of worship now. Moreover, White's labels for different ways of worship are hard to match with labels derived from looking at current worship styles.

And so, I developed an alternative way of trying to label and distinguish between Protestant ways of worship. I developed this alternative taxonomy by identifying three points at which I see Protestants actually having different approaches to worship. One point deals with the content of worship, specifically the story about God's saving activity. There are worship services whose content stresses the personal or individual nature of God's dealings. I call those "personal-story" churches. In contrast, there are churches whose worship content highlights the larger, more cosmic nature of God's actions. I call those "cosmic-story" churches. In contemporary worship services, I usually find a very strong "personal-story" approach.

The second point of difference deals with how worship decisions are made and the authority that individual congregations can claim for themselves. This point is thus about liturgical polity. Congregational polity churches are able to determine everything for themselves. In contrast, connectional polity churches have things like denomination-wide worship books or music books that they start with and have to be accountable for.

Finally, there are differences about where the worshiping people most commonly expect to find the presence of God in worship. I assess this point of difference by looking at where congregations spend most of their time in the service, what gets the best sight lines, and what gets the greatest allocation of resources. That usually indicates where the people expect to experience the presence of God. This connection to experiencing God's presence in worship is why I label this point of difference as being about the "sacramental principle." I see three main choices: a musical sacramental principle; a word sacramental principle; and a sacrament (i.e. the Lord's Supper) sacramental principle. If I was to redo my original article today, I would add a fourth: a fellowship sacramental principle, meaning the people look to their own fellowship as the primary place they expect to encounter God.

14. When you use the phrase "sacramental principle" in your taxonomy, are you referring specifically to the sacraments, or to something broader?

The important thing to remember is that by the word *sacramental* in the phrase "sacramental principle" I don't always mean *the* sacraments of baptism and the Lord's Supper. I mean something broader: the normal means by which people experience God's presence and activity in worship and expect to experience God's presence.

15. I couldn't agree more with your words, "there are churches whose services balance music-organized and Word-organized sacramentalities and churches whose services balance Word-organized and

table-organized sacramentalities. Less likely are churches that combine music-organized and table-organized sacramentalities. Less likely, too, are churches that combine all three." Unfortunately, it is the same for Korea. What do you think is the reason for this situation?

The reason that there are lots of music- and word-organized churches on the one hand and music- and table-organized churches on the other hand is due to continuing trajectories for Protestant and Roman Catholic worship from the sixteenth century. Protestant forms of worship usually lost a weekly emphasis on Communion and placed their emphasis on the reading and preaching of Scripture and on congregational singing, thus becoming music- and word-organized churches. Just consider how much space, good sight lines, and resources are given to music making and preaching in most Protestant congregations. If Protestant worship in Korea is like this, it is because this is the form of worship that the first Protestant missionaries brought with them to Korea.

In contrast, Roman Catholic worship has always emphasized the Lord's Supper (known as the Eucharist) and has been making strides in restoring strong congregational singing or other music making. What has been harder for Catholicism, with some exceptions, is the expectation of strong biblical preaching from all of its pastors. Thus, I would say that Roman Catholic worship has tended to be music- and sacrament-organized, with a much stronger emphasis upon the sacrament.

16. What is your opinion on calling it "traditional worship" before contemporary worship appeared? What are the positive aspects and weak points? I would also like to hear what kind of worship you are ultimately pursuing, please.

What many Protestants call "traditional worship" is not really all that traditional when compared against a broader history. That comparison can take place at either the level of a particular liturgical tradition's broad history or at the level of comparing against ancient practices. For example, there are several significant ways in which either "traditional" Presbyterian or Methodist worship of the twentieth century is not really like the ways Presbyterians or Methodists worshiped in earlier centuries. Specifically, earlier Presbyterians would have received Communion while seated around tables in order to emphasize the meal quality of the Lord's Supper. In addition, Communion was often done yearly but followed a period of intense spiritual preparation and examination. (That is why revivals sometimes broke out at times of Communion in individual congregations.) Or consider Methodists. Early Methodist worship tended to be very loud and boisterous with all the singing done fervently but without any musical instrument. A sedate form of Methodist worship where quiet and physical passivity was considered reverent is a development of the late nineteenth century. What should be considered true traditional worship for a Methodist or Presbyterian? The way it originally was done or the way that it was done at the beginning of the twentieth century?

In addition, any of the Protestant ways of worship are very different in several significant respects with what Christian worship was like in the first five centuries of church history. Should a way of worship practiced in the twentieth century be called "traditional" if it differs significantly from the worship of the earliest Christians? The difficulty in answering these questions is why I say that so-called "traditional worship" is often not all that traditional in actuality.

As for the kind of worship I am pursuing, I most appreciate services that tell a full and robust story of God's activity in Jesus Christ. I want to hear about God's activity before Jesus, God's activity during the life and ministry of Jesus (with an emphasis upon his death and resurrection), God's activity now, and God's activity when Jesus returns. Every aspect cannot be explored exhaustively in every service, but every worship service could give a sense that there is this breadth and scope of the story and should unfold it over time.

I also am drawn to services that have a full and rich prayer life in the services. There is lots of prayer and lots of different kinds of prayer. And when prayers are read from a book, those who lead the prayer do more than just read what is written; they actually are in awe of the opportunity and stewardship of talking to the living God. In terms of the breadth of prayer, I also appreciate it greatly when a congregation intercedes for the world broadly, not just their own felt needs. We are a priestly people and we have a stewardship to intercede for the world.

I also desire a robust sacramental life in a congregation. Tying administration of the sacraments to the church year is an easy way to reinforce their connection to major saving events in the ministry of Jesus. Connecting baptism and the Lord's Supper to an actual loving fellowship of people and to the ministry of preaching are other ways to achieve robustness. I am not talking about having to have a lot of formality or ceremony.

Finally, I am drawn to services in which there is strong congregational participation, especially in the singing. We humans were made for this:

to praise and worship God, not just watch someone else doing it. I think there is particular spiritual power in hearing a congregation that is singing with great strength. For me personally as a worshiper, I can best participate in a service in which the music includes some sort of rhythm section, whether a bass guitar or a drum kit.

Selected Bibliography

Park, Andy, Lester Ruth, and Cindy Rethmeier. *Worshiping with the Anaheim Vineyard: The Emergence of Contemporary Worship*. Grand Rapids: Eerdmans, 2017.

Ruth, Lester. *Early Methodist Life and Spirituality: A Reader*. Nashville: Kingswood Books, 2005.

Ruth, Lester, ed. *Essays on the History of Contemporary Praise and Worship*. Eugene: Pickwick, 2020.

Ruth, Lester, ed. *Flow: The Ancient Way to Do Contemporary Worship*. Nashville: Abingdon, 2020.

Ruth, Lester. *A Little Heaven Below: Worship at Early Methodist Quarterly Meetings*. Nashville: Kingswood Books, 2000.

Ruth, Lester. *Longing for Jesus: Worship at a Black Holiness Church in Mississippi, 1895–1913*. Grand Rapids: Eerdmans, 2013.

Ruth, Lester. "A Rose by Any Other Name." In *The Conviction of Things Not Seen: Worship and Ministry in the 21st Century*, edited by Todd E. Johnson. Grand Rapids: Brazos, 2002.

Ruth, Lester, and Lim Swee Hong. *A History of Contemporary Praise and Worship: Understanding the Ideas That Reshaped the Protestant Church*. Grand Rapids: Baker Academic, 2021.

Ruth, Lester, and Lim Swee Hong. *Lovin' on Jesus: A Concise History of Contemporary Worship*: Nashville: Abingdon, 2017.

Ruth, Lester, Carrie Steenwyk, and John D. Witvliet. *Walking Where Jesus Walked: Worship in Fourth-Century Jerusalem*. Grand Rapids: Eerdmans, 2010.

6
MELANIE ROSS

Melanie Ross majored in music education at Messiah College, pursued a master's degree in religious studies at Yale University, and obtained a doctorate in liturgical studies from the University of Notre Dame in Indiana. Since 2012, she has served as Professor of Liturgical Studies at Yale University and is currently recognized as one of the most prominent scholars in North American worship studies.

Particularly noteworthy is her book *Evangelical Worship: An American Mosaic*, published by Oxford University Press in 2021. This work has garnered significant attention and admiration not only from liturgical scholars but also from lay and nonspecialist readers in North America.

Dr. Ross is widely recognized as a leading figure who will guide the liturgical studies community in the future. While researching the history and theology of evangelical worship, she is also engaged in the significant task of seeking reconciliation between liturgical worship and evangelical worship. She is a scholar whose future research and contributions are eagerly anticipated.

Interview with Melanie Ross

Hello, Professor Ross. It is a great pleasure to speak with you. I would like to express my deep appreciation for your contributions to the field of worship studies, particularly for your work bridging evangelical and liturgical traditions. Your scholarship—especially your recent book *Evangelical Worship: An American Mosaic*—has provided insightful perspectives for both academics and church leaders alike. I believe this conversation will be a meaningful opportunity for many readers to better understand the richness and complexity of evangelical worship today.

1. Yale Divinity School has an Institute of Sacred Music in the master's program. Would it be good for students who are interested in worship studies, or is it a specialized course for music majors?

Yale has an Institute of Sacred Music (ISM), which is an interdisciplinary graduate center dedicated to the study and practice of sacred music, worship, and the arts. Students admitted to the ISM are jointly admitted to either Yale Divinity School or Yale School of Music, from which they receive their degrees. Our students have many interests—some of them are musicians, but we also have many who come to study visual arts, literature, and liturgical studies. All students create connections between their chosen fields and explore the role of the arts in human flourishing. For example, church musicians learn more about the theological and liturgical contexts of the traditions in which they will work. Musicians learn not only the notes on a page for a Bach aria or work of Britten or Palestrina, but also the importance of the sacred texts on which these works are based. Pastors learn to make connections between theology and the arts in order to enhance their ministries. The liturgical studies program offers a sustained and broad-ranging education in historical, theological, and practical aspects of worship. We offer lots of electives to ensure that students not only gain a broad understanding of worship and approaches to its study, but also that they encounter the remarkable diversity of liturgical patterns in the Christian tradition.

2. Could you tell me about the academic tradition of Yale's liturgical studies department? What are some of the distinctive features that differentiate Yale's liturgical theology department from other universities, such as the University of Notre Dame?

Our liturgical studies students study all practices of worship—textual and nontextual. So, you may find us interrogating practices of liturgical dance just as much as ancient manuscripts that offer prayers from the fourth or fifth centuries. We inquire into the past of liturgical practices, and because we are a part of a divinity school, we also talk about theological claims and meanings in worship. How do we study these things? There are dominantly three approaches: (1) a historical approach that asks, "What actually happened and what can we know?" (2) a theological approach that asks questions about the God-sustained truth in worship practices, and (3) a practice-oriented approach that asks, "What happens on a Sunday morning and what could we do better? What could happen differently?" In many ways, our program is very similar to that of Notre Dame, but a major difference between them is that Notre Dame offers a PhD in liturgical studies, while Yale's highest degree is a masters.

I owe a tremendous debt to the scholars who studied evangelical worship before me—particularly James F. White, who in the 1990s was one of the first liturgical scholars to insist that evangelical worship was a phenomenon worthy of academic study. I've also been deeply influenced by scholars like Todd Johnson, Lester Ruth, and John Witvliet: giants in the field who have studied evangelical worship much longer than I have, and on whose shoulders I stand.

I think there are at least three unique things that have shaped my intellectual journey and might make my work interesting to others. The first is my ecclesial tradition. Many of the scholars who paved the way before me had strong ties to a denominational tradition: Wesleyan, Reformed, etc. By contrast, I grew up in a nondenominational church, and I'm still keenly interested in ecclesial communities that are "generically evangelical"—they are self-governing, more focused on biblical principles than denominational polity rituals.

A second, related, thing that makes my work unique is that I am committed to the method of liturgical ethnography. In addition to studying the historical evolution of a church's liturgical rites and the systematic theologies that govern their worship, I spend time "on the ground" in local congregations, talking with leaders and congregants to better understand the culture that shapes their practices. These small, circumscribed, closely grained studies of evangelical worship are vital, especially for understanding communities that don't rely on ritual texts like a Book of Common Prayer for the structure and content of their services.

Finally, I am committed to ecumenical dialogue across lines of difference. I've studied at evangelical, mainline Protestant, and Roman Catholic universities, and I believe strongly in what the scholar Richard Mouw has called a "hermeneutic of charity" over a "hermeneutic of suspicion." Good scholarship will always give the other at least some benefit of the doubt, especially when that "other" is a fellow Christian. No matter how much I might disagree with another Christian, I must remember that above all, my sisters and brothers want to be faithful followers of Jesus. I hope that this spirit of generosity always shines through in my writing.

3. Some liturgical theologians, for example, Gordon Lathrop and Frank Senn, point out the weaknesses of the worship in Evangelical churches or megachurches. That is to say, like American religion in general, their worship tends to be individualistic and gnostic. What do you think about this claim?

In the past, some liturgical theologians have argued that evangelical worship tends towards Gnosticism because it celebrates individuals and their processes of decision-making and because it is overly concerned with salvation and the escape of the fleshly conditions of life.

I find the comparison of Gnosticism and evangelicalism problematic on a number of accounts. If you read the gnostic gospels, you discover that they are comprised mostly of post-resurrection collections about the sayings of Jesus, and that these sayings challenge, puzzle, and even provide conflicting information about a given subject. The topics shift rapidly, with little meaningful connection between them, and the community that develops in this gospel is in no way analogous to a church.

The evangelical churches I have studied are much more incarnational. For example, one of them developed the motto: "Becoming like Jesus, head, heart, hands, knees and feet." This theological position rejects Gnosticism and affirms the post-Vatican II emphasis that spirit and flesh, body and soul, are not competitors.

4. Could you give an example? What do you think are the strengths and weaknesses of evangelical worship and liturgical worship?

I think a helpful analogy for considering the relationship of evangelical churches to liturgical churches is to think about the relationship between the Synoptic Gospels and the book of John.

Synoptic is the Greek word meaning "having one view," and there is indeed a clearly discernible relationship among the first three gospels. However, the Fourth Gospel overlaps with the Synoptics in only about ten percent of its material and has been dubbed the "nonconformist Gospel of the bunch." John represents an adventuresome Christianity which freely goes its own way and explores new avenues of expression. (For more on this, see Raymond Brown's book, *The Churches the Apostles Left Behind*.)

The Synoptic Gospels describe Jesus as the builder, founder, or cornerstone of the church. By contrast, John prefers more personal images: Jesus is the shepherd who tends to the sheep that belong to him by name. Jesus is the vine from which Christians receive life.

The Fourth Gospel is best understood in conversation with the unified witness of the Synoptics. Similarly, evangelical Christianity stands in need of important correctives from the unified witness of the liturgical traditions. For example, a strictly "me and Jesus" spirituality could cause evangelicals to question whether there is any real need for community, corporate liturgy, or sacraments. At the same time, the Gospel of John reminds readers of the Synoptic Gospels that an individual relationship with Jesus is a necessary component of sound ecclesiology. In the same way, evangelical churches can remind other traditions that in addition to providing pastoral care, liturgy, and sacraments, a church must bring people into some personal contact with Jesus so that they can experience in their own way what made people follow him in the first place.

Seen through this Johannine-Synoptic lens, my hope is that the relationship between evangelical and liturgical churches can be seen as mutually encouraging and mutually corrective.

5. In your recently edited book, *Historical Foundations of Worship: Catholic, Orthodox, and Protestant Perspectives*, the chapter entitled "Evangelical Practices of Worship" was short but very impressive. Even in the evangelical camp, there are positions that emphasize pragmatic and methodological practices in worship, such as Charles Finney (and later megachurch movements such as Willow Creek), and positions that emphasize the essence of worship more, such as John Williamson Nevin and Tozer. You compared them historically, and it naturally makes us think about which path we should take. What do you think of Charles Finney's or the megachurch's claims about worship? What are their pros and cons?

One of the great challenges megachurches face is that of making a Sunday morning worship experience engaging—even entertaining—for thousands of churchgoers without watering down the theological message. James K. Wellman Jr., Katie E. Corcoran, and Kate J. Stockly address precisely this dilemma in their seminal work, *High on God: How Megachurches Won the*

Heart of America. Integral to their argument is the work of sociologist Émile Durkheim, who posits a fundamental paradox: as *homo duplex*, humans desire to be unique autonomous beings, but we can only accomplish this in and through community. Megachurches "work" not because they help people reason their way out of the tension between individuality and community, but because they meet their "emotional needs." After their five-year study of twelve megachurches across the United States, the authors argue that megachurch leaders create an environment and a set of emotion-laden interactions that pull visitors in and keep them coming back.

Specifically, the authors detail their theory of a "Megachurch Ritual Cycle": six megachurch practices linked to six core emotional desires: (1) belonging and acceptance are provided by inviting websites, familiar architecture, and an "ultra-friendly welcome team," (2) a "wow" factor is achieved through the music and lighting of worship services, (3) a reliable leader is established by the charismatic pastor in the talk or sermon, (4) deliverance is obtained through the altar call, (5) purpose is met through service groups, and (6) a recharge of emotional energy is attained through midweek small groups.

Megachurches create the "wow factor" during musical worship in a number of ways. Cameras scan the audience and project images of people worshiping, raising their hands with closed eyes, crying, singing, or smiling. Seeing individuals around oneself (or a close-up shot of someone on the projection screen) facilitates the recognition of a shared experience and mood, which contributes to the growing sense that something is happening. As one megachurch attendee reflected, "There is just nothing more powerful than when 10,000 or 11,000 people [are] singing at one time." Robust congregational singing can also be evangelistic: one member of a megachurch I studied recounted bringing an unchurched friend to a Sunday morning service, praying that the visitor could sense that "we [the congregation] are singing with *everything we have*. We are worshiping God." Megachurches succeed because they understand how to create, motivate, and charge their congregations with emotional energy that stimulates intense loyalty and the desire to keep returning for a recharge.

But size isn't always the best measure of success, and megachurches need to grapple with important questions. What unintended messages about power and economics are being projected? What does it mean for a pastor to preach about the priesthood of all believers when his face is on a jumbotron? In a culture that is obsessed with making and spending money, how can we promote excellence in worship, but not promote the idea that it takes hundreds of thousands of dollars to worship God well? Contemporary culture appears to be obsessed with measuring things by size and by numbers. But of course, God is loving enough to tell us lots of countercultural stories about numbers: going after one and leaving the ninety-nine, for example (Luke 15:3–7), dwelling on a single sparrow (Matthew 10:29), or numbering the hairs left on one's head (Matthew 10:30). As one popular saying (often attributed to Albert Einstein) puts it, "Not everything that counts can be counted, and not everything that is counted counts."

6. You explained the appearance of YFC youth rallies in the United States in the 1960s, how the evangelism rally changed the worship of young people in local churches, and how eventually they became independent from worship with adults. This led to the disconnection between generations and "juvenilization of evangelical worship." I found your points insightful. Korea is also walking a similar path. In the 1980s megachurches had a great influence even on small churches, and in order to gather young people, separate worship and worship that was disconnected from tradition were held. There are many cases in which a disconnection between generations has occurred; failure to deliver one generation's faith to the next generation eventually leads to a weakening of the Christian faith and communal aspect of the church. What efforts are American evangelical churches making to overcome these things? For example, intergenerational worship could be an alternative, but are there any other notable options?

This is a huge and important question, and there's no one-size-fits-all answer. I've always appreciated the philosophy of my friend Tim Stafford, who serves as the music minister at Moody Church in Chicago. Tim is committed to the possibility of an eighty-year-old and a twenty-two-year-old sitting next to each other in the pew and having a shared experience. He plans music for worship between three continuums: ancient and modern, simple and eloquent, familiar and new. Christians should value their church's rich history and inherited songs, without isolating themselves from the revitalizing forms of the young. In the same way, there is immeasurable value in singing simple songs that bring forth a childlike heart of faith while also appreciating demonstrations of God's creative nature in more complicated works of musical art. Finally, what is familiar to some may be new to others, and everyone needs both in their routine for healthy growth.

I think this kind of long-term perspective is important, particularly since the lifespan of worship music has declined dramatically. In a 2022 study entitled "Worship at the Speed of Sound," Southern Wesleyan University professor Mike Tapper and his colleagues studied the accelerating pace of creation, distribution, ascent, and decline of congregational worship songs. They discovered that in the mid-1990s, a hit worship song had a lifespan of about a dozen years, rising for 4–5 years before hitting a slow decline. Today's new songs have comparably steeper rises, diminished peaks, and more rapid falls. For example, the popular worship song "In the Secret" entered the CCLI charts in 1999, peaked in 2003, and disappeared in 2009. By contrast, the song "Overcome" entered CCLI in 2018, peaked in 2018, and disappeared in 2019. One danger of catering exclusively to teenagers' musical tastes and preferences is that they may never learn that it's healthy, from an aesthetic point of view, to sometimes *not* like something and still remain open to trying it.

7. I am Presbyterian and have been greatly influenced by Reformed theology in doctrine and evangelicalism in worship practice. When I participate in worship services of various denominations, I feel that liturgical worship is static but weighty, while evangelical worship is light. Sometimes I feel that liturgical worship is cold and evangelical worship is passionate. I think the worship of each church exists at some point between this coolness and passion. Is this division of mine too artificial? In North America recently, why is the liturgical church shrinking and the evangelical church growing? Could it be related to the style of worship?

It's an interesting contrast, although I might want to nuance your two categories a bit. After all, there are many evangelicals in denominational traditions who would argue that worship that uses a prayer book can still be warm and passionate!

My colleague Lester Ruth at Duke has suggested that we move beyond distinctions like "liturgical" and "nonliturgical" churches and instead talk about "personal story churches" and "cosmic story churches." No pure form of either church strictly exists, but churches tend to lean toward one end of the spectrum or the other. "Personal story" churches have worship that focuses upon the story of each individual and God's work in his or her life. "Jesus has done this for me, I benefit from what he has done, and return worship in response." On the other end of the spectrum there are "cosmic story" churches: their worship focuses on the acts of God in salvation history, from creation, through covenant and redemption, to the promise of God making all things new at the end of time. I think the healthiest churches find a way to help worshipers juxtapose their personal story with the cosmic story of salvation. They find the sweet spot in the middle.

8. I would like to focus on your recent book *Evangelical Worship*, published by Oxford University Press. Why should we distinguish between fundamentalism and evangelicalism when discussing worship?

To answer this question, some American historical background might be helpful. The movement that eventually came to be known as fundamentalism rose to national prominence in the 1920s. Fundamentalists stressed belief in the virgin birth, Christ's divinity, the inerrancy of Scripture, and the literal truth of the Bible's recorded miracles. Whereas modernists were optimistic about human nature and progress, fundamentalists underscored human sinfulness and proclaimed the imminent return of Christ. Many fundamentalists took a staunch separatist stance, insisting that it was necessary to leave denominations that had become too liberal or modernist.

As the Second World War came to an end, it was becoming clear to some conservative Protestants that the fundamentalist strategy of oppositionalism and separation had been counterproductive. Many conservatives had grown weary of fighting, especially given the fundamentalist tendency to split not only from liberals, but also from each other. New leaders like Carl F. H. Henry, Harold John Ockenga, and Billy Graham launched the National Association of Evangelicals (1943), Fuller Theological Seminary (1947), and the publication *Christianity Today* (1956). These conservative Protestants called themselves "neo-evangelicals"—later, simply "evangelicals"—and had a friendlier attitude towards science, an increased emphasis on scholarship, and a growing willingness to converse with liberal theologians.

Tensions between evangelicals and fundamentalists peaked in the late 1950s, when Billy Graham accepted an invitation from the Protestant Council of the City of New York—a coalition that included many non-fundamentalist Christian churches—to hold a revival in the city. Fundamentalists were furious: Graham seemed to be giving his blessing to liberalism. When pressed to defend his decision to work with mainline Protestants and Roman Catholics in New York, Graham noted that Paul was sponsored at Mars Hill by the Stoics and Epicureans and that Christ preached in a synagogue.

By the time of the opening meeting of Graham's New York City crusade on May 15, 1957, the division between fundamentalists and evangelicals had passed the point where reconciliation was possible. Hardline fundamentalists boycotted Graham for recruiting liberal churches and charged him with preaching a watered-down gospel. Cooperation of fundamentalists and evangelicals—common during the 1940s, but subject to increasing tension in the early 1950s—had finally broken down. From this point on, institutions would begin to assume an explicitly "fundamentalist" or "evangelical" outlook.

Fundamentalism took a political turn in the 1970s and 1980s when conservative Protestants became active in American politics. The key figure during this time was Jerry Falwell, televangelist, Independent Baptist pastor, and founder of Liberty University. Falwell and other religious conservatives were alarmed by a number of national developments, including the civil rights movement, the women's movement, the gay rights movement, and US Supreme Court rulings that banned institutionally initiated group prayer and Bible reading in public schools and that affirmed the legal right to abortion. In 1979, Falwell founded the Moral Majority—a political lobbying group that advanced conservative social values. Falwell's strategy for uniting cultural conservatives was enormously effective: the Moral Majority quickly grew to several million members and is credited with helping Republican Ronald Reagan win the 1980 presidential election. It remained a strong force for the next decade, but dissolved in 1989 after several prominent evangelists, including Jim Bakker and Jimmy Swaggart, became embroiled in scandal.

The distinction between "evangelical" and "fundamentalist" is significant when discussing worship. Many American evangelical churches align themselves with the conservative theology of fundamentalism but worry about the entanglement of church and politics. As the pastor of an evangelical church in one of my studies wisely noted, "Laws are limited in their power; they cannot make people good, nor can they make godly families. The Christian message must be more radical than any governmental policy could possibly be." Many evangelicals worry that the unwise intertwining of evangelicalism and right-wing politics creates a stumbling block to many who might otherwise be open to the message of Christianity.

9. You studied various evangelical worship styles. What do you see that all evangelical worship has in common?

The question of what makes worship identifiably "evangelical" is disputed. Sunday mornings across the evangelical spectrum can include everything from hellfire preaching and altar calls to responsive readings and contemplative prayer to upbeat praise music and speaking in tongues. So instead of pointing to one specific practice as common across evangelicalism, I like theologian Kevin Vanhoozer's picture of evangelicalism as a boat that is securely tethered. Evangelical theology is "anchored" by its Trinitarian theology and by its emphasis on the cross and resurrection. But from that anchor there is also a "rope" that gives the church delimited flexibility, and that rope is catholic tradition.

To put it differently, there are at least three levels of doctrine that allow evangelicals to maintain a healthy tension between unity (on essentials) and diversity (on nonessentials). First-level doctrines are the things on which the communion of saints has formed a consensus, the things that Christians at all times and places must confess. These doctrines, preserved in the New Testament, put Jesus's death, burial, and resurrection at center stage and represent the agreed upon universal judgements of the church.

Second-level doctrines are the doctrines on which evangelicals have not reached full agreement. They treat aspects of salvation history (i.e., the image of God, sin, justification) that must be affirmed, though there is some scope for different interpretations. Debates about second-level doctrines represent points of significant "regional" difference between evangelicals—points important enough to be required for membership within a church or denomination—yet theological disagreement about them does not impede cooperation between evangelicals of different stripes. Finally, there are third-level doctrines. Differences over them are not damaging to the gospel or divisive to congregational life.

The evangelical congregations may have several "second-level" and "third-level" doctrinal differences that show up in their worship (i.e., some are more Reformed in their theology; others are more Wesleyan; some evangelicals are strongly influenced by Pentecostalism and are open to miraculous healings and speaking in tongues during worship; others are not). While these debates are significant, they do not undermine the unity-in-plurality that is the evangelical movement. Just as many members with different gifts make up the one body of Christ, so do many faithful readings make up the full catholicity of evangelical worship.

10. In your book *Evangelical Worship* you express doubts about the application of "Frontier worship" in James White's classification to all evangelical worship. I'd be grateful if you could elaborate a bit more on this.

According to the prevailing scholarly paradigm, the roots of contemporary evangelical worship can be traced back to the nineteenth century: a time when there was a great need to convert the largely unchurched American population. Liturgical scholar James White traced the roots of the Frontier tradition to the nineteenth century, a time when there was a great need to convert the largely unchurched American population to Christianity. Revivalist Charles Finney—a man White nominates as the most influential liturgical reformer in American history—put worship to work doing just that: making converts. Finney developed a three-part liturgical order that eventually came to dominate American Protestant worship: preliminary songs that softened up the audience, a fervent sermon, and an altar call for new converts. White's suggestion that the origins of "seeker services" and the "church growth" movement could be traced to nineteenth century revivalism has proven extraordinarily influential in liturgical studies. It provided mainline scholars with a way of understanding and critiquing the new evangelical worship trends that were creeping into their denominations. Most of these scholars agree with White's depiction of Frontier Christianity as an irresistible black hole that swallowed up the distinctive characteristics of other liturgical traditions.

My concern is that White's assessment represents a highly selective reading of the evangelical tradition, one that is more interested in the movement's discontinuities from historic Christianity than its ecumenical contributions. This lopsidedness can be attributed to the fact that liturgical historians and theologians seldom move beyond Charles Finney's *Lectures on Revivals of Religion* to probe how evangelical theology and practice had either developed before that work or matured in the nearly two hundred years since its publication.

Describing all acts of worship before the sermon in nondenominational churches as a "warm ups" or "preliminaries" also strikes me as unnecessarily pejorative. For example, I studied a large evangelical church in Milwaukee, Wisconsin, where approximately one third of the congregation's members are minorities from seventy different ethnic groups. The church is passionate about encouraging diversity among believers and unity between all ethnic groups. One of the ways the church actively fosters these connections is through music. To cite one memorable example, a few years ago the church's worship pastor worked with an ethnomusicologist at a nearby university to set the lyrics of the hymn, "In Christ There is No East or West," to Chinese harmonies. The adult choir then spent several months working with a language tutor from the congregation in order to sing the verses of the hymn in both English and Mandarin Chinese. A Midwest church choir that devotes half a year to learning a song in Mandarin Chinese clearly does not have pragmatism at the top of its theological priority list!

11. How would you define evangelicalism?

On the academic side of things, I've always found David Bebbington's definition of *evangelical* to be a helpful starting place. Bebbington says that evangelicalism is comprised of four distinctive traits: *conversionism* (the belief that lives needed to be changed), *activism* (the expression of the gospel in effort), *biblicism* (a particular regard for Scripture); and *crucicentrism* (a stress on the sacrifice of Christ on the cross). None of these traits would, on its own, distinguish an evangelical from any other kind of Christians. But the combination of all four together, in one time and place, is distinctive to the evangelical movement.

For a different, more experiential, definition of evangelicalism, I think about this story. My friend Jacob is a staff member at a large, nondenominational evangelical church. Not long ago, Jacob was introduced to a Jewish rabbi. The two men enjoyed each other's company and wit and quickly struck up an unexpected friendship. They started meeting once a month at a local coffee shop, with no particular agenda. One morning, the two were sitting across from each other, exchanging their usual banter, when the rabbi suddenly set down his mug and turned serious. Stroking his beard, he looked straight into Jacob's eyes, and asked a piercing question: "You want me to accept Jesus, don't you?" The challenge came out of nowhere, and Jacob was taken aback. He sputtered the first thing that came to mind: "Of course not! I'm not here to try to evangelize you!" The rabbi nodded in acknowledgment but persisted. "I know. But somewhere, deep down, you want me to accept Jesus, don't you? Be honest." Jacob did a quick internal inventory. In his heart of hearts, he recognized the rabbi was right and admitted as much to his new friend.

Now that the subject had been broached, Jacob was curious. He asked the rabbi whether he, a nondenominational pastor, was going to heaven. "Yes," the rabbi replied, without hesitation. "I'm 100 percent sure. You're a godly man who shows God to others." Jacob began to protest. "I don't keep any of the kosher laws, I don't . . ." The rabbi cut him off. "You have a different ladder to climb than I do as a Jewish man. Your ladder is a Gentile ladder. But you evangelicals always want us to accept Jesus."

To me, that's the definition of evangelicalism in a nutshell: we want people to know and accept Jesus.

12. I think the most important part of a hymn is the lyrics. It is critical to examine how the lyrics express biblical and theological messages. However, with the variety of music genres, deciding which tune or rhythm is suitable for public worship seems to be a very complex matter. What should the standard be for selecting worship songs or congregational hymns? How can we overcome the severe generational gap in church music?

I think that there is a way in which songwriting is a lot like preaching. Good preachers know that it's not enough to say to the congregation, "I have the truth of God's word up here in the pulpit, and it's your job to listen." Instead, the pastor has to present the material in a way that makes the congregation want to listen—in other words, *how* you say it is as important as *what* you say. A similar truth is at work in songwriting. Sound doctrine, while vitally important, is not enough by itself. If you have the best lyric in the world, it won't go anywhere without a good melody. A great melody makes a congregation *want* to sing just as much as a great pastoral communicator will make a congregation *want* to listen to a sermon.

Selecting music for a congregation is a vitally important job, and there's no one-size-fits-all answer about how to do it. But recently, I've been reflecting on two important things. The first is how much contemporary worship music is dependent on a lead singer and intricate syncopation in order for the congregation to follow along. If you take the drum away, the song falls apart. We need to teach our congregations melodies and lyrics that can be sung with just voices and no rock band. One of the reasons that hymns have endured for as long as they have is that they can be sung in a variety of circumstances: with full orchestration, around a piano in a family's living room, or with no instruments at all at a dying person's bedside. We need contemporary songs that have that kind of versatility.

The second thing I've been thinking about is how much relationships matter in music making. I once heard of a worship committee that regularly asked different parts of the church body, "What song is important to you right now?" They got responses from the seven-year-old Sunday school class, the men's fellowship group, the women's prayer circle, and from missionary families that the congregation supported around the world (to cite just a few examples). Each week, the worship leader highlighted the song from a particular group: "This morning, we are going to sing 'Song X,' which is especially meaningful to our high school students in this season." I think this is a beautiful example of a congregation setting aside its individual musical preferences and uniting across generational differences. They were literally singing each other's songs.

Selected Bibliography

Ross, Melanie. "Assessing an Emerging Church." In *Doing Liturgical Theology: Method in Context*, edited by Jason McFarland and Stephen Burns. Leuven: Peeters, forthcoming.

Ross, Melanie. *Evangelical Versus Liturgical? Defying a Dichotomy*. Grand Rapids: Eerdmans, 2014.

Ross, Melanie. *Evangelical Worship: An American Mosaic*. New York: Oxford University Press, 2021.

Ross, Melanie. "The Influence of the BCP on Other Liturgies." In *The Oxford Handbook of the Book of Common Prayer*, edited by Paul Bradshaw, Luiz Coelho, and Ruth Meyers. In progress.

Ross, Melanie. "Liturgies Beyond the Reformation: Anabaptist, Quaker, Methodist, Pentecostal, Evangelical." In *Cambridge Companion to Christian Liturgy*, edited by Joris Geldhof. In progress.

Ross, Melanie. "Megachurch Movements." In *The Oxford Handbook of Music and Christian Theology*, edited by Emmett G. Price III and Timothy H. Steele. Submitted.

Ross, Melanie, and Mark A. Lamport, eds. *Historical Foundations of Worship: Catholic, Orthodox, and Protestant Perspectives*. Grand Rapids: Baker Academic, 2022.

Ross, Melanie, and Simon Jones, eds. *The Serious Business of Worship: Essays in Honour of Bryan D. Spinks*. London: T&T Clark, 2010.

7
GORDON LATHROP

Gordon Lathrop is a pastor and religious educator of the Evangelical Lutheran Church in America. He earned a master's degree from Luther Theological Seminary in 1966 and a doctorate from the Radboud University in Nijmegen, the Netherlands. From 1975 to 1984, he taught liturgy at Wartburg Theological Seminary in Dubuque. Then, from 1984 to 2004, he taught liturgy and theology at Lutheran Theological Seminary in Philadelphia. He has honorary doctorates from the University of Helsinki, the University of Iceland, and two American seminaries. He was a Lutheran World Federation Scholar (1966–69), served as president of the North American Academy of Liturgy (1984) and as president of Societas Liturgica (2011–13). His trilogy, *Holy Things*, *Holy People*, and *Holy Ground*, is considered foundational to the development of liturgical studies.

Interview with Gordon Lathrop

Thank you, Dr. Lathrop, for accepting the interview. It is a great honor to discuss liturgical studies with one of the top scholars in North America who is the recipient of the Berakah Award, which is the highest honor in the area of worship. I was very glad to meet you at the NAAL reception, and I remember your warm hospitality.

When I was studying liturgical studies at Garrett-Evangelical Theological Seminary in Chicago, I read your trilogy, *Holy Things*, *Holy People*, and *Holy Ground*. Your books impacted me greatly. Your work is deep and profound; therefore, I could not understand everything. But I think these books are historic works. On behalf of readers, I would like to ask several questions if you don't mind.

1. Are there any liturgical theologians or books which have greatly influenced you?

Probably the two most important for me have been Alexander Schmemann, especially his *Introduction to Liturgical Theology*, and the nineteenth-century German Lutheran pastor Wilhelm Löhe, especially his *Three Books on the Church* and his *Agenda* for North America. Some of the other liturgists important for me are (in alphabetical order) Louis-Marie Chauvet, Mary Collins, Anscar Chupungco, Nicolai Grundtvig, Robert Hovda, Graham Hughes, David Power, Gail Ramshaw, Don Saliers, and Gerardus van der Leeuw. In addition, these writers have mattered to my work (in chronological order): Ignatius of Antioch, Irenaeus, Augustine, Martin Luther, George Herbert, Austin Farrer, Dietrich Bonhoeffer, Mary Douglas, John Dominic Crossan, Edward Schillebeeckx, Richard Hays, and Timothy Wengert. As you can see, they are not all liturgical theologians nor are they all contemporary scholars.

2. I am curious about your journey to become a liturgical scholar. How did you come to study liturgical studies and how did you develop your academic capabilities?

My doctoral studies were in New Testament and hermeneutics. My dissertation was on the Gospel according to Mark. My advisers at the Catholic University of Nijmegen (now Radboud Universiteit in the Netherlands) were Bastiaan van Iersel and Edward Schillebeeckx. I am a Lutheran, but I wanted very much to do graduate studies in an ecumenical context, and the people in Nijmegen welcomed me. When I returned to America to take up pastoral ministry, two things happened: I was asked to participate on several drafting committees that were preparing what was ultimately published as the *Lutheran Book of Worship* (1978) and I translated from the Dutch Herman Wegman's *Christian Worship in East and West: A Study Guide to Liturgical History* (New York: Pueblo, 1985). Both of those events immersed me in liturgical study on my own. Then, in 1975 I began to be the chaplain—and then to teach liturgy—at Wartburg Theological Seminary in Dubuque, Iowa. I have always considered myself to be a pastor, with a biblical and ecumenical formation, who cares about the liturgy and who also has taught. When I went to the Lutheran Theological Seminary at Philadelphia in 1984, where I taught until 2004, it was also to be chaplain as well as to teach liturgy. One other thing: I have come to think that critical biblical studies are one of the best preparations to think about Christian liturgy. That is certainly so for Lutherans. Luther himself was a Bible scholar.

3. The Korean Protestant Church emphasizes the sermon as the most important aspect of worship. As a result, lay persons have a tendency to think, "Because I heard the sermon, I have successfully finished the worshipers' duty." You emphasize that while juxtaposing the elements of worship, these *ordo* **form a holistic meaning. What kind of relationship between the sermon and the other elements should be considered desirable?**

I believe that Christian worship involves gathering around the crucified and risen Jesus Christ—that is, gathering in the grace of the holy Trinity—through word and sacrament. God gave us two gifts for this gathering, and they work together. As Paul says, the holy communion "proclaims the Lord's death until he comes." Thus, the eucharist *preaches*! And as both Ezekiel and the elder John say, a preacher must speak the scripture that he or she has "eaten": it is bitter "lamentation and mourning and woe," but it is also "sweet as honey" (Ezekiel 2:8–3:3)—it is both law and gospel, both admonition and life-giving comfort. A good sermon might be as if we could *eat and drink* what is said and so live! There always should be a faithful sermon at the Sunday liturgy. The sermon is important. But there also should always be a celebration of the Lord's Supper. Both. More: the church's discipline of scripture reading, the lectionary, is important. So is the discipline of intercession for all the world. If the sermon is the only "most important" thing, then the preacher becomes far too central and the assembly of the body of Christ—"Christ existing as congregation," as Bonhoeffer says—is increasingly disregarded. Christ feeds us at both word and table, together. And both things are double in character: the word is not just the preacher speaking; it is also people from the assembly reading the lectionary aloud, an important ministry, and people from the assembly subsequently praying for the life of the world. And the supper is not just the pastor's thanksgiving; it is also the assembly sharing the food and remembering the poor. Having Christ's gift at the table next to the sermon helps to urge the preacher to speak Christ's gift in words, using the terms of the texts of the day, not simply to talk about anything he or she wants. There are a lot of preachers who do not "directly deliver God's message." I think we can often trust the Lord's Supper to deliver that message more directly. For my ideas about preaching, see my *Proclaiming the Living Word: A Handbook for Preachers* (Minneapolis: Augsburg Fortress, 2018).

4. I would like to discuss your trilogy and introduce your work, which has attracted a lot of attention, with Korean readers as well. I hope it will be translated into Korean in the future. It would be appreciated if you could briefly explain the characteristics and key points of each book.

Holy Things starts with the Bible and then thinks about how God uses ordinary things to gather us into the celebration of the gospel of Christ. It proposes a simple ordo—drawn from Luke 24 and Nehemiah 8, among other places—of gathering, word, meal, and sending. It then ends with a consideration of the relationship between that ordo and both Church Order and World Order. *Holy People* takes up Church Order again more extensively, thinking about assembly, about ecumenism, and about liturgical inculturation. *Holy Ground* thinks more extensively about World Order—about how liturgy gives us a sense of the world but also about the dangers of that "world making"; then it goes on to think about liturgical ethics and liturgical poetics. The titles of the three books are actually paradoxical or ironic: only Christ is holy. Yet, by the Spirit poured out from Christ, ordinary things are used for God's purposes, sinful and needy people are made into the assembly of God, and our broken worldviews suffice to let us walk in loving service to our neighbors. For an accessible introduction to the ideas that are found in the trilogy see my *Central Things: Worship in Word and Sacrament* (Minneapolis: Augsburg Fortress, 2005).

5. The relationship between liturgy and cosmology seems to be an essential concept for your work. It seems that cosmology influences the formation of the liturgy in an area, and at the same time the liturgy (or liturgical practice) also shapes the people's cosmology. What do you intend readers to focus on through this relationship?

Early in *Holy Ground* I write about how Platonism had an established worldview that privileged rich philosophers. The Platonic dialogue *Timaeus* makes that clear. For the *Timaeus*, the sky is eternal, and philosophers simply have to look at the stars and follow the stars to learn order.

Indeed, in the book people who are blind cannot be philosophers. And, for Timaeus, the sky is the very Son of God. But in the Gospel according to Mark 10:46–52, the son of Timaeus is blind. Christ heals him and he learns God's mercy and life-giving grace by following Jesus, not the stars. Jesus, who goes to the cross, is the Son of God. When Jesus is baptized, the sky is torn open. When he dies, the temple curtain is torn open. According to Mark, the gospel of Jesus Christ gives us an utterly different way to see the world. When Christian liturgy is faithful, the liturgy forms us in that way to see the world—to see and experience God's mercy on the earth; to come to life with Christ; to remember the poor of the world; to serve our neighbors. Many of us have been formed in ways to see the world that are as unhelpful and closed as the way in the *Timaeus*. Christ also tears open those worldviews so that grace and service can pervade our world. I hope that reference assists anyone who wants to engage *Holy Ground*. Start with reading pages 25–38.

6. From the point of view of one who emphasizes the structure of worship, how do you evaluate contemporary worship, which has recently been in the spotlight in the evangelical world? Of course, even in contemporary worship there is the word, the Lord's Supper, and a major ordo. Also, would you define the word *ordo*?

For me, *ordo* is the "shape of the liturgy," the pattern for communal liturgical celebration as an event that can be outlined, an event that an assembly knows how to do. And, for me, the deepest characteristic of this ordo is the juxtaposition of events, as word next to sacrament, of which I wrote in response to your question 3. For more on ordo, see my *Saving Images*, chapter 5. I am actually quite sorry that we use the terms "contemporary worship" and "traditional worship." All worship that is faithful will be both: *traditional*, in that we receive the gifts of God we use in worship from the past—as Paul received the Lord's Supper from the Lord (1 Cor 11:23) and as we all receive the Scriptures—and *contemporary*, in that those gifts are full of the presence to our own current time of God's grace in the risen Christ. But if what is meant by "contemporary worship" is worship led by a praise band, then I would want to caution a congregation using this pattern to be careful that the event does not become simply an entertainment, with the assembly watching others do the singing and with word and sacrament overshadowed. Such worship can then become neither traditional nor contemporary.

7. Your idea that the elements of worship form meaning by juxtaposition seems to be an excellent one. I would appreciate it if you could explain this in more detail.

I began to think about this idea when I read in Alexander Schmemann's *Introduction to Liturgical Theology* his proposal that the first mark of the Christian ordo was the Sunday "eighth-day meeting" held side-by-side with prayer on the seven days, what he calls "liturgical dualism." Christian meaning arises from these two things interacting together, again like *word* and *sacrament* together. *Juxtaposition* is like John Ciardi's definition of poetry: a poem is one part against another across a silence. So is good liturgy.

8. Depending on the denomination or church, the elements or order of worship are different, so they are juxtaposed differently. In this case, even if each is juxtaposed, the meaning will be different. How does the differing placement of the elements of worship relate to this idea of juxtaposition?

While details in denominational worship patterns may differ, I think the great outline of the ecumenical ordo belongs to us all. What I mean is the pattern you can see in Luke 24—the risen Christ gathers us together; the scriptures are all interpreted as about him; we encounter him in the breaking of the bread; we go to tell others—or the pattern you can see in Nehemiah 8—the assembly gathers and the book of the scriptures is brought; God is praised as the book is opened; the scriptures are read and interpreted; we express what we have heard by praying with mourning for the needy world; we share the meal; and we send portions of food and money for those who have none.

9. I think your opinion is excellent: "Juxtaposition does not abolish the old things . . . while juxtaposing old things and new things, it produces more profound meaning." However, I have two questions: Does the juxtaposition automatically guarantee the formation of meaning? Isn't it necessary for a more systematic and organized explanation on the principle of formation of meaning?

No, juxtaposition does not automatically lead to the production of meaning. And such meaning as it may produce is not always good. Ritual juxtapositions can indeed propose ideas that are not according to the gospel. But when a congregation faithfully uses the scripture, looking there for what "drives Christ," as Luther says, and faithfully uses baptism and the Lord's Supper, being gathered there by Christ into new life, then the juxtapositions can work to speak the good news of God. That speaking will happen in the assembly and is the primary theology of the liturgy, the primary way the liturgy speaks of God. But, of course, we will also need secondary reflection on this theology, reflection that helps call us again and again to reforming our worship so that the juxtapositions do speak the gospel. And we will still need the vocation of systematic theology to help us think through Christian meaning in our present time.

10. In the midst of the pandemic, online worship, online communion, and online baptism have become issues. I'm curious about your personal opinion on this topic. Also, I would be grateful if you could tell us about your prospects for worship in the future?

I am grateful that we have had electronic means to stay in touch with each other during this difficult time. Such electronic means are especially good for conversations or meetings for study. But they are not good for worship. At best they can only provide a memory of worship. And they have very significant dangers: not everyone has access to them, and they can fool us about what is "real." For Christian liturgy we need the bodily presence of each other, we need to be able to sing together, and we need the communal celebration of the sacraments. You can read more of my response to this current quandary in the article, "Assembly: A Biblical-Liturgical Reality We Will Need Again" (*Worship*, April 2021, 129–47), or in the just-published book, *The Assembly: A Spirituality* (Minneapolis: Fortress, 2022). My hope for the future is that we will recover *assembly* in strength—what Dietrich Bonhoeffer called "Jesus Christ existing as congregation" and what Louis-Marie Chauvet called "the Christians' primary mark" and "the fundamental sacrament of the risen Christ."

11. Usually, liturgical scholars are very interested in sociological research, but your writings seem to put a lot of emphasis on the Bible. How can our worship become biblical worship on a deeper level? Although each denomination claims that their worship is biblical, there are various differences in actual practice of the liturgy. Can it be said that the difference in Bible interpretation also affects the difference in worship format?

You are quite right. See above my answer to your question 2. See also my recent books, *The Four Gospels on Sunday: The New Testament and the*

Reform of Christian Worship (Minneapolis: Fortress, 2012) and *Saving Images: The Presence of the Bible in Christian Liturgy* (Minneapolis: Fortress, 2017). See also chapter 1 in *Holy Things*. I think that using sociological research has been helpful to liturgical studies. I have myself sometimes used, for example, the work of Victor Turner and of Arnold van Gennep. But I think that careful and critical biblical studies, especially when they seek for "what drives Christ," can be more helpful to our assemblies in understanding and deepening their participation. Of course, difference in biblical interpretation will lead to difference in worship format and content. That is why I have written about "critical biblical studies" and looking for "what drives Christ." It strikes me that awareness of biblical metaphor, the "rebirth of biblical images" in speaking of Jesus Christ, as Austin Farrer said, and biblical "intertextuality," the constant reuse in the scriptures of earlier passages and images, are both hugely important for deepening biblical worship. So is awareness that the books of the New Testament—especially Paul and the Gospels—were written to be read in assemblies and to have an influence on assemblies.

12. Liturgical writer Aidan Kavanagh explains the relationship between liturgical theology and systematic theology as "theologia prima" and "theologia secunda." Likewise, you explain while using the terms "primary liturgical theology" and "secondary liturgical theology." Are there any differences between your thought and Kavanagh's thought on this subject? Also, in North America, can we say that liturgical theology has priority over systematic theology? In Korea, liturgical theology does not have an academic status that can compete with systematic theology and is even known as a subdivision of practical theology.

My thought is indeed very much like the thought of Aidan Kavanagh, and I do appreciate his writing. See my introduction to his work in Dwight Vogel, *Primary Sources of Liturgical Theology* (Collegeville: Liturgical Press, 2000), 89–90. I have, however, added to my own work the concept "pastoral liturgical theology"—the kind of thinking about liturgy that seeks to renew and reform it (see *Holy Things*, 7–8). And I am not so certain as Kavanagh was, with his lifelong commitment to *conversion* as the heart of Christianity, that encountering the "crisis" of the liturgy will radically change us. In regard to the academic status of liturgical theology, North America is not much different from Korea. I do hope that liturgical theology can be regarded as a worthy discipline among you. Still, we are not called to worry about status, but simply to take courage to do our work faithfully and joyfully.

13. Is there any difference between the present Lutheran eucharistic thought and Martin Luther's eucharistic thought?

Current Lutheran thought on the eucharist is substantially in continuity with Luther, especially as regards the presence of Christ in the eucharist: by the gift of God and the power of the Spirit, the risen Christ gives us his body and blood, on, in, and under the bread and cup of the Supper: this bread is the body of Christ; this cup is the blood of Christ—that is, God gives us the means to encounter the living presence of Jesus Christ, his body, and God gives us the life that flows from him, his blood. But Lutherans today understand that we have come to significant rapprochement with Roman Catholics, with the Orthodox, and with many other Protestants in saying this. We are not at all as ecumenically divided on eucharistic presence as we once were, though we may say the matter differently. And, many Lutherans today have shifted a bit from Luther on eucharistic praying. There was a brief eucharistic prayer *in nuce* in his *Formula Missae*, but not at all in his *Deutsche Messe*. There was however, a much more robust eucharistic prayer in the Swedish Lutheran liturgy of the mid-sixteenth century. But since the late nineteenth century, Lutherans have been recovering richly biblical forms of thanksgiving at the table. In that, they are much like Anglicans, Presbyterians, and Methodists in the current time. As Philip Melanchthon wrote in the sixteenth century, "we retain the mass," and we do so now also in this way.

14. Your book, *Holy People*, deals with liturgical ecclesiology. You consider the church a "liturgical assembly." I totally agree with your opinion. Worship is the central act of the church; people have a duty to serve in worship. So then, can I say that we should study the development of ministers (or church office) with respect to people's liturgical roles? What are the merits and weak points in this perspective?

Yes. Excellent. We should indeed so study. And I do not know any weak points in this perspective. We ordain ministers so that they might serve in the assembly as presiders. Church office is for the sake of assembly. Pastors are not "lone rangers" for the gospel. Their whole vocation is to serve the assembly in word and sacrament and in calling people to turn toward the world in love and assistance. More about this idea is to be found in my books, *The Pastor: A Spirituality* and *The Assembly: A Spirituality*, as also in *Holy Things*, chapter 8.

15. I understand that you have held an important role in the World Lutheran Council. You have also had a great influence on the writing of the Nairobi Statement, which deals with the relationship between worship and culture. Can you tell us about the process of your work? And, decades later, does it still have the same significance? Is there something that needs to be developed in more detail?

The Nairobi Statement was produced by the Worship and Culture Study Team of the Lutheran World Federation, and it was the result of several study and discussion meetings of that group. You can read about those meetings and read the papers presented in the three volumes of LWF studies, beginning with *Worship and Culture in Dialogue*, edited by Anita Stauffer, who was also the chair of the group. There were also ecumenical participants, chiefly Anscar Chupungco, perhaps one of the most important scholars ever on liturgical inculturation. A more recent work, which reconsiders the LWF Statements and does so with many contributions from ecumenical voices, is *Worship and Culture: Foreign Country or Homeland?* edited by Gláucia Vasconcelos Wilkey (Grand Rapids: Eerdmans, 2014). I think the Nairobi Statement is still important and useful in the churches, but—along with some of the writers in the Vasconcelos Wilkey book—I also think we need to add the phenomenon of the wide hybridity of cultures (most of us now live in a mix of cultures) and the reality of postcolonialism (the domination of Western culture has to be rethought) to the categories that statement proposed.

Selected Bibliography

Lathrop, Gordon. "Assembly: A Biblical-Liturgical Reality We Will Need Again." *Worship* 95 (April 2021): 129–47.

Lathrop, Gordon. *The Assembly: A Spirituality*. Minneapolis: Fortress, 2022.

Lathrop, Gordon. *Central Things: Worship in Word and Sacrament*. Minneapolis: Fortress, 2005.

Lathrop, Gordon. *The Four Gospels on Sunday: The New Testament and the Reform of Christian Worship*. Minneapolis: Fortress, 2011.

Lathrop, Gordon. *Holy Ground: A Liturgical Cosmology*. Minneapolis: Fortress, 2003.

Lathrop, Gordon. *Holy People: A Liturgical Ecclesiology*. Minneapolis: Fortress, 1999.

Lathrop, Gordon. *Holy Things: A Liturgical Theology*. Minneapolis: Fortress, 1998.

Lathrop, Gordon. *The Pastor: A Spirituality*. Minneapolis: Fortress, 2011.

Lathrop, Gordon. *Saving Images: The Presence of the Bible in Christian Liturgy*. Minneapolis: Fortress, 2017.

8
E. BYRON ANDERSON

E. Byron Anderson studied music and psychology at Carthage College and pursued a Master of Divinity and music studies at Yale University. He obtained his Doctor of Philosophy degree under the guidance of Dr. Don Saliers at Emory University.

After starting his teaching career at Emory's Candler School of Theology, he taught worship at Christian Theological Seminary in Indianapolis, Indiana, from 1996 to 2003. Following that, he assumed a position at Garrett-Evangelical Theological Seminary in Evanston, Illinois, where he has been teaching liturgical studies for almost twenty years and until 2016 served as the Director of the Music Ministry program.

As an outstanding liturgical scholar, Dr. Anderson has served as the president of the Liturgical Conference as well as the Societas Liturgica. Within the North American Academy of Liturgy (NAAL), he actively participated as the convener of the Liturgical Hermeneutics group for an extended period, working alongside not only Don E. Saliers but also esteemed Berakah Award recipients such as Ed Foley and Lawrence Hoffman.

Anderson has made significant contributions to the development of liturgical theology through works like *Worship and Christian Identity* and *Common Worship: Tradition, Formation, Mission*, along with numerous articles.

Interview with E. Byron Anderson

I appreciate the opportunity to meet with you. You are one of the top scholars in liturgical theology. You have served not only as the president of The Liturgical Conference but also as the president of the Societas Liturgica. With outstanding theological depth, you contributed to the development of liturgical studies through various articles and books. Although the scope of the study of worship is wide and each scholar has a slightly different emphasis, you have a deep knowledge in systematic and liturgical theology. Your writing is very unique, and your work weighs heavily through its consilience with Christian ethics. Thank you very much for agreeing to the interview.

1. Your resume is quite unique. You graduated from Yale with a Master of Divinity and Music major, and later earned a PhD at Emory University under the guidance of Dr. Don Saliers. I remember that James Fowler, an outstanding educational psychologist of the time, was also on the committee for your thesis. I would be grateful if you could explain your academic background.

In many ways, my formation as a scholar has been consistent since my undergraduate degree, when I was an organ major as well as a psychology major. During college, I was working as a church organist and a crisis intervention counselor. In seminary, my initial focus was on church music and music ministry but found my interests expanding to focus on pastoral ministry and, thanks to my teachers Jeffery Rowthorn and Aidan Kavanagh, on liturgical theology. After seminary I served as a pastor in several United Methodist churches (I am an ordained elder in the United Methodist Church), where I had responsibilities for music, Christian education, and youth ministry. That pastoral experience began raising and shaping a series of questions about the relationship between Christian worship and formation. I also discovered during this time in pastoral ministry a vocation as a teacher and writer, which Dr. Don Saliers encouraged me to explore more fully by pursuing the PhD. I had earlier met Dr. James Fowler at a conference on faith development in children, so had become familiar with some of his scholarship as well. The program I entered at Emory, now called "Person, Community, and Religious Life," had a strong focus on practical theology and religious education, as well as faith and moral development. Fortunately, the program was shaped in such a way to enable me to combine these emphases with work in liturgical theology and ritual studies. As you know from your work with me at Garrett, these combined emphases continue to influence my research and writing. They are especially reflected in my dissertation and first book *Worship and Christian Identity* and, to some extent, in my most recent book *Common Worship: Tradition, Formation, Mission*.

2. **Like Professor Don Saliers, you seem to have excelled in both systematic and liturgical theology. Not only that, but you seem to have a deep knowledge of philosophical hermeneutics. Why is hermeneutics important in the study of liturgical theology? Why did you work for a long time in the liturgical hermeneutics group as a convener at the North American Academy of Liturgy?**

I do not have as strong a background in systematic theology as I would like, but research and teaching in liturgical and sacramental theology requires that one become conversant with and continue to study some of the major themes in systematic theology, including Christology, the Trinity, anthropology, and, of course, grace and the means of grace. Although I was introduced to key scholarship in hermeneutics during my doctoral studies, my work in hermeneutics has developed more intentionally since I completed that doctoral work, largely in conversation with colleagues in the Liturgical Hermeneutics seminar of the North American Academy of Liturgy (NAAL). Those conversations have pushed me to read more deeply in hermeneutics and in philosophies of pragmatism, reading Gadamer and Ricoeur as well as the American philosopher Charles Sanders Peirce and the French sociologist Pierre Bourdieu. The work of Peirce and Bourdieu have been especially influential on my understanding of the place of habit and habitus in human intellectual and spiritual formation. My continued participation in the NAAL Liturgical Hermeneutics seminar has enabled me to engage conversations that bring together theology, hermeneutics, aesthetics (especially music), and ritual action. My colleagues in that seminar continue to help shape my continuing study and research. More importantly, they press me to keep asking "Why does this matter?" in all of our talk about ecumenical liturgical reform and renewal.

3. **Can you briefly give an example of analyzing worship documents and worship in the church through hermeneutics?**

Perhaps one of the contributions that a hermeneutical approach to liturgical study has provided in recent years is the understanding that as liturgical scholars we are not dealing simply with a "text" (that is, with printed words) but with an event—or what theologian David Power calls a "language event"—combining scripture, prayer, and ritual action. This approach has also called attention to the contexts in which these texts are enacted (whether a small rural church or a megachurch, whether a simple "meeting house" or an elaborate gothic building, whether homogeneous or diverse congregations) and how these contexts shape our experience and interpretations of these "texts." More, it invites us to attend to the styles of music, the kind of liturgical art, the acoustical character of the space (reverberant or dry), the gestures and movement of worship leaders and worshipers—all of which contribute to the ways that we make meaning of Christian worship. Philosopher Paul Ricoeur many years ago wrote about "meaningful action as text," helping us expand our notion of what a "text" is and how we go about interpreting it. This approach shapes assignments I give to students in my worship classes and my expectation that they pay attention to the particular community with or for whom they are shaping and leading worship: Who are these people? Where do they gather for worship? How is that worship space shaped? How do they participate in the "work of worship" together? How do they speak and sing and move? It is only after answering these questions that they can then begin to think about the patterns of worship in the congregation and denominational tradition.

4. If we look at worship in the church from a hermeneutical point of view, is there any danger that this will become a kind of eisegesis?

Looking at Christian worship (or scripture, or theological texts) from a hermeneutical point of view is to acknowledge first and foremost that all of us—liturgical scholars as well as the average person in the pew—engage in interpretation. Such interpretation is how we find and make meaning in our lives. I think the danger, if there is one, comes when we limit our interpretive frameworks either by some literal reading of a text or liturgical practice (including, for example, the creeds of the church, eucharistic prayers, and hymn texts), or assume that these texts have no history in either their development or interpretation, or by assuming that what a particular denomination says about one of these texts is what every member of that denomination believes about the text. A hermeneutical approach reminds us that we never engage a symbol and its meaning without the mediation of an interpreter—whether that interpreter is a theologian or not. Therefore, part of the work of a hermeneutic approach to liturgical studies, part of the task in such an approach, is to make explicit the interpretive lenses we are using in our research and to make explicit the commitments we as interpreters bring to that work. As Mark Searle argued in his proposal for "pastoral liturgical theology" some forty years ago, liturgical scholars need to know something of the history of the development of our liturgical texts and practices; we need to know how the church has received and interpreted and practiced those texts; and we need to ask critical questions about those interpretations and practices.

5. Like the aphorism *lex orandi lex credendi*, there seems to be a mutual tension between liturgical theology and systematic theology. In Korea, it feels like systematic theology suppresses worship studies. Theology should check the worship service, but sometimes the richness and vitality of worship is lost. What is the desired relationship between these two? How can we provide a worship service that harmonizes the richness, vitality, and theological soundness of the worship site?

Perhaps one starting point is to remember that this aphorism—"the law of prayer (*lex orandi*), the law of belief (*lex credendi*)"—is itself an abbreviation of a larger argument about the relationship between prayer and doctrine. Liturgical scholars have put it to both good and problematic use through the ages. I also find it helpful to remember, as I remind my doctoral students, that the aphorism finds its origin in a theological argument about the universal need for grace, an argument supported by the church's liturgical practice of praying "for all manner of people" (1 Timothy 2:1–3), an argument that because we pray for "all manner of people" all people are in need of grace. However, I also remind them that by paying close attention to church history, especially the histories of theology and liturgy, we discover that there has always been a mutual and reciprocal relationship between prayer and belief. As the fourth century theologian Evagrius claimed, "the one who prays is a theologian and a theologian is one who prays." Prayer and belief are necessary companions in an ongoing conversation. For example, we need to remember that, on the one hand, the Apostles' Creed was first a liturgical text, emerging from the church's baptismal practices and expressing the faith of the church we profess in baptism. On the other hand, the Nicene Creed was first a doctrinal text, addressing problems of belief and only later incorporated in the church's worship. As another example, we could explore the ways in which the early church offered its doxology to God—often in the Western churches "to the Father, through the Son, in the Spirit" and in the Eastern churches "to the Father, and the Son, and the Spirit"—and how this doxology in prayer has shaped our thinking about the Trinity.

6. You have been interested in the connection between worship and Christian ethics and have been researching how worship shapes the faith of individuals and communities, how worship shapes an ethical self, and how it leads to social participation. Recently among Korean Protestants, there have been critical voices of self-examination pointing out that the appearance of faith in the church has not led to structural reform and transformation of society and that public trust has been lost. How can we connect our confession of faith in worship (orthodox faith) to the level of right life (orthopraxis) in the process of forming believers' faith?

The French theologian Louis-Marie Chauvet writes about the need for liturgy and scripture to be "verified"—to be tested for their truthfulness—by ethics. What he means by this is that what we pray for and how we live our daily lives are intimately connected. For example, if we pray for peace, but do not work for peace, then our prayer is "untrue" (or perhaps "unfaithful"). If we pray for the dignity and rights of all people, but do not treat all people with dignity or equal rights, our prayer is untrue or unfaithful. If we pray in such a way that suggests God will solve everything, we forget the purposes of the incarnation, death, resurrection, and ascension of Christ and of the outpouring of the Holy Spirit that makes us disciples in the way of Jesus and children of God, with responsibilities for our brothers and sisters, for "the least of these" in our midst; our prayer is then untrue or unfaithful. Perhaps this is only to say that if we are not engaged in *orthopraxis*—right action—we cannot consider ourselves to be *orthodox*—which concerns not only "right belief" but also "right worship."

The public has lost its trust in religious leaders—certainly among many in the United States—because they see the inconsistency between words and actions in the churches and from the churches' leaders; they see the hypocrisy of a faith that separates prayer, belief, and ethical action. Perhaps one way to say this is if Christian faith is portrayed as only reinforcing the individualistic consumerism of so much of Western society, or the ideology of one political party, then why should anyone be interested in the Christian faith or joining the church?

7. It seems that the decline of the church worldwide is serious. It feels like the pace of decline has accelerated due to the COVID-19 crisis. The United Methodist Church is one of the largest denominations in the

United States, but the number of pastors, seminarians, and members seems to be decreasing. How do you evaluate this phenomenon? And is there any good way to improve the number and vitality of the next generation?

I would argue that the church is *not* declining worldwide, but primarily in the European and American contexts. It is growing rapidly in South America, Africa, and parts of Asia. The causes of this decline have received much scholarly attention as well as denominational anxiety. For us in the United States, I think it goes back to what I said in response to the previous question about the loss of trust in religious leaders as well as in the church. Young people in the United States see many vital ways to engage in the work of ministry, many of which do not seem to require the church or the church's approval. Many of these young people have become "prophets outside the city," calling the church to account for its lack of care for the poor, its history of racism, its discrimination against women, and, as is true in my own United Methodist Church, its lack of welcome to the gay and lesbian community. There is a vitality among these young people that I think has the potential to help refashion the church. I also think this decline is a result of the dominant individualism we find in Western cultures and the ensuing tendency to recreate "spirituality" in our own image. Religious participation, sacramental life, and Christian worship are all communal practices that summon us into relationship with God and with our neighbors. To be "religious" (as well as "spiritual"), is to bind ourselves to a community of belief and practice.

8. **I know that you are a musician belonging to the organ guild and have deep knowledge of music theology. Music is receiving a lot of attention in contemporary worship, but it seems that there are many different opinions about what kind of music should be used in worship, what hymns should be sung, and whether there are restrictions on the use of musical instruments. What hymns in your opinion should we sing? What makes a hymn good? What should the standards for the use of music in church be?**

There is no short answer to these questions, so I only offer some basic points. Let me first say that the church has always had disagreements about the place of music in Christian worship. In his *Confessions*, the fourth-century theologian Augustine outlined what came to be the three prominent positions that emerged in the Protestant reformation from

Luther, Calvin, and Zwingli concerning the place of music in worship. (Augustine's conclusion seems to be rather Lutheran, arguing in part that music is necessary in worship to help move our "weak minds" to worship. Several of Jeremy Begbie's books on music and theology helpfully explore these positions more fully.) Given that there has always been such disagreement, the question then becomes how we make decisions about what music to use in worship. Here, too, I start with a reminder: most church hymnals of the past one hundred years are examples of "blended worship music"—gathering the church's song as it is has emerged over the centuries, testing the fittingness of both texts and tunes in Christian worship, exploring where and how to best make use of music. Christian hymnody has always been a practice of blending old and new tunes with old and new texts, as the musical language of one time is carried through, altered, or abandoned by another and as texts migrate to new cultures. As a result, each new edition of a denominational hymnal helps test new texts and tunes. Making our discernment more difficult today is the fact that over the past sixty years there has been an explosion of new hymns and songs for worship, all needing to be tried and tested.

All of that being said, I do have some basic criteria that can be helpful. A good hymn or song *text* must be well-written and coherent; it should express some Christian truth; and it should enable a congregation to sing—that is, it should be created for communal rather than individual singing. A good text needs to provide an expression of the church's faith and, therefore, needs to be consistent with the beliefs and doctrines of the denomination. A good hymn *tune* must be singable by an average congregation (not an individual solo voice), structured to carry us through the tune from beginning to end and have a regularity of rhythm. A good tune must also match in some way the emotional character of the hymn text; we know, for example, that a strong text of praise is weakened by a tune that is contemplative or sorrowful and a contemplative text is defeated by a strong, energetic tune.

9. You have been teaching not only PhD students but also MDiv students for a long time. How do the students you taught in your first days compare with the students you are teaching in 2022? As one of your students, I am very curious.

As I think back to my own seminary experience at Yale in the 1980s, one of the significant changes I see in mainline Protestant seminary students in the United States (as this is my primary point of reference) is that fewer seminarians have been formed by a life in the church, by its traditions, patterns of worship, or repertoires of hymns and songs. An increasing number of students come to seminary today requiring basic formation in scripture, Christian doctrine, and Christian practice. At the same time, those students are suspicious of the church (for reasons I mentioned earlier about the loss of trust), of the church's traditions, and of denominational structures. Seminary students today are also more anxious about their futures in ministry. In the 1980s and 1990s, at least in the United Methodist Church in the US, seminary graduates were almost guaranteed some form of pastoral appointment. That is no longer true today, with many small churches closing or unable to financially support a full-time pastor. This is pressing students not only to consider whether pastoral ministry is appropriate for them but also to consider whether they will need to be prepared for a bivocational ministry, that is, for some additional work outside of the church to enable a living. (Of course, I realize that many pastors in other parts of the world have long understood that they will need to support themselves outside of the church.) While the world has changed, posing new questions and challenges to the church, not everything has changed. Seminarians today, as in the last half century (and more), come with a passion for justice, for human rights, for care for the sick, the poor, and those in need, and for care of the earth. They, like most people in our pews, are wondering what it means to be a disciple of Jesus.

10. What kind of worship do you seek? Please also share your thoughts on the church's traditions and contemporary changes.

I am increasingly aware that some of the many problems in Protestant worship result from an (often) implicit clericalism which suggests that Christian worship is or should be shaped according to the pastor's desires, tastes, and expectations. While there has always been some variation in the patterns of Christian worship as they have emerged through church history, many pastors—especially those in traditions not shaped by formal prayer books or directories for worship—seem inattentive to or disregarding of both history and theology in the shaping of worship. In current US culture, we also seem to be "captive to the always new." Because our consumer culture leads us to expect that everything should always be the most "up-to-date" (our appliances, phones, and computers, our phone and computer operating systems), we think the same of worship, that worship must be always changing and updated. In this "captivity to the new," we lose sight of the role of ritual in the formation of persons and communities, the kind of stability it provides in times of great change and anxiety, and the ways in which it helps us "negotiate" the many transitions in our lives.

What do I look for in worship? I look for a community with church leaders who respect a denomination's traditions and practices of worship, who care for and steward well those traditions, who work carefully to integrate prayer, song, preaching, and sacrament. I look for church leaders who do not think they are the focal point of worship and who are focused on helping us encounter God in Christ. I look for leaders who take Paul's words to the Corinthians to heart—that we are "servants of Christ and stewards of God's mysteries" (1 Cor 4:1). I look for a community that respects and celebrates well the sacraments of baptism and eucharist as well as marriage and funeral services. I look for a community that continues to explore and learn new (and old) hymns and songs.

11. In Korea, there have been many studies on the worship theology of the sixteenth-century Reformers such as Luther, Calvin, and Bucer, but research on Wesley's contribution to worship and sacraments seems to be relatively minimal. In the case of North America, can you explain what kind of research has been conducted on this subject and what kind of research is needed?

John Wesley did not write much about worship, and what he did write about worship and the sacraments was often adapted from others' work in the Anglican tradition. We often forget that both John and Charles Wesley remained Anglican priests throughout their lives and were committed to the Anglican church's sacramental and liturgical life, even as they worked to reform and revitalize the church. They did not believe that the church's sacramental rites and forms of worship were subject to the individual judgment of a pastor but that sacrament and worship were a matter of "common authority" of the church. Their concern about the church was not with its forms of worship, but about the character of the people who participated in that worship. Having said this, I would note that there has been much good scholarship on Methodist and Wesleyan theologies of worship and the sacraments, especially over the past seventy-five years. There have been numerous fine studies of the Wesleys' hymns as both theological and liturgical documents—for example, the work of J. Ernest Rattenbury in the 1940s remains a significant contribution. Karen Westerfield Tucker has provided a definitive history of American Methodist worship. There have been several significant studies related to the meaning and practice of baptism and eucharist that engage both Wesleyan and contemporary ecumenical theologies—for example, the recent volume edited by Jason Vickers entitled *A Wesleyan Theology of the Eucharist*. Of course, my own work remains in close conversation with the Wesleyan Methodist tradition in my explorations of the baptismal renunciations and praying the eucharist.

12. I would like to talk about your recent book, *Common Worship: Tradition, Formation, Mission*, for a moment. I think that it would be good to be translated and introduced in Korea in the future. Please briefly explain what motivated you to write the book and the key points of the book.

Although it is written very much from my own American Methodist context, I think it would be great to see the book in translation. However, I would be more interested in seeing others take up the themes I explore in the book in conversation with their own contexts and traditions. *Common Worship* brings together research and writing I had been engaged in over about ten years. It continues my emphasis on the relationship between worship and Christian formation as well as my long commitment to ecumenism and ecumenical liturgical renewal. The primary question the book seeks to answer is how we might talk about "common worship" (especially in a divided church) as a means toward and as evidence of our engagement with Christ's prayer "that we may be one." The book looks at five primary themes and oppositions that I thought had been neglected in discussions of liturgical renewal: tradition and contemporaneity, habit and freedom, canon and ordo, unity and diversity, participation and mission. In the book I argue that our current postmodern context requires that we attend to the "and" in each of these pairs, that we cannot limit ourselves to one item in each pair, and that each requires the other for faithful worship. As I note in the introduction to the book, learning to deal with "both/and" (habit *and* freedom, for example) confronts us with our own incompleteness, an incompleteness often hidden by the presumptions expressed by "either/or" (for example, that worship is *either* traditional *or* contemporary).

13. It seems that there are many different worship traditions in Christianity. From a synchronic and diachronic perspective, the theology and practice of worship are very diverse. It seems that often theologians and believers are very critical of other worship traditions. How can we maintain the unity of the church in the midst of such diversity of worship? Also, what should be the relationship between cultural diversity and liturgical unity in the contemporary context?

With both this question and the next, I am inclined to suggest reading my chapter on unity and diversity, and my chapter on participation and mission in *Common Worship*. These are big questions! Fortunately, the next meeting of Societas Liturgica in August 2023 will focus on the relationship between worship and ecumenism. I'll offer just a few comments here. First, we are suspicious and, often, critical of things we do not know or understand. We remain isolated from one another rather than learning from one another. This is why organizations like Societas Liturgica and the North American Academy of Liturgy are so important—they require that we listen to and learn from each other. I think this is also why the work of the Faith and Order Commission of the World Council of Churches has been so important over the past century. Second, although there has been much diversity in worship practices throughout the history of the church, I do think there have been some normative patterns and practices evident in that history—what Lutheran scholar Gordon Lathrop and others would call the ecumenical ordo that includes gathering on the Lord's Day to hear God's word proclaimed in scripture and preaching, gathering about the Lord's Table to give thanks and share in holy communion, and baptizing and receiving persons into the body of Christ. How we embody those patterns and practices in each time, place, and culture requires a willingness to be accountable to one another as well as to be respectful of each other. Perhaps one of the roles of liturgical scholars is to help churches and denominations ask of themselves some hard questions: If this is the tradition of the ecumenical church, why do we, or why should we, do something different? Does our limited vision contribute more to the division of the church than to its unity?

14. One of the main highlights of the Second Vatican Council was "active participation." This word *participation* seems to be a term not only for physical presence but also for mental and spiritual presence. It seems, then, to have a deeper philosophical meaning. I would appreciate it if you could explain this idea of participation.

Here, too, a full answer would require a book. In fact, there have been several fine books written about the meaning of "active participation." I also discuss it in my chapter on "Participation and Mission" in *Common Worship*, as well as in an article published prior to the book. Let me start with a quote from the Roman Catholic theologian Kevin Irwin, which I use in both the book chapter and article. Irwin writes: "The notion of 'participation' is frequently used to describe our active involvement in the act of worship: in word, song, gesture, and silence [such that] through these sacred rites, symbols, and celebrations . . . we experience the very life of Christ, we participate and share (take part in and become part of) his paschal saving mystery" (Kevin Irwin, *Liturgy, Prayer and Spirituality* [New York: Paulist Press, 1984], 127). Those of us who have written about liturgical participation have argued that our enhancement of participation by the whole gathered worshiping community is a starting point, rather than the goal, of liturgical renewal and reform. Our goal is not simply "active participation" in worship—people reading scripture, praying and singing together, receiving the bread and cup at the Lord's Table—but a deepening participation in the Body of Christ that is the church, and, ultimately, participation in the divine life through communion with God. Such an understanding of participation is consistent with my own Methodist theological tradition which would argue that faithful participation in the means of grace—in worship and especially in the sacraments—is not only a means toward perfection, toward sanctification, and toward God, but also an experience of and participation in God. This is what participation seeks.

15. Lastly, I would be grateful if you could share your personal views on online communion, online baptism, and online worship, which have become issues during the COVID-19 era.

Answering this question could also fill a book or two! Karen Westerfield Tucker (Boston University School of Theology) and I wrote a short article several years ago, before the pandemic, to address some of these questions for the United Methodist Church. We argued, and continue to argue, against online celebrations of the sacraments, especially of Holy Communion. In the article we concluded that such celebrations "fail to embody a 'holy communion' of the church and undermine the incarnational character of the Christian faith." Our experience during the pandemic has only strengthened this belief for me. I do believe that the use of Zoom and streaming platforms have given people a new kind of access to church, but that access has made them primarily "observers" of worship rather than full participants. Christian worship, as I suggested earlier, is a communal event requiring our embodied presence with and as the church. Such presence is most fully evident when we greet one another as a body in Christ's name, sing and pray together, confess our sins before God and one another, exchange the sign of peace with friends as well as strangers, and partake from a common loaf and cup. Such presence is neither evident nor possible when an individual simply joins in an online presentation. When online, even with a platform such as Zoom, we lose sight of the fact that the communion intended at the Lord's Table is not only a communion between the individual and God but especially a communion of and with the church as the assembled people of God. Much of what is presented as online worship is little different from what we experienced earlier in the twentieth century with radio and TV broadcasts—an emphasis on preaching and music performed by professional ensembles, with little attention to the active participation of the congregation or the communal practice of the sacraments.

Nevertheless, I and other Methodist colleagues have argued that some forms of Christian worship *might* lend themselves to some forms of online participation, including, for example, some patterns of daily prayer, some devotional practices such as *lectio divina*, some forms of catechesis, instruction, and evangelization. Notice my repeated use of "some." Not all forms nor all platforms are appropriately engaged online. It requires careful discernment, not simply a response based on expediency or convenience. (Luke 14:15–24 suggests that Jesus had some harsh words for those who refused to come to the banquet because it was inconvenient!) What congregations did in response to the pandemic should not become either normal or normative; these were exceptional circumstances and should be understood as such. As pastors and scholars, we have much work to do to think through the strengths and weaknesses of these media platforms when used for Christian worship as well as to the long-term consequences of their use. How do they change our understanding of the sacraments? How do they reinforce an individualistic and consumerist approach to worship and the sacraments? How do they shape our understanding of the body of Christ? What does it mean to *be* church (not just to *attend* church)? These questions are only starting to be explored; few of them yet have clear answers.

Selected Bibliography

Anderson, E. Byron. *Belief and Belonging: Living and Celebrating the Faith—A Teaching Companion*. Collegeville, MN: Liturgical Press, 1993.

Anderson, E. Byron. *Common Worship: Tradition, Formation, Mission*. Nashville: Foundery Books, 2017.

Anderson, E. Byron. *The Meaning of Holy Communion in the United Methodist Church*. Nashville: Discipleship Resources, 2015.

Anderson, E. Byron. *Worship and Christian Identity: Practicing Ourselves*. Collegeville, MN: Liturgical Press, 2003.

Anderson, E. Byron, ed. *Worship Matters: A United Methodist Guide to Ways to Worship*. 2 vols. Nashville: Discipleship Resources, 1999.

Anderson, E. Byron, and Bruce Morrill, eds. *Liturgy and the Moral Self: Humanity at Full Stretch Before God*. Collegeville, MN: Liturgical Press, 1998.

Yust, Karen Marie, and E. Byron Anderson. *Taught by God: Teaching and Spiritual Formation*. St. Louis: Chalice Press, 2006.

9
DAVID HOGUE

David Hogue is Professor Emeritus of Pastoral Theology and Counseling at Garrett-Evangelical Theological Seminary in Evanston, Illinois. He is ordained as Minister of Word and Sacrament in the Presbyterian Church (U.S.A.), and served in parish ministry, hospital chaplaincy, and pastoral counseling settings. He has also been active in denominational and presbytery work, as well as consulting and education.

Dr. Hogue is the author of *Remembering the Future, Imagining the Past: Story, Ritual, and the Human Brain* and several book chapters and journal articles exploring the intersection of ritual, liturgy, pastoral care and counseling, and the neurosciences. He has been particularly interested in the ways rituals enable life transitions and provide opportunities for healing and reconciliation for faith communities and other groups. His interest in brain research eventually led to broader study of the ways in which our bodies participate in rituals.

He received his PhD from Northwestern University in religious and theological studies and an MDiv from Christian Theological Seminary, as well as an MS in education from Indiana State University (counseling) and a BA in music and English from Greenville University.

Interview with David Hogue

Thank you for agreeing to the interview. I feel very fortunate to have met you at Garrett Seminary and to have taken your class. It was a "God's move" that there was a course called "Ritual Studies" in the PhD coursework in liturgical studies. If I had not studied ritual studies, I would not have been able to properly study liturgical theology, and my articles published in various international journals would not have been properly written. Thanks to you, Dr. Hogue, I became interested in rituals and brain studies. Through today's interview, we would like to discuss why ritual studies is necessary to properly study the liturgy, what books to read to study ritual, the thoughts of major scholars, and what the recent research trends are.

1. I would be grateful if you could explain the meaning of ritual studies. Usually, when reading books on liturgy and worship, words such as *liturgy*, *rites*, *ritual*, and *ceremony* often appear. These words seem to have some things in common but also have their own differentiated characteristics. *Ritual* is not easy to define clearly, but I'd appreciate it if you could explain it simply for the sake of the readers.

This is a great question to begin our conversation! It would be helpful if there were a clear, straightforward definition that ritual scholars agreed to. But that is not the case. Scholars have proposed multiple answers, but they often raise more questions than they answer. Most would probably agree that rituals are practices *repeated over time*; they carry an *authority* that comes from outside the participants (e.g., God, or the ancestors); we think of rituals as maintaining or *conserving the values* of a community on one hand and *transforming or liberating* them on the other. But can rituals be enacted by an individual or must it be a group? Can new rituals be developed, or must they be inherited from the past? Are we human beings naturally "ritualizing animals," or are some people ritualizers and others are not? Are rituals optional? Is it possible for anyone to truly understand the rituals of a group very different from their own?

Ritual scholar Ron Grimes argues that we are wrong to think of rituals as nouns, as "things," but should think instead of them as a verb: ritualizing. That, he says, is a practice all human groups undertake as they *make sense of the world*, particularly the environment they live in, *organize their social lives*, and *pass their deeply held values on* to future generations.

Early in my own work in this area, I found two definitions particularly helpful. The first is from family therapist Onno van der Hart. He says, "Rituals are *prescribed symbolic acts* that must be *performed* in a certain way and in a certain order and may or may not be accompanied by verbal formulas. Besides the formal aspects, an experiential aspect of rituals can be distinguished. The ritual is performed with much *involvement*. If that is not the case, then we are talking about empty rituals. Certain rituals are *repeatedly* performed through the lives of those concerned; others, on the contrary, are performed only once (but can be performed again by other people)."[*]

The second is by anthropologist Roy Rappaport in *Ritual and Religion in the Making of Humanity*. Ritual, he says, is "the performance of more or less invariant sequences of formal acts and utterances not entirely encoded by the performers."[†] This concise sentence highlights three important dimensions of ritual: (1) Rituals are not written documents, descriptions, or instruction manuals; rituals are activities, practices, performances. (2) Rituals have formal patterns (templates) that must be followed, either in minute detail, or more generally, allowing adaptations based on local circumstances. (3) Rituals have their origin (and therefore authority) from others and from times past.

2. Your major area of study is pastoral counseling. However, I think that you taught the subject of ritual studies at Garrett despite the presence of prominent North American scholars such as Ron Anderson, Frank Senn, and Ruth Duck who reveal that you have a great recognition in this field. Why were you interested in ritual studies? Is there any relationship between pastoral counseling and ritual studies?

I believe I was, indeed, the only faculty member from outside the field who was active with our liturgical faculty in teaching and advising. My field of pastoral theology (care and counseling) focuses on studying the "care of souls," or sometimes, the "cure of souls." What are the practices of religious and other communities that promote healing and wholeness, and what are the practices that wound or alienate? Pastoral theologians, like all practical theologians, have great interest in theological anthropology: what are human beings that God is mindful of us (Psalm 8)?

---

[*] Onno van der Hart, *Rituals in Psychotherapy: Transition and Continuity* (New York: Irvington, 1983), 5–6.

[†] Roy A. Rappaport, *Ritual and Religion in the Making of Humanity* (Cambridge: Cambridge University Press, 1999), 24.

In hindsight, I suspect my interest in ritual was lifelong. But I became acutely interested during my early PhD coursework in cultural anthropology (where I learned to discern and value cultural differences). Later, my interest in the neurosciences led me to emerging scientific literature on the ways the brain participates in ritual practices and the ways those experiences bind a group of people together. I began to realize that our brains are not isolated within our skulls; they enable (and require) our engagement with others.

More recently my interest has broadened to the ways our human bodies are engaged in ritual practices that go far beyond the power of words. Our brains constantly receive feedback from what our bodies are doing, what they are experiencing. That has elevated my appreciation of what we are doing in worship—how we are moving and acting—even beyond what we are saying or hearing. Our brains, after all, are part of our bodies.

So, my interest in ritual and liturgy is deeply related to my concerns for the well-being of persons, of congregations and communities, and for the practices of our faith. As a pastor, I want to know how worship and other practices of the church contribute to human wholeness, to faithful living, to human flourishing within the body of Christ. As a pastoral counselor, I want to know the same things—and to evaluate how clients are making use of the resources of their faith.

3. If people study anthropology or religious studies, it seems that rituals exist in other religions, sometimes with many similarities to Christian rituals. It sounds like a tough question, but I wonder what makes a ritual a Christian ritual? What is the difference between Christian rituals and rituals of other religions?

Ritualizing is, indeed, a deeply universal human activity; we know of no cultures that lack evidence of practices we would call rituals. Some scholars, like Roy Rappaport and Catherine Bell, even argue that ritualizing is what makes us human, what sets us apart from other animals. Others, like Tom Driver, argue that even our pets have rituals!

So, the fact that we Christians also ritualize is deeply reassuring. The Incarnation demonstrated that our humanity, our creatureliness, our physical bodies, are created and loved by God—so much that God came to dwell among us in human form. We Christians speak of resurrection of the body rather than a separation of body and soul at the time of death.

What our bodies do is important; and in worship, our bodies participate deeply in the life of God.

Our Christian worship practices are ritual practices. We repeat them, we call on them during life transitions (birth, marriage, death), we follow formulas for them, we believe them to be received from tradition, and ultimately, from God. Worship is much more than ritual, of course. Some have achieved the status of sacraments—initiated by Christ, drawing us into the community of faith, and sustaining us with Christ's own body. I think of "ritualizing" as the human side of our worship experience; it is the ways we are endowed to respond to God's graceful initiative toward us.

As you note, some of our rituals have been adopted from other faith traditions (e.g., the Seder, and even baptism); some have probably been modeled on other cultural traditions, like Confirmation, one of the few adolescent rites of passage that we currently employ (at least in the United States). There are universal human needs that our Christian faith responds to, even when that means adopting or "sanctifying" non-Christian traditions. What makes rituals Christian is our understanding of them: what they mean, what they accomplish, how they fulfill God's purposes for us and for our world. Christian rituals, we believe, align us with God's intent for us as followers of Jesus Christ, and for the world God created.

4. Traditionally, the Protestant tradition seems to have a negative reaction to the words "ritual" and "ceremony." There seems to be an antipathy toward many rites and ceremonies of Roman Catholicism, and sometimes there seems to be a thought that formalities or complex ceremonies undermine the centrality of God's word. Why are ritual studies necessary? I would appreciate it if you could explain why Protestants need to study ritual and rites as well.

Our suspicion of rituals and ceremony is rooted in our history. The Protestant Reformers in Europe rejected the abuses of the Roman Catholic Church and its authority over the spiritual lives of clergy and believers alike. The Reformers saw a need to remove the rituals, art, and even music—the aesthetics—that symbolized for them the church's corrupted power. This was in part because they believed all Christians had direct access to God; rituals and art should not stand in between us. Calvin and his followers went even further than Luther and others in their distrust of ritual, as leaders attempted to understand a Christian church without a pope, without a powerful hierarchy. The centrality of preaching the word overshadowed the role of sacrament and ritual in the congregational lives of Reformed Christians.

It might have been necessary for early Reformers to swing the pendulum that far as they worked out the identity of this new movement and separated themselves from the Roman Catholic Church. In proclaiming the "priesthood of all believers," the role of clergy changed dramatically—from sole "owner" of sacramental practice to teacher and interpreter. We are taught that rituals are hollow, thoughtless, repetitious, and even boring (see van der Hart's description of "empty rituals"). But today many of us mourn the loss of communal spiritual discipline, of tradition, of beauty—many of our worship practices that we owe to the early church and even to what we know of the life of Christ. In the United States, clergy from several Protestant denominations have been reclaiming some of those liturgical and ritual practices of the earlier church, such as the liturgical year, confession, and healing of the sick.

Understanding ritual is critical for Christian leaders for several reasons. First, we human beings are ritual creatures. In various ways we order our lives, our priorities, and our faith through regular practices—not just in our words and thoughts but in our habits and actions. We are formed as Christians by what we do at least as much as by what we learn and say. And if we ritualize thoughtlessly—without understanding and evaluating the ways we are being formed and forming others—we miss out on a rich resource for our faith. And worse, we risk forming ourselves in ways that are destructive. James K. A. Smith (in *Desiring the Kingdom* and other volumes) does an excellent job of outlining the ways our unreflective practices shape us in unanticipated ways, and the importance of paying attention to the habits we are consciously or unwittingly forming.

Our distrust of ritual has, I am convinced, blinded us to the prevalence of ritual in our lives and the power of ritual—for good or for evil. We overlook the rituals in our lives. For instance, the church of my youth regularly involved us in practices I now understand as rituals: the altar call, the testimony meeting, the prayer meeting. We would have refused to call them rituals, but they shaped us deeply, and understanding how they work can help us harness their power for good and limit their power for harm.

5. Why are ritual studies essential in the study of liturgical studies? Recalling my own opportunity to learn about ritual studies through your class, I would appreciate it if you could explain why the ritual

studies perspective is important in addition to the historical, systematic, and biblical perspectives in the understanding of liturgical studies.

I hope I have addressed this question in part in the last question, but there is more to be said. The fields of theological study you listed are among those we call "classical disciplines." They are concerned with the cognitive, intellectual understandings we need to have of our faith tradition, and they are very important to ministry. Other fields, those in practical theology, are focused on the practices of religious communities and of individuals—liturgy, homiletics, pastoral care and counseling, Christian Education, administration.

In the United States and Europe, the distinctions between theory and practice—the "what" and the "how"—is being questioned. We learn the "what" by doing, and we learn the "how" by standing back and evaluating what we have been doing. Ritual studies is part of that reflection—how do we understand what we are doing when we worship, when we sing and pray, when we partake in the Lord's Supper?

Many are concerned about how Christianity "translates" from one cultural setting to another. We've become aware of the impact of colonialism and cultural appropriation of earlier missionary endeavors; at times the church has committed spiritual abuse when we believed we were following Jesus's command to "go into all the world and preach the Gospel." We urgently need to learn how the Gospel can be communicated in ways that respect cultural differences and appreciate their spiritual value rather than imposing a Western value system on the rest of the world. Ritual studies is one way we can explore those differences.

Ministry education draws on multiple disciplines beyond theological and biblical studies. The social sciences, such as psychology, sociology, economics, anthropology, and ritual studies, deepen our understanding of religious experience, of living in faith communities, and how people grow and heal. These disciplines should never replace those of theology and bible; they should, however, broaden our understanding of them, and of their relevance to the persons and communities we serve.

6. I still remember the books I read in your class: Mary Douglas, *Purity and Danger*, *Natural Symbols*; Van Gennep, *Rites of Passage*; Catherine Bell, *Understanding Rites*; Victor Turner, *Ritual Process*; Clifford Geertz, *Interpretation of Culture*; Ronald Grimes, *Deeply into the Bone*; d'Aquili and Newberg, *Mystical Mind*; . . . etc. Is there any particular reason for choosing these books?

First, I am delighted how well you have appreciated and recalled these classic texts! They have certainly been important to my own understanding of ritual, and I believe they are well worth reading and rereading.

The primary reason for including these texts is their impact on the field of ritual studies and other disciplines over the decades. One can't read far in the literature without encountering their names and their concepts. It would be difficult or impossible to understand ritual without at least an initial understanding of their work. Secondly, each text has a particular lens on ritual—it may be the ways ritual is deeply intertwined with culture (Douglas, Geertz, Turner), with ecology (Rappaport), with ritual structure (van Gennep), or with the physical realities of ritual participation (Grimes, d'Aquili and Newberg). They also span a range from the late nineteenth century to more current writers. This is helpful in understanding how our notions of ritual have evolved over the years.

Finally, these texts are particularly relevant to liturgical studies, and their authors' names will be familiar to most liturgical scholars. Each one informs, in some way, our understanding of our own liturgical practices, and has implications for those practices.

6. Van Gennep's *Rites of Passage* is considered to be a truly monumental work in the study of rites and rituals. Van Gennep explains the process of ritual in terms of separation, limen, and aggregation. Please explain this in more detail.

Van Gennep's work is indeed seminal in ritual studies; many consider him a primary founder of the field. His three-part structure of separation, liminality, and incorporation (or reentry) provided an early template for understanding adolescent rites of passage, relying primarily on anthropological field study undertaken by other scholars in less developed populations. The structure has become a model of major transitions over the lifespan, emphasizing a clear removal from earlier cultural roles (e.g., childhood), into a period of isolation and trial (a "liminal" or threshold in-between time), and finally a reentry into the society formed for a new role (e.g., as an adult.)

It describes a process of transition—of moving from one social/psychological state to another—and emphasizes the need for "time out" and self-examination before assuming the roles of his or her new identity. It has deepened our understanding of Christian conversion, of the catechumenate, and later of the Roman Catholic Church's Rite of Christian

Initiation for Adults (RCIA). Van Gennep's work did highlight one powerful function of ritual—assisting individuals in transition from one life stage to another while limiting the potentially disruptive results of such changes. It provided a road map—and a road—from one stage to the next. For twenty-first century Western Christians, it has also pointed to our lack of culturally recognized rites of passage for adolescents—except, perhaps, for obtaining a driver's license or graduating from school.

Even more important than his work itself was its impact on later ritual scholars such as Victor Turner and Joseph Campbell. Turner in particular expanded the notion of liminality to describe whole groups of people who live at the margins of a society.

As powerful and intuitively appealing as the model is, we should exercise caution in applying it to all rituals. First, van Gennep described the process of particular rituals—rites of initiation for adolescents—and not for *all* ritual processes. Second, the model more accurately described male transitions than female transitions. Finally, it attempted to describe less-developed tribal cultures and will not necessarily be as descriptive of late-modern industrialized societies.

7. Van Gennep's theory has clearly influenced many liturgical scholars. His well-known framework of separation, liminality, and aggregation has offered a valuable lens for interpreting rituals of transition—such as Christian initiation, weddings, and funerals—by drawing attention to what occurs both before and after the central ritual event. Building on your previous response, I would like to ask a few follow-up questions. How do you assess the strengths and limitations of Van Gennep's theory? Some critics have noted its resemblance to thesis-antithesis-synthesis logic, raising the question of whether its structure might be too schematic or reductive for certain ritual contexts. Moreover, there are many rites of passage in the church today—some inherited and others underdeveloped. What, in your view, are the functions and merits of rites of passage in congregational life? And how might we renew or reimagine these rites in ways that are pastorally meaningful and theologically sound?

I touched on several of these great questions above. Each one deserves a fuller exploration, but that would go well beyond the limits of our time and space here.

First, it is important to acknowledge that van Gennep's model can inform many of the life passages that twenty-first century Christians (and others) experience in Western countries. Our culture, and even our churches, lack powerful rituals that could highlight the importance of these transitions, and ease them as well. How to do that, though, is complicated by the religious and ethnic pluralism in the United States, by the doctrine of separation of church and state, by the diversity of Christian denominations, etc.

But let me briefly discuss two areas of pastoral interest. We have celebrations of many life events—birth, marriage, and death in particular. But we lack rites of passage for adolescents in Western societies. Other cultures, of course, have transition celebrations like the bar and bat mitzvah in Judaism or the quinceañera in Mexico and elsewhere. Lacking popular or even secular rituals to mark this important transition, the Christian church has an opportunity for ritual innovation and for developing rites within congregations and denominations that could fill this gap. I've heard of churches, for instance, that mark a teenager's new driving status by handing them a set of car keys during a regular worship service, pointing out both the privileges and the responsibilities that go with their new status. Perhaps even more powerfully, I know a Baptist congregation (which does not practice infant baptism) but which had many members from other Christian traditions where their children had been baptized. Rather than practice "re-baptism," the pastor developed a beautiful Confirmation service where these Christians affirmed their baptisms as infants. That service was held the week after the "adult" baptisms and became so popular that the young Christians baptized just the week before asked to be included in the new Confirmation service!

Church membership is another important transition. At least in the United States, though, Protestant church membership has become a more casual, less demanding process than in the Roman Catholic Church, for example, or even in other social groups like lodges and political parties. The social sciences tell us that we value more highly those groups that require more from us in order to belong; groups that require more effort to join become more valuable to us. Of course, we risk making it so difficult to join that few would be willing to pay the price. But van Gennep's work suggests to me that we would deepen the meaning of church membership if we expected more of those wishing to join. These steps might be as simple as extended membership preparation, including the history of the church and the congregation; participation in a social service event or small group in the church; perhaps even a sponsoring member or family, much like we provide for confirmands.

8. What was interesting while reading Victor Turner's book, *Ritual Process*, was the "transition phenomenon of ritual process" and "communitas." Turner uses the expression "liminal" (in Latin, *limen* means a threshold) to mean people, by doing ritual, moving from one phase to another phase. The participants at this stage of transition are neither in a previous state nor in a subsequent state, nor are they subject to any previous or subsequent rules or positions. Turner described the group of participants in this transitional stage as an anti-structure community. I would be grateful if you could explain structure, anti-structure, liminality, and communitas for the reader. I would also be grateful if you could give an example of how these ideas can be used when we explain "initiation into the church" and change through various ceremonies.

Turner's development of liminality is an interesting and complicated one. I will try briefly to sketch what I have taken from his work.

First, van Gennep introduced the term as a *temporary* time/space between one status and another—especially between childhood and adulthood. He understood that each society had roles and expectations of adults that were different from those of children. The roles are part of the society's "structure"—their routine ways of relating to each other, their mutual expectations, their daily habits and activities, the level of responsibility each has. During liminality, the rules are suspended; participants are no longer children, but not yet adults; they form ways of relating that are fluid and less predictable—a period of "anti-structure." Once the former children have experienced liminality, they then return to the previous structure, but now with the status and responsibility of adults.

Turner translated this understanding to groups of people within larger societies who functioned at the margins. He described the monastic movements in Europe (e.g., the Franciscans) who operated outside normal ecclesiological structures but under the blessing of the church. They were less temporary than van Gennep suggested, but their original marginal status eventually led to a new structure of their own, particularly once they were endorsed by the church. Turner believed these "marginal" groups fulfilled important functions for the larger church. "Communitas" was his word for the sense of belonging, often felt ecstatically by participating members.

I'm not sure that Turner's development says as much about Christian initiation as van Gennep's. But it could suggest that we carefully examine the roles and expectations we have of members, for instance, and how we look at those who want to be a part of our congregation but don't fit the "molds" we have fashioned. For instance, how might differently abled children or adults enrich our decision-making and our worship? How might the unhoused change our perceptions of what God is up to, or what might we learn from those who have recently come to faith, or who don't want to turn their whole lives over to the church? Can we develop new ways of belonging that are more flexible, more diverse?

9. I think that Clifford Geertz's book *Interpretation of Culture* also provides a good perspective for the study of ritual. In interpreting culture, he rejects the Western-centered traditional/modern dichotomy and emphasizes ethnographic and empirical research. He insists that interpretation of culture is not simply looking at the culture of the group from the perspective of an outsider but from the perspective of an insider, through "thick description" work; it can be an interpretive science that seeks meaning, not merely an experimental science that seeks rules. I would appreciate it if you could explain "thick description," what advantages it has in interpreting the culture of a particular group, and what points to keep in mind.

You have described it well. "Thick description" is a term that applies to the ways most anthropologists work, though Geertz gets credit for developing the notion most clearly. Rather than observing and interpreting behavior from the outside, it requires understanding what the actions, like rituals, mean to the participants, how they interpret them. For Geertz, this also meant understanding cultural meanings in great detail and breadth, both those shared with others and those particular to individuals. For instance, he conducted fieldwork primarily in Indonesia and included in his writing the different ways in which time is experienced and the meaning of birth order in families. Thick description involves suspending judgment and studying deeply the symbolic meaning of actions, language, and belief.

In the social sciences we find a parallel in qualitative research—the study of individuals, groups, or settings in depth, in contrast to quantitative research which focuses on measuring social variables like religious practice, charitable giving, or political views. Quantitative researchers can then compare those numbers, either with other groups or before and after some intervention, such as an education program or sermon series. Quantitative research can be generalized—applied to other groups—while qualitative research is focused on in-depth study of one group or institution. Each type of research has its place. Qualitative research, like thick description, provides a richer contextual picture of groups, but is not focused on determining which is better or worse.

10. Then, from Clifford Geertz's point of view, how can an understanding be reached in order to observe the worship and ceremonies of a specific church or age group through thick-description work? Also, what are the benefits, and what are the limitations?

In graduate school, we were required to undertake a brief study of some small group. I sang in the church choir in a large church my family and I were attending. I participated in rehearsals and worship services, observing the ways members and the conductor interacted with each other, and listening to the ways they talked about what this group meant to them. I offered no interpretation to others (until I wrote up my study for class), though I did attend carefully to how I was welcomed as a newcomer, how I experienced the music and the interactions among members, what changes in group dynamics I observed over time, and what it was like to leave the group. I also looked at the history of the congregation, its demographics, and its theological commitments. It was a very small "thick description."

Anthropologists talk about their work as "participant-observers." They do not stand apart and make judgments about what is going on; they experience being part of the group over time. Rather than focusing on being "objective," they attend carefully to their own experiences as well as to what they learn about the experiences of other participants. Since people become self-conscious when being observed by outsiders, becoming an insider leads to greater trust, more openness, and more authentic understanding.

Ethnographic research methods have been helpfully used to study congregations and other faith groups. One excellent resource is pastoral theologian Mary Clark Moschella's 2008 volume on *Ethnography as a Pastoral Practice: An Introduction*.

11. While learning ritual studies with you at Garrett, I remember watching the *Avatar* movie that was released at the same time. From the point of view of ritual studies, there was not only ethnographic knowledge but also many examples of formative effects of rituals and symbols incorporated in this film. I thought about how rituals move the hearts of the congregation, creating emotional empathy and motivating them to act as one force; how communal rituals create, maintain, and transmit memories; how ritual forms communal identity; how it can grow people into warriors. I thought that the content I read in the books on ritual studies was intensively concentrated in this movie. Rituals seem to have

formative power. However, I do not think that rituals have magical powers. There are also wrong rituals. For example, the Nazis in Germany had rituals, and there was the power of rituals found in the communist revolution as well. How can we distinguish between good and bad rituals? Are bad rituals eliminated by natural processes or time passing? How can a congregation remain neutral and coolheaded without being swept away by crowd psychology?

You have highlighted at least two really important dimensions of ritual. First, as I've mentioned, ritualizing is a natural dimension of being human. We are created to make sense of our world, and navigate it, through ritual as well as through language; it is a feature of our biology. Genesis 1 outlines not only the Creation, but a seven-day liturgical cycle of work and rest. While we are more aware of some of our rituals than of others, our daily lives, as well as our church calendars, are marked by ritual.

That said, since ritual is "normal" or natural, it is morally neutral. Rituals can be used for good or for evil. The intense use of ritual in 1930s and 1940s by the Nazis to mobilize the German people to conquest and genocide is one of the more dramatic ways in which ritualizing binds groups of people together and moves them toward predesigned goals—even against their better judgment. Our Christian rituals can also shape us to believe that we are superior to others or can promote attitudes toward the world that are destructive rather than life-giving. This is, in fact, the strongest reason we have to understand ritual's power—to make use of ritual for God's purposes rather than selfish or nationalistic outcomes.

12. Why did anthropology or ethnography mainly study primitive tribes or people in undeveloped areas to understand the structure of people's thinking?

There were many reasons, though earlier anthropologists and other social scientists believed in a basic human nature that became more complicated and less visible with the dawn of industrialized societies. Human behavior, they believed, could be seen in its purer form in smaller, less developed communities which they imagined were closer to the kinds of groups our own ancestors inhabited. Finding isolated tribes, untouched by "civilization," would, they believed, provide a simpler sample of human cultural interactions.

More recently, scholars have questioned the validity of that belief, and explored whether we can so easily apply those convictions to larger, more developed societies like our own. For example, industrialized societies rely more on specialization—groups or individuals learning skills that they then trade with others for goods and services. While this has made field work and analysis more complicated, it undoubtedly will help us come closer to helpful insights. At least as importantly, we must realize that our society is not necessarily more "advanced" than so-called primitive societies. Each social structure is uniquely adapted to its own setting.

13. The book *Mystical Mind* by d'Aquili and Newberg was also very interesting. It was a masterpiece for these two leading medical researchers of the time to explain the human experience of religion in terms of neuroscience and neurophysiology. In other words, discussions on how the human brain is involved in religious experience and how the human brain interacts with human emotions and cognition were explained. What is your evaluation of this book? Is it possible to scientifically explain the "mystical mind?" There are many subjective parts of human faith and passion, so is it reasonable to objectify the structure? I would also appreciate it if you could explain the relationship between "conscious," "subconscious," and human rituals in the book.

My own interest in this whole area of ritual and liturgy blossomed about the same time that I was discovering the neurosciences. Like ritual, I see the functions of the brain as the human side of the divine-human encounter. d'Aquili and Newberg have followed in the steps of earlier scholars known as biogenetic structuralists, who combined brain sciences with anthropology and argued that our brains are "hardwired" for ritual. Ritual participation promotes a sense of social cohesion—of bonding together. In ritual our heart rates and even our brain functions synchronize with those of other participants; we become part of a large whole. This is probably related to Turner's notion of communitas.

Our brains, they argue, have evolved to make sense of the world, of ourselves (including our bodies), of our social connections, and of God. It is our brains that experience transcendence, connection with others, and the physical realities of the world. This is an oversimplification, but our language about God is rooted in the brain's left hemisphere (for most of us), and our passions, intuitions, and feelings emerge from the right hemisphere and other structures beneath the brain's outer shell or cortex. Our brains and bodies may become aroused by threats around us or by the excitement of seeing a loved one; they may also be calmed as our bodies experience safety and comfort, returning to rest. When both occur at the same time, d'Aquili and Newberg believe we experience the ecstasy of religious experience.

This book is only one of several attempts to understand how our brains and faith intersect. Because we think about God, talk about God, worship God, feel God's presence, and participate in religious communities, faith is a very complex matter, involving our whole selves: our intellects, our passions, and our bodies. So, it is not surprising that there are no simple correlations between religious experience and brain functions.

Much work has been done in this area since this 1999 volume, so it is scientifically dated. The book has been criticized on several fronts, including their conviction that we can build a universal theology "from the bottom up," beginning with the brain as a roadmap. If this were possible, they believe it would diminish or eliminate much of the world's conflict. In emphasizing the commonalities of the world's religions, they overlook the significant differences between them, the cultural differences that shape our experiences of God, and the many other influences on our religious beliefs.

As I have worked in this field, I have also increasingly come to see the whole body as a site of God's activity rather than just the brain. In fact, much of the brain is dedicated to "reading" the body—its physical position, its state of arousal, its health and well-being. I am intrigued to understand more fully how our bodies shape our experiences of the world, of each other, and of God as our brain works constantly to make sense of how our bodies are responding to the world around us. This is particularly relevant to liturgical study, since our movements, our gestures, our eating and drinking, all shape our intellectual and emotional faith experiences.

The notions of consciousness and the unconscious were highlighted by the work of Sigmund Freud in the late nineteenth and early twentieth centuries. He believed that the conscious mind pushed painful memories out of our awareness; healing involved recovering those memories and integrating them so that they had less power to shape our thoughts and behaviors. Recent neuroscience describes the unconscious quite differently. We are conscious of only a small fraction of what our minds are doing—the tip of the iceberg—but it is activity within the brain, rather than repressed memories, that is too complicated and hidden for us to be aware of. It is here, I would argue, that much of our ritual experience shapes us—a present but invisible resource that is formed over time by extended practice. What we do shapes us as effectively as what we think and believe. We may be conscious of learning a new spiritual practice, but over time, it becomes automatic—a critical part of who we are.

Theologically, this work in neuroscience has called into question the distinctions between body, mind, and soul. Many of us are returning to a Hebraic emphasis on the unity of the person. Greek influences in the early life of the church thought of body, mind, and soul as operating in two or three different realms; when death occurs, the soul leaves the body and returns to God. This resulted in a distrust and even denigration of the body, and of women's bodies in particular. Yet Christian faith speaks of the resurrection of the body, when we are raised again to be united with Christ.

14. You also wrote *Remembering the Future, Imagining the Past: Story, Ritual, and the Human Brain* (Eugene, OR: Wipf and Stock, 2003) from within the context of brain research. You were interested in the connection between ritual and brain studies twenty years ago. I would appreciate it if you could introduce the motivation for writing this book.

Thank you for the book promotion! This volume grew out of my early attempts to make sense of the ways the brain sciences might enhance or strengthen our understanding of both spiritual practice and pastoral care. It would have been tempting to just scratch the surface and find "easy" connections. But the neurosciences are complicated enough that it required coursework, study, and thought to probe more deeply. This book was an attempt to introduce the possibilities of the emerging neurosciences for counseling and other religious practices. I also hoped to provide just enough scientific context to invite others to think along similar lines.

At a personal level, I suspect that my childhood religious training—which distrusted the body and promoted spiritual "purity" as the highest good—was a deep (unconscious?) motivation to learn more about the body. I have learned to value the body's wisdom.

15. Research such as neuroscience and brain study is recently in the spotlight. What benefits can be given to the field of pastoral counseling or liturgical studies through these studies? I would appreciate any practical examples you use.

The neurosciences have contributed to my work in both pastoral care and liturgy in at least two ways. The first, I believe, is the most important. It concerns the unity of body, soul, and mind. In my teaching, research, and ministry I find myself thinking differently, more holistically, about human beings. What will engage their bodies as well as their minds? What will inspire and arouse as well as what will give comfort or healing? How can we follow Jesus's commands to "fear not," while remembering that realistic fear is necessary to our survival. What can we do, what habits and spiritual skills can we practice that will bring about the love of God and neighbor? I have been drawn back to Psalm 8 on many occasions: what are we human beings that God is mindful of us?

Second, at the practical level, there are countless insights the sciences offer. Because our bodies have their own internal rhythms, what does it mean if we speed up or slow down a practice like singing a favorite hymn, or familiar prayer like the Lord's Prayer? How can we make use of the brain's feedback from the body by involving movement, gesture, and posture in our worship experiences? How can we listen to the body's response to early trauma in ways that promote healing and diminish the destructive power of memory?

The clearest practical matter for me, however, has involved memory. We now know that the brain does not store memories of events in single "files" of information. Instead, the brain automatically breaks down our experiences into sights and sounds and smells and feelings, storing each of these in different locations in the brain. When we remember, then, we are not calling up an unchanging memory; we are reconstructing the memory as we recall it. This can be disconcerting since we rely so much on our memory and its accuracy. But it also means that our memories can change; each time we recall them, we have opportunities to enrich them. We may add forgotten details, or find a new perspective on the event, or diminish the memory's harm by retelling the story to a trusted friend, pastor, or therapist.

That also deepens my appreciation for how liturgy and ritual work: they are ways we remember—not just in our minds, but in our bodies. We recall the stories of the Gospel and the dramatic characters in the Old Testament. We find personal connections with those stories as our brains imagine ourselves in those stories; we will likely find new meanings in those stories as we recall them at different points in our lives. And we are transformed in the process.

16. Roger Sperry's split-brain experiments, various types of memory through brain research, the relationship between memory and

participants' identity, and mirror neurons, which you had previously taught in class, were very informative. Through this knowledge, I remember gaining insight into how important Christian rituals, such as the Lord's Supper, can affect the memory and identity of the participants. What are some needed precautions when applying the knowledge of neuroscience to the field of theology? Is science value-neutral? What attitude should theologians and pastors have in the dialogue between science and theology?

Another critically important question. There is a temptation to idolize the sciences, to see scientists as the new "priests and prophets." During the recent pandemic, we often heard the mantra to "follow the science." As persons of faith, it is critical that we respect the sciences for what they reveal (e.g., masks and vaccinations save lives) while also recognizing the difference between knowledge and wisdom.

First, the sciences can appear to reduce "truth" to what can be observed and measured through our five senses. That is an advantage when we are looking at diseases, climate, or the physical universe in which we live. It can be a detriment when we are dealing with matters of faith and meaning, even with what we should do about our dilemmas.

In my early chaplaincy training, it became clear to me that the medical profession knew much about healing and extending life. When patients faced terminal illnesses and quality of life became questionable, the physicians' impulse commonly dictated prolonging physical life. That is understandable, given medicine's vocation, but too often the needs of patients, their families, and even their financial resources were overlooked. Our faith tells us that physical life is to be cherished but not idolized; there is more to life than this world dreams of. Fortunately, social and medical attitudes toward death have been changing.

Our society worships technology not only for its ability to heal illness, but to enhance human functioning. We now have at our fingertips more computing power than massive mainframe computers did in the 1960s. Our memories get less exercise now that we can Google any information that we need; we no longer need to remember. At its extreme, this worship of technology has given birth to a movement called posthumanism, or transhumanism. If our brains are simply sophisticated computers, why could we not upload all our memories into a huge hard drive; immortality would be within our reach if our minds (or our selves) didn't depend any longer on our mortal bodies. There are many who dream of such a future.

Our faith teaches us that we are mortal; only God is immortal. Physical life has boundaries: we are born, we live, grow, love, and suffer, and we die. Even death, we proclaim, cannot separate us from the love of the eternal God. To live without limits is a denial of our creation by God. Though most of us fear death and won't welcome it before its time, we live out our lives knowing that time itself has limits. We shall pass, but others will come to take our places in God's world. And we will live forever in God's memory.

In short, we need to respect the sciences for what they offer us—understanding of our bodies and our world, methods of healing, relief from pain—but we also need to recognize the questions science doesn't answer: what does life mean? What is it for? How shall we best live? Better wisdom is found there in our faith.

17. At the height of the COVID-19 pandemic, debates over the propriety of online worship and communion became hot issues worldwide. What is your opinion? How can we evaluate practices such as online worship, communion, and baptism from a ritual studies point of view?

Such a timely topic! We have all had to rethink such critical issues over the past few years and try to discern faithful responses. I was serving as interim pastor of a congregation when the pandemic changed our lives forever. In the space of two days, we had to decide how to handle in-person worship, balancing our need to be together with the risks to worshipers, especially older members. It was not an easy decision, but we decided Saturday night to cancel; I made my sermon available via email. The next week we were providing recorded worship services that members could watch. Our learning curve was steep!

Though most of us returned to in-person worship months ago, many congregations continue offering services online; many will do so indefinitely. This has helped many who could not, or should not, attend services for health and safety reasons or who are traveling; they have been able to participate from a distance.

But it has also raised important questions like those you mention. I have friends and respected colleagues on different sides of the issue. Since you asked for my opinion, I will say this: while I value accessibility for worshipers who cannot attend, I believe ours is an embodied faith—Jesus's life, death, and resurrection emphasize the goodness of our physical world that is worth redeeming. Since childhood I have recalled the command to "forsake not the assembling of yourselves together" and Christ's claim that "where two or three are gathered together in my name, there am I in the midst of them." I do not experience that profound, physical connection when I watch a service on television or my computer screen. But as a Reformed theologian, I also recognize that my own limits do not restrict God's power!

Selected Bibliography

Hogue, David A. "Brain Matters: Neuroscience, Empathy, and Pastoral Theology." *Journal of Pastoral Theology* 20, no. 2 (2010): 25–55.

Hogue, David A. "Brain Matters: Practicing Religion, Forming the Faithful." *Religious Education* 107, no. 4 (2012): 340–55.

Hogue, David A. "Catching the Dog's Own Tail: An Essay in Honor of Catherine Bell." *Religious Studies Review* 36, no. 3 (2010): 175–81.

Hogue, David A. "How I Learned to Stop Worrying and Love the Brain." *Religious Education* 106, no. 3 (2011): 257–61.

Hogue, David A. "Re-membering Our Body of Work." *Journal of Pastoral Theology* 29, no. 1 (2019): 1–11.

Hogue, David A. *Remembering the Future, Imagining the Past: Story, Ritual, and the Human Brain*. Eugene, OR: Wipf and Stock, 2009.

Hogue, David A., Herbert Anderson, and Marie McCarthy. *Promising Again*. Louisville, KY: Westminster John Knox, 1995.

10

WILLIAM WILLIMON

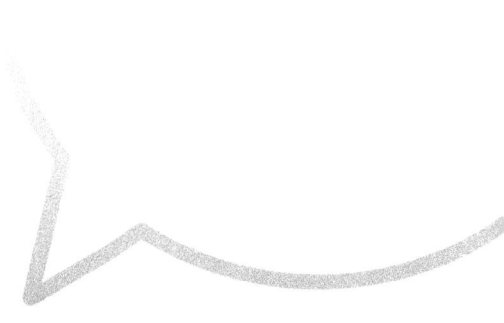

William Willimon is a pastor and theologian of the United Methodist Church. After graduating from Wofford College in 1968, he received a Master of Divinity from Yale University Divinity School and a Doctor of Theology from Emory University in 1973. He has taught for many years at Duke University and served as Dean of the Divinity School. In 1996, he was selected as one of the twelve most outstanding preachers in the English-speaking world by Baylor University. He is widely known through works such as *Resident Aliens: Life in the Christian Colony*, coauthored with Stanley Hauerwas, a colleague at Duke University. In addition, works such as *Worship as Pastoral Care*, which emphasizes the importance of rituals in the process of faith formation, have received much love from readers.

Interview with William Willimon

Professor Willimon, it is an honor to meet you. Your reputation is widely known not only in North America but also in Korea. Currently, nine of your books (including coauthors) have been translated into Korean. They are widely read by seminarians, pastors, and believers. I really appreciate your time to attend the interview.

1. Could you please tell us about your background as a theologian?

I studied religion in college and theology at Yale Divinity School with further graduate work at Emory University. I then served as a Methodist pastor in South Carolina.

2. When I read your books, I could sense that your fields of interest are very diverse. For example, your book *Worship as Pastoral Care* seems to indicate that you have a great deal of interest and insight into the rites and ceremonies of church. Whereas *Resident Aliens*, which you coauthored with Stanley Hauerwas, illustrates a deep insight into Christian ethics. *Pastor: The Theology and Practice of Ordained Ministry* also shows in-depth teaching on pastoral theology, and *Sunday Dinner* and *Remember Who You Are* give valuable teaching on sacramental theology. In this regard, I want to ask you a couple of questions. What should we call your area? Are you a pastoral theologian, a pastoral counselor, a practical theologian, or a worship scholar? What kind of academic and pastoral background do you have that enabled you to conduct such diverse research?

I suppose I'm a pastoral theologian. I think that my brain works like a pastor's. I am interested in so many different topics because ministry is about everything. I think that it's not good that the academic study of religion has become so very specialized. Pastors have to be interested in a broad range of topics because, in a sense, God is not about "spirituality" or "religion." God is about everything. Therefore, our minds must be expansive, and we've got to be generalists rather than specialists.

3. Now, I would like to ask a question about your book *Worship as Pastoral Care*. This book was published in Korea in 2017, and the first printing sold out as soon as it came out. I have read this book as a must-read while I was doing my PhD at Garrett-Evangelical Theological Seminary. I must say that it's a book full of valuable insights. For the Protestant Church of Korea, there is not much interest in rituals and ceremonies yet. Can you tell us why the rituals and ceremonies are important for our life of faith? What motivated you to be interested in this field?

I am so flattered that my books have a readership in Korea. It is wonderful for me to be a partner with the growing, dynamic Korean church. I'm humbled. Many Protestants say, "We aren't into rituals and ceremonies" when, in reality, ritual is a part of any continuing human gathering.

Ritual is patterned, predictable, purposeful behavior. Isn't it interesting that some of the most important times of our lives—like birth, death, marriage—are so heavily ritualized? Rituals help us cope with mystery and change. All churches are "ritualized," even those who don't admit that they are. In a way, Protestants who think they don't have a Book of Common Prayer or prescribed rituals need to be even more attentive to their rituals and ceremonies, asking themselves questions like, "Are our rituals, that we go through on Sunday morning, functional or not? Do they help us do work with God that we need to do, or do they hinder us from this work? Are they biblical? Do they help us meet God or do they enable us to avoid God?"

4. According to your book, it seems that the rituals and ceremonies play a very important role in the process of forming faith. However, in the Protestant tradition, which emphasizes preaching over the rituals and ceremonies, there seems to be some objection; they have a tendency to think that ritual or ceremony belong to the Roman Catholic Church, not the Protestant church. How can I persuade people who hold this position?

Of course, preaching itself is also a ritual—patterned, purposeful, predictable behavior. Just try to preach in a church that's not of your tradition and you will be quickly told, "That's not really a sermon." Also, when someone in the congregation dies, we don't just preach. We do a wide range of rituals in church and out, everybody knows how to respond. Rituals help us to do work that's difficult to do (such as confronting death and bereavement) but work that needs to be done. They tell us how to behave when life is falling apart. They tell us what to do first, then second, then third in order to move closer to God. Sure, Protestant churches don't have as many noticeable rituals as a Catholic church, but even a Pentecostal church has rituals—certain predictable patterns for speaking and acting that they use every Sunday.

5. The United Methodist Church seems to have produced many outstanding liturgical theologians. For example, James F. White, Don E. Saliers, E. Byron Anderson, Karen Westfield Tucker and, of course, you, Professor Willimon. Is there any secret for such an outcome? Garrett, Drew, and Boston University—affiliated with the United Methodist Church—showed a great interest in the liturgy by opening a doctoral program in liturgical studies. I am curious as to why the United

Methodist Church is showing such interest and investment for studying liturgy (or worship matters).

Interesting question. Not sure why so many Methodists have been liturgical scholars. Maybe it's because Methodism is both Protestant and Catholic, coming out of the Anglican church. Maybe we are a bridge between so-called "liturgical" and "nonliturgical" churches, borrowing some from both. I hope it's also because Methodists want to be part of the universal church. Let's remember that there are more people having the Lord's Supper every single Sunday and using the lectionary and going through ritual (that is, Roman Catholics) than those of us who don't.

6. Your book *Preaching and Worship in the Small Church* seems to have great implications for the current Korean church. In this book, you wrote, "Unlike large churches that carry out various ministries, small churches should focus their capabilities on the most basic and core ministries that the church has to undertake, which are worship, sermons, sacraments, baptisms, weddings, and funerals." I think it's an excellent statement. A small church should not simply benchmark a large church but develop on its own strengths. Now, a question pops up in my mind: In order to excel at worship services, sermons, baptisms, weddings, and funerals, how crucial is the lead pastor's competence?

I think the pastor's leadership is crucial for every aspect of the church's life. It's hard to imagine any congregation that outpaces its pastor's leadership capabilities. Frightening thought but still true to my experience. Following Jesus, being faithful to his mission, is just too difficult to do without leadership!

7. How can seminarians or people who want to be a pastor learn about the ceremonies such as baptisms, weddings, holy communion, and funerals in depth? While Korean churches and seminaries emphasize preaching, there are few curricula about worship and its practice. How can the senior pastor learn or develop their ability to preside over or plan these rites and ceremonies?

Well, as you note, there are lots of good resources out there for reading. Also, I think it's helpful for pastors-in-training to visit other church families, to observe, and to participate. Protestants are free to borrow, adapt. For instance, I know lots of new, young, evangelical congregations in the US who are now having communion every Sunday, who are using incense and processing with crosses. That's new to them, but the young folks in their congregations don't know if it's new or old, it's just helpful to their own development as Christians. I think we are in a time of greater borrowing and experimentation. We are free to adopt practices that we find to be helpful and nourishing of faith.

8. Related to the previous question, I would like to ask a question about worship service. How should a lead pastor plan out the worship service? Small churches have a common difficulty: the lack of human resources. For example, it's hard to find a musician or even a pianist. So, it seems that it is not easy for the lead pastors to plan and lead the worship services under such circumstances. For a leader of a small church, what does it mean to focus on the competency of worship? How can we plan a worship service well and lead it gracefully? Could you give us some tips?

I think worship should be planned. By the pastor in smaller congregations, with help from musicians and others in larger churches. I like it when small congregations see their small size as an opportunity rather than a lack. Small congregations don't need to act as if they are second-rate churches with bad music. Use music that is appropriate. Adopt a style of leadership that is appropriate to the scale of the congregation. Remember, Jesus ended his ministry, its summit, with the Last Supper where he presided, not by strutting around with a microphone on a stage, but as a gracious, welcoming host at a table. A small congregation can do that better than a large one. However a pastor leads, it must be with a sense of expectation, responsibility, and care, realizing that this service is most people's major encounter with Christ for the week.

9. The disappearance of the next generation in churches is a global and a current issue. The United States seems to be no exception. In a way, it seems like you lived the golden age of the American church and theology. What do you think of the current situation? For the future of the church and the next generation, what can leaders and members of the church do? When I was studying for my PhD at Garrett Theological Seminary, I felt that the number of pastors enrolled in the United Methodist Church was insufficient. In rural parts of America, a pastor often serves several churches. How can we overcome this crisis?

Maybe I was fortunate to have lived in the church of the past few decades. On the other hand, maybe the present church, with its challenges, is more of an adventure to lead. We have got to be flexible, experiment, and find a way to keep up with Jesus as he moves toward a new generation. He WILL have a people, he WILL have a witness, and he WILL reclaim his world. So, the question is not IF Jesus shall reign, but whether or not he will reign with us as part of his reign!

10. It seems that the matter of worship posed the biggest issue in the church during the COVID-19 pandemic. Pastors, theologians, and church members have had heated discussions about online worship, online baptism, and online sacraments. I want to ask what your thoughts are on this matter after observing the actions of churches over the past two years. I am also curious to know your personal theological reflection as a theologian and pastor.

These have been incredible years of experimentation and innovation. Among my questions are:

- Is your congregation's website publicly presenting who you aspire to be? If the main feature of your front page is a picture of your building, that's a sure sign of looking at your church from the inside out. The website should be inviting, pitched to those on the outside.
- Social media ought to be used but ought not to be a substitute for in-person worship and study. Your online worship is a wonderful accommodation to some of your members who, for reasons of health, mobility, or geography, can't be physically with the congregation. Online worship is best seen as a prelude to, a means toward in-person worship participation. During the pandemic some of us made the mistake of telling our congregations, "Online worship is just as good as being here." No, it isn't. In a time of shrinking in-person life and expanding of virtual life, your congregation has an opportunity to be a prime place for person-to-person, God-to-person encounters. Sunday worship at your church could be just what people are yearning for, even though they may not know it.

11. You are an outstanding preacher, being selected as one of the best preachers in North America. How did you prepare to become a good preacher? Please give us your own know-how, especially to those who want to become good preachers.

I listened to other preachers. I tried to get in deep with scripture. I tried to work hard on my craft. The Holy Spirit did the rest. Don't know if I'm a "great" preacher, but I at least try to be faithful.

12. The annual seasonal sermon (according to the Christian year) is a great burden for the pastors, since congregations can remember what the pastor preached for several years. But, it is not easy to prepare a fresh sermon because of our lack of knowledge about the Christian year. How can we prepare well for the seasonal sermons, for example, Christmas, Easter, Trinity Sunday, Ascension Sunday . . . ?

There are now more resources for the biblical preacher than ever before, particularly resources tied to the common lectionary. Use those resources. I also think there is so much preaching on the web on platforms like YouTube. View those to help stimulate your creativity.

13. If there are any scholars or books that have had a great influence on you, please tell us. What motivated you to become interested in pastoral theology?

Walter Brueggemann has always been a great help to me in my work. I vividly remember when his book, *Prophetic Imagination*, came out. It was most influential on my work. I've also been helped by all of the preaching books of Tom Long, particularly his *Witness of Preaching*. I also admire the preaching books of Barbara Brown Taylor.

I think my interest in theology comes from my days in college when I first took a college religion course and found that theology was interesting, much more interesting than philosophy!

14. Could you please introduce me to how to do lectionary preaching? In Korea, preaching methods using lectionaries are not well known. Also, there are several texts in the lectionary in a specific week. There are some connections among texts, but sometimes it is hard to find some relationship among the texts (first, second, third readings). I would appreciate it if you could explain the process of preparing a sermon with these texts.

I have found the lectionary a wonderful way to preach from a wider array of scripture than I would preach if left to my own devices. The lectionary encourages me to explore areas of the Bible that are challenging and daunting for me.

I generally only preach from one of the assigned texts. I think it's hard to do justice to the unique voice of a given text while attempting to mix it with other texts. So, I usually stick with just one text, more often than not the assigned gospel.

15. I would like to ask a question about your book *Word, Water, Wine, and Bread*. In chapter 6, you point out the shortcomings of the Reformers' thoughts on worship. You point out that the Reformers were creative and sensitive in matters of faith and doctrine but lacked creativity in the area of worship. You insist that while the Reformers succeeded in enhancing the participation of worship among congregations, their worship was somewhat personal and subjective. You evaluate the role of the congregation in worship as still being passive. It seems that you evaluate the sixteenth-century Reformers as having failed in the liturgical and worship matters. Is this a correct understanding of your book? Some reformed churches or denominations insist that we should follow a sixteenth-century Reformer's worship theology (or practice). What do you think about that?

I think it's true that the Reformers were mostly interested in doctrine and, with the exception of someone like Zwingli, didn't spend much effort changing the liturgy. They felt that scripture had been neglected, but, interestingly, they didn't seem to think that the liturgy needed to be reformed to make it speak a wider array of scripture.

The heavily penitential emphasis upon sin and the passion of Christ that characterized medieval Catholic liturgy continued in the liturgies offered by Calvin and Luther. They did not know that this penitential emphasis was an "innovation" the church had made in the early Middle Ages, not the oldest liturgical practice.

Modern liturgical innovation has generally tried to recover a wider, broader use of scripture in its liturgies for baptism and the eucharist so that they emphasize the whole, full sweep of salvation history, not just the cross and sin aspects.

16. Your book *Remember Who You Are* has had much attention and concern among Korean believers. The book has been evaluated as explaining well the deep meaning of baptismal theology and practice. I especially think chapter 9 and chapter 10 are very impressive. In chapter 9, you connected baptism and death, and in chapter 10, you connected baptism and Christian identity. It was excellent!! Related to these, I would like to ask two questions.

(1) How can we remember well the baptism which we received a long time ago? I know there is baptismal renewal in North America, but what are other ways we can continually remember our baptism?

I'm amazed and gratified at the Korean response to my work. That's wonderful. In the renewal service, when you are urged to "remember your baptism and be thankful," that is more in the sense of "remember who you are," "remember that you are owned and claimed by Christ" more than an historical recollection of a past event. In a sense, at whatever age we are baptized, we keep living into an understanding of our baptism, we keep finding new significance as the Holy Spirit, given to us in baptism, keeps working in us and leading us into deeper truth about Christ. So "remember your baptism" is a call to keep moving forward and to keep exploring Christ.

(2) As you mentioned, baptism is very closely connected to Christian identity. We know the *Apostolic Tradition* shows three years of education for people. However, in current times, there is a very short time of education. Would you tell me your opinion? How long should we teach catechumens? What sort of curriculum is necessary?

I think at a minimum this says that instruction of baptismal candidates is needed. The church needs to articulate to baptizands what the church believes happens in baptism and the ways in which the church considers baptism to be a gift of God through the church. How long? In a sense, it's hard to do too much preparation. I would think two or three sessions at least. On the other hand, some of the most important education related to baptism comes after baptism. I think that postbaptismal instruction may be more important than prebaptismal instruction. When you think about it, the whole Christian life is a long process of postbaptismal instruction, of waking up and discovering deeper significance in your baptism.

17. Your book *Sunday Dinner* was also translated into Korean. Your book establishes what is the Lord's Supper, and why this is important and beneficial for us. Currently, I heard that, in America, "dinner church" has appeared, and these churches have grown enormously. What do you think the reasons are for the success of these churches? How can we connect the Lord's Supper and dinner table fellowship?

I have heard about these dinner churches but know nothing about them. I would say that it makes sense to connect our human meals with the Lord's Supper, to keep being reminded that God comes to us in meals and that God uses the ordinary stuff of everyday life to meet us. Calvin says somewhere that God never forgets that we are animals, so God comes to us most vividly in something that all animals do—eat!

I used to say that a church ought to try to have some of the feeling at the Lord's Supper (joy of being with one another, delight in fellowship, and food together) that they have at other picnics and congregational dinners.

When I was in Seoul a few years ago, I vividly remember the wonderful dinner that we had with a congregation in a church basement. I knew no Korean, but in the meal and the laughter and joy, I felt very close to and very loved by the people there.

Jesus knew what he was doing when, at the end of his earthly ministry, he said, "This is what it all means. Have some bread, have some wine."

Selected Bibliography

Hauerwas, Stanley, and William H. Willimon. *Resident Aliens: Life in the Christian Colony*. Nashville: Abingdon, 1989.

Willimon, William H. *A Guide to Preaching and Leading Worship*. Louisville, KY: John Knox, 2008.

Willimon, William H. *Lectionary Sermon Resource: Preaching the Psalms*. Nashville: Abingdon, 2019.

Willimon, William H. *Lectionary Sermon Resource: Year A, Part 1* and *Year A, Part 2*. Nashville: Abingdon, 2019.

Willimon, William H. *Lectionary Sermon Resource: Year B, Part 1*. Nashville: Abingdon, 2017.

Willimon, William H. *Lectionary Sermon Resource, Year C, Part 1* and *Year C, Part 2*. Nashville: Abingdon, 2018.

Willimon, William H. *Listeners Dare: Listening for God in the Sermon*. Nashville: Abingdon, 2022.

Willimon, William H. *Pastor: The Theology and Practice of Ordained Ministry*. Nashville: Abingdon, 2002.

Willimon, William H. *Preachers Dare: Speaking for God in the Sermon*. Nashville: Abingdon, 2021.

Willimon, William H. *Remember Who You Are: Baptism, a Model for Christian Life*. Nashville: Upper Room, 1998.

Willimon, William H. *Sunday Dinner: The Lord's Supper and the Christian Life*. Nashville: Upper Room, 1998.

Willimon, William H. *Word, Water, Wine, and Bread: How Worship has Changed Over the Years*. Valley Forge, PA: Judson, 1980.

Willimon, William H. *Worship as Pastoral Care*. Nashville: Abingdon, 1982.

Willimon, William H., and Robert L. Wilson. *Preaching and Worship in the Small Church*. Nashville: Abingdon, 1980.

11
PAUL WESTERMEYER

Paul Henry Westermeyer was born in 1940 in Cincinnati, Ohio. He holds a BD degree from Lancaster Theological Seminary, an MSM degree from Union Theological Seminary in New York, and a PhD from the University of Chicago under the guidance of Martin Marty.

Westermeyer is a pastor in the Evangelical Lutheran Church in America (ELCA) and has achieved great fame as a church musician, theologian, educator, and author. He served as Professor of Church Music at Luther Seminary in St. Paul, Minnesota, for twenty-three years. Prior to that, he taught at Elmhurst College in Illinois for twenty-two years.

Westermeyer served as president of the Hymn Society in the United States and Canada and as editor-in-chief of The Hymn, a publication of that society. He also served as national chaplain for the American Guild of Organists. In addition to the Christus Victor Prize awarded by the Liturgical Institute of Valparaiso University, he has received many other awards. He has written numerous articles about the nature of church music and the vocation of church musicians. His representative works include *Te Deum*, a detailed account of church music from the Old Testament to the present.

Interview with Paul Westermeyer

It is a great pleasure to meet you, Professor Westermeyer. You are well known as a master in the field of church music, especially in music theology. Although music is becoming a greater part of modern worship services, many church pastors and worshipers seem to be in a state of confusion as to which music is appropriate for worship service and which hymns or gospel songs to choose. I would like to express my sincere gratitude for this interview with you, professor, as one who has influenced the North American academy and religious circles for a long time.

1. I would like to ask you a question about one of your books that is considered a masterpiece in music theology. I read your book *Te Deum* and was astonished by the extensive research that you poured into this book. Please tell me how you wrote and prepared this book. And if it is translated into Korean, what should the Korean readers focus on while reading?

When I was teaching a course about church music at Elmhurst College in Elmhurst, Illinois, I assigned students readings on closed reserve at the college library. They repeatedly said to me, "Would you give us a book with this material in it between two covers so that we don't have to keep going to the library to get it?" I said to them, "There's no such book." They replied, "Then write one." I had not planned to do that but began to think about it and to work on it. *Te Deum* was the result. It took a number of years to complete, so it was not published until after I had left Elmhurst College to teach at Luther Seminary in St. Paul, Minnesota.

I should probably explain what made *Te Deum* possible. It was the result of a long quest and study. When I was in high school, and even before that, I began asking questions about church music. Pastors from various backgrounds and traditions said to me, "Keep studying theology, and you'll get over the music." Musicians, on the other hand, also from various backgrounds and traditions, said to me, "Keep studying music, and you'll get over the theology." I didn't "get over" either one and found it hard to find sources where church music was studied with musical, theological, and liturgical insights.

At Elmhurst College, as an undergraduate student (BA, Music, Organ), I had a splendid music professor, T. Howard Krueger. He was the first person who took my questions seriously. He was a music theory expert, not a theologian, but he was a faithful Christian who was conversant with the academy and the church. He helped me find the places and people where I could get help.

Trying to find places for graduate study with an interdisciplinary program in church music was the problem at graduation. I did not find a ready-made program, but I did find places that were open to the interdisciplinary study and had the necessary resources for it: Union Seminary in New York (MSM, Choral Conducting), Lancaster Seminary in Pennsylvania (BD), and the University of Chicago Divinity School (MA and PhD, Church History), with Martin Marty as my advisor.

I don't think there is a Korean translation of *Te Deum*. There is a translation in Chinese by Fang-Lan Hsieh. It is published by Grace Publishing House in Taipei, Taiwan. Korean readers should focus on the same things readers in any language should focus on—trying to learn all they can about church music from as many times and places as possible and then use what they learn in the most faithful and constructive ways possible in their traditions, places, and languages.

2. Looking at the works of Augustine and Calvin, they seemed to recognize the power of music used in church. At the same time, they warn about the side effects and possible risks in church music. What is your opinion on this matter?

Both Augustine and Calvin were aware of the power of music and sought to keep it from becoming idolatrous. Augustine knew that words with music can stimulate more ardent piety than words alone, but he also knew that music can call attention to itself. He vacillated between the value of music and its danger, finally permitting music as long as the meaning of the words and not the singing is the most important thing. Calvin in his sixteenth-century Geneva restricted sung texts to congregational Psalms in syllabic unison settings without instruments or polyphony.

Augustine knew he could be too strict or too lax. He is very perceptive and needs to be heeded, but no good is done if reading his comments drives you into a corner in a mental institution. Calvin's danger is to write off the value of choirs and God's gift of the musical arts. I think Luther and the church catholic have a more constructive position which, as Gordon Lathrop might say, is that music like all things in worship is to be "broken" to the word of God and sacraments. What that means is not solved by legalistic pronouncements, but by the gracious use of music, as J. S. Bach and others would tell us, for the glory of God and the good of the neighbor. The word "broken" is positive, not negative. In this context it has the sense of "opened to," "used and developed constructively with its characteristics and underlying capacities," or something like that.

3. Knowing that there are two sides to church music, what kind of music should churches use in the worship service? What are the criteria that churches should look for when choosing church music?

I'm not sure what you mean by two sides, but I think what I just said answers the question. The criteria are for the glory of God and the good of the neighbor. This is not about either legalistic restrictions or about anything goes. It's not about writing off pleasure or embracing its dangers. It's about using God's gift of music wisely, constructively, and faithfully. That means learning all we can learn from our sisters and brothers before us from many times and places, with their checks and balances. It's not about idiosyncratic desires of any one person or time and place, but about what faithfully sings the church's song of God's grace around word, font, and table in our assemblies here and now.

4. Church music helps to form faith through repeated practices, to convey theology through lyrics, and to play a role in offering. Yet, it seems that there are many cases where church music is used only functionally and as an auxiliary means. Is church music essential in worship? If so, what is the most important role or influence that music plays in worship?

I probably hinted at an answer to this question in the last answer. Music sings the church's song of God's grace around word, font, and table, for the glory of God and the good of the neighbor. Whether music is essential in worship is answered by the church's practice: the church sings and can't help from singing in response to what God gives us. As Luther says, God is present everywhere in the creation, but God is present to and for us in the celebration of word and sacraments. The church as a whole has responded to this gracious gift by singing at this celebration and then by going out from it to our various vocations in service to one another.

Yes, church music helps to form faith through repeated practices, it does convey theology through lyrics, it plays a role in offering, and it is functional. And, yes, music is often used as if these "functions" are unimportant and music is an irrelevant "auxiliary." This situation helps to explain why music and musicians can be used as scapegoats and treated badly and disposably.

The role and influence of music are multifaceted, given the nature of music. It is hard to describe their multifaceted reality with a single category of most important role and influence. One can perhaps get at this or point to it by noting that the church's music sings the grace, love, mercy, and forgiveness of God in a communal song of praise, prayer, proclamation, story, and gift.

5. Everyone will agree that the lyrics are important in hymns. However, there seems to be no standard for musical form, beat, tempo, etc. Traditionally, conservative churches are more closed, whereas contemporary churches seem to be very open to hymn selection or music style. What are your thoughts on this?

Styles vary across time and even in the same period. Forms, meters, tempos, and musical syntaxes as a whole are not always the same. This is to be expected in different linguistic, ethnic, and cultural groups where histories and memories are different. In the same time, place, and culture, there are also different memories and histories. Different ethnic groups, for example, do not erase their histories when they have moved to countries different from their ones of origin. That is a good thing when used well. The trouble comes when churches in the same time and place use styles as tools to beat up on other churches with different styles.

Rather than focus on style, the place to begin is by figuring out what is fitting and makes the most constructive sense in context, with the resources that are available in that time and place. So, for example, congregational music has to be congregational. Strophic forms, folk song, and memory banks are important. Choral, organ, and other instrumental music has to take these factors into account in the sense that the music is being made for and with a worshiping congregation. It is not a concert or a time to show off technique, though technique and the finest possible standards in a given context are important. But a choir can do all sorts of music that a congregation cannot do, provided it fits the place in the church year, the service itself, and the occasion. So, for example, a piece that is beyond a congregation's capacity to perform but within that congregation's capacity to understand is appropriate for the choir, but not for the congregation.

This can be surprising. On one Pentecost Sunday I decided to use a piece that fit the day. It was an aleatory piece with unusual sounds. I was concerned about doing it, but thought the congregation I was serving could handle it. It turned out that I was right. After the service a woman in the church who thought she was the most unmusical person in the world sought me out with deep thanks. She said, "That was the most meaningful piece I have ever heard." It would not have been appropriate or have received that response on almost any other Sunday, but on that day it was quite important for her and for other people in that congregation.

6. The importance of music in modern churches seems crucial. The emphasis on praise is almost equivalent to the sermon. Sometimes it even seems to be as important as the sacraments. In the history of church music, was there a time when music was more important in church than today? How do you view this contemporary trend in church music?

The importance of music in modern churches is no more nor less crucial than always, but we live in a period where the church is systemically stuck in imitating the culture's warfare. That can make music seem more crucial than normal and has led to crucial mistakes like making it the same as or equivalent to word and sacraments.

I don't know how to compare our age to past ages about this particular form of our broken human tendency to engage in warfare. Music has been a source of dispute before, though the nature of the dispute changes. Our dispute is propelled by the culture's predisposition to view the market as god. The church collapses into that position and uses music the way the culture does, to sell things. Music becomes a device to sell Christianity which becomes one more product on the shelf of products. The message of God's love and grace which the church sings is denied in our version of works righteousness.

7. A few years ago, there was a debate on the use of EDM (Electronic Dance Music) and drums in worship among Korean churches. What are your thoughts on using EDM in worship? Drums have already been used in Korean churches for a long time. What do you think about the use of drums in public worship?

Drums, like all other forms of music-making, can be used well or poorly. The issue is not the instrument, but how we use it. It can be used fittingly or not fittingly. The electronic component, however, is especially prone to misuse whatever instrument it is used with.

Electronic components of twentieth century composition that are associated, for example, with aleatory forms can be used well, but anything recorded that is used as the rhythmic control of a congregation's singing makes big trouble. The congregation's song is a living thing that changes with seasons, temperatures, surrounding sounds in the environment, the health of the congregation, a death or celebrative occasion sometime before a regular worship service, etc. Congregational song requires live leadership with sensitive leaders who know how to listen and respond.

8. One of the issues in modern Korean churches is uniting all generations to worship together. However, I feel the generational gap the most when it comes to the music of the church. There is a difference between the music that each generation prefers. How can we reconcile musical differences? I think arranging the song could be an alternative. For example, rearranging old hymns in a modern style could appeal to all generations. I would like to hear your thoughts on this matter.

Generational gaps are among the things we in our sinful condition use to divide us. There are good reasons to have some things that are generationally specific, but the weekly worship of the church is not one of them. It is among the church's constructive countercultural contributions to our common life.

Yes, we can and should arrange our music in various ways. But that arranging needs to be for everyone, not for one group, any one set of preferences, or what fits my individual likes and dislikes. Its reason for being is not to attract people or to cater to likes and dislikes. My individual favorite hymn or a particular group's favorite hymn is likely to be irrelevant. Music that is worth doing for the worship of the community as a whole is not spur of the moment or driven by individual tastes. We may experiment with good intentions, but what we compose may or may not have lasting value beyond our moment. And we will not decide whether it does or not, the same as those who preceded us did not decide what we have kept from what they gave us.

The music of the church lives with the checks and balances of past and present, young and old, multiple cultures, and multiple likes and dislikes, in a community of love, mercy, grace, and forgiveness through word and sacraments.

9. I believe that church musicians play an important role and provide great help in planning and officiating worship services. I wonder what the differences are between the roles of church musicians and the

officiators/preachers and how they can collaborate. Also, how should church leaders or pastors approach musical literacy?

You are right. The roles are important but different. They can be and need to be distinguished. Our tendency to collapse everything into one thing gets us in trouble. It denies the beauty and possibility of our life together.

In the gathered body, the ordained clergy is called to preach the word of God and preside at the sacraments. In the gathered body, the church musician is called to help the people of God sing the song of the church. In the gathered body, the congregation is called to sing. Then, the congregation is called to scatter to their various vocations in the world as clerks, bakers, secretaries, truck drivers, managers, family members, committee members, doctors, lawyers—whatever each person is called to do, with and for his or her neighbors.

10. In Korea, there are no hymnals specific to each denomination; there is just one hymnal common to Korea. I wonder if a hymnal for each denomination is necessary and what role it plays.

That's a good question. The value of a denominational book is that it can relate specifically to a certain group. The value of a common book is that it has the possibility to be more ecumenical. If it's a service book and hymnal, however, not just a set of hymns, each group has to have some kind of separate service book. Agreement between groups about pretty detailed confessional and liturgical matters is not likely.

11. It may sound absurd, but I think there is a similarity between Gregorian chant and rap music. Of course, chants were used for worship and praise, whereas rap music is for externally expressing sharp and intense human psychology. However, chanting is allowed during worship, while it seems that the use of rap is not allowed. What are your thoughts on this matter?

There may be a similarity, but the associations and character of the two are very different. I'm not sure it would be possible, at least as a general rule, to find rap fitting for worship, especially if rap is for what you say it is for. Though human psychology and expressions related to it, like everything else in human life and experience, are not absent from worship, "expressing sharp and intense human psychology" is not the intent of worship or music for it.

12. It is not an exaggeration to say that the "praise and worship" style dominates the beginning part of worship in Korean churches. Regardless of the denomination, a band-style praise team leads the beginning of worship with contemporary gospel songs, followed by the traditional worship ordo, beginning with the call to worship. This practice seems to raise some questions of where to start the worship service. In addition, the order of worship and praise is often misunderstood as a time to prepare for worship. Some people also say that it feels like the worship service is split into two parts. Do you have any advice for how to address the situation the Korean churches are going through?

It would appear that you are describing two theologies with two practices. The two are hard to reconcile. What is called "praise and worship" has Pentecostal, free church roots. It takes a form where praise leads to worship. Praise is congregational singing for about an hour that leads to worship or "high praise" or "high worship." The second part exhibits gifts of the spirit and movement, but it is not the "traditional worship ordo" you reference which I assume is a Protestant preaching service with the Lord's Supper sometimes.

There is no way to "solve this situation" without changing one or both of the theologies and their practices. If you look at this from a broad historical point of view, this is another instance where a sectarian movement displaces, tries to displace, or at least unsettles a more catholic one. The sectarian movements have short life spans because of fewer or no checks and balances from other times and places, and the more catholic ones have longer life spans with at least some checks and balances built in even if they are not sought. If a strong leader comes along, there will be movement in one direction or the other, but high-level historical forces in a long-term catholic direction will have some control no matter what happens. Much or all of this will happen long after most of us are dead.

13. Although it depends on the church's situation, architecture, and theological considerations, where do you think it is most appropriate to place the choir seats in the church? It seems that Pentecostal churches locate the choir seat behind the pulpit, whereas Lutheran churches put it behind the public seats or in a loft where it can be hidden. Some churches locate it at a 45-degree angle to the left or right, while in some churches it seems to sit with the public. Is there an intention or meaning hidden in each position of the choir seat?

There may or may not be a conscious intent in how churches get constructed, but the architecture has implications and an influence no matter what. If the choir is in a position that is like a concert performance, a concert-like performance will tend to be elicited. If it's in a position where it can help the congregation sing, it will tend to help the congregation sing.

The congregation will hear the choir best if the choir is behind the congregation in a balcony or on an elevated position of some sort. And back there it cannot show off visually. In the front, showing off can be curtailed by directors and choirs who know what they're doing, and visual cues can be given. If the choir is hidden so it can't show off but also can't be heard well, there's double trouble.

My preference is the back where the choir is heard well, and is located with, not against, the congregation. I prefer to avoid the temptation visual cues bring in spite of their value, and I think organists and choirs can give musical cues if they are sensitive and think about it.

14. Martin Luther and John Calvin emphasized the importance of public engagement in singing. Some extremists even say that church choir is unnecessary because public singing is more important. What do you think about this issue?

Well, Luther did not junk choirs. He valued them along with the congregation's singing. That's why there are so many choral settings of hymn stanzas. A typical Lutheran way of singing hymns is to give some stanzas to the choir in alternation with the congregation. That gives the pastor and musician a chance to work together constructively to highlight a given stanza that will emphasize a certain theme in the sermon, and it gives the congregation needed breaks, especially if the hymn is a long one.

Luther and Lutherans also kept choral music beyond hymnody as well as hymns with the liturgy and Psalms in metrical and chant settings. When you add the organ and other instruments to this, you add further possibilities plus freestanding pieces in relation to all the rest. This gives all sorts of possibilities.

Calvin allowed only metrical settings of Psalms by the congregation with no choirs, no instruments, and no chant. If one wanted to do something else at home, that was fine. But the weight and majesty of worship before God in church required the restrictions he imposed. The Genevan Town Council restricted this even more severely. Calvin wanted the Lord's Supper weekly in a word and table sequence, but the Town Council thought that was too "Catholic." So, the part of the service that had the physical stuff of bread and wine plus actions was curtailed along with the balance of word and table and the danger of words alone pushing to the tyranny of words.

Luther and Calvin as well as the churches that followed them represent two quite different positions. Both are completely public. The Lutheran one pushes in an evangelical catholic direction, the Calvinist one in a direction that is nervous about anything "catholic," with a lowercase c as well as an uppercase C.

15. These days, there seems to be a lot of new styles of worship, such as jazz Vespers. What do you think about the movement to use jazz or various styles of contemporary music in worship?

Why not use jazz? It can work very well. It can also work poorly. The questions are what is fitting for worship, and how to do it in this particular time and place in relation to the wisdom of the whole church catholic and the grace of God in word and sacraments. This is not about legalistic fictions. We can figure it out.

Selected Bibliography

Westermeyer, Paul. *Church Musician*. Minneapolis: Fortress, 1997.

Westermeyer, Paul. *Church Musicians: Reflections on Their Call, Craft, History, and Challenges*. St. Louis, MO: Morning Star, 2015.

Westermeyer, Paul. *A High and Holy Calling: Essays of Encouragement for the Church and Its Musicians*. St. Louis, MO: Morning Star, 2018.

Westermeyer, Paul. *Hymnal Companion to All Creation Sings*. Minneapolis: Fortress, 2023.

Westermeyer, Paul. *Hymns of Lent*. Minneapolis: Augsburg Fortress, 2003.

Westermeyer, Paul. *A Large Catechism: Understanding Music in the Lutheran Tradition*. Minneapolis: Lutheran University Press, 2017.

Westermeyer, Paul. *Let Justice Sing: Hymnody and Justice*. Collegeville, MN: Liturgical Press, 1998.

Westermeyer, Paul. *Rise, O Church: Reflections on the Church, Its Music, and Empire*. St. Louis, MO: Morning Star, 2008.

Westermeyer, Paul. *Te Deum: The Church and Music*. Minneapolis: Fortress, 1998.

Westermeyer, Paul. *With Tongues of Fire: Profiles in 20th-Century Hymn Writing*. St. Louis, MO: Concordia, 1995.

12
RUTH MEYERS

Ruth Meyers is a liturgical theologian representing the Episcopal Church in the United States. After majoring in special education at Syracuse University, she taught elementary school students for five years. Following the completion of her Master of Divinity degree at Seabury-Western Theological Seminary, she earned her master's and doctoral degrees from the University of Notre Dame in liturgical studies. Her completed doctoral dissertation in 1992 focused on the development of baptism and Christian initiation rites in the revised 1979 Episcopal Book of Common Prayer.

Meyers served as the chair of the Episcopal Church's Standing Commission on Liturgy and Music from 2010 to 2015 and contributed to the Marriage Liturgy Task Force from 2016 to 2018, conducting in-depth research on the history and theology of Christian marriage. Recognized for her scholarly contributions and research depth in this field, her article "Marriage and Funeral Liturgy as Rites of Passage" was published in the *Oxford Encyclopedia of Religion* in 2016. With a deep interest in the relationship between worship and mission, she published *Missional Worship, Worshipful Mission* in 2014.

From 1995 to 2009, Meyers taught liturgy at Seabury-Western Theological Seminary in Evanston, Illinois, and from 2009 to the present, she has taught liturgy at the Church Divinity School of the Pacific and the Graduate Theological Union in Berkeley, California. Additionally, she served as the president of the North American Academy of Liturgy (NAAL) in 2003 and 2004.

Interview with Ruth Meyers

Nice to meet you, Professor Ruth Meyers. I am personally honored to have an interview with someone who is known as a leading liturgical theologian of the Episcopal Church in the United States. In 2008, when I was studying at Calvin Seminary, I read your article, which offered me valuable insights into the liturgical practices and theological framework of the Episcopal Church. I am grateful to finally have a theological conversation with you after fourteen years.

1. What is the relationship between the Episcopal Church of America and the Anglican Church of England? Could you explain the similarities and differences between the two in terms of institution and theology? Also, please tell us the number of members, the number of churches, and the seminaries of the Episcopal Church in the United States.

The Episcopal Church and the Church of England are both part of the worldwide Anglican Communion, which includes 42 member churches and an additional 5 "extra-provincial" churches. Churches in the Anglican Communion have their roots in the Church of England, which separated from Rome during the sixteenth century. Many of the churches were founded by missionaries from England, some by missionaries from the United States or Canada. We take counsel together in the Lambeth Conference of bishops, which has met about every ten years since 1867, and the Anglican Consultative Council, which includes bishops, clergy, and laity from each member church, and has met about every 3 years since 1971. Decisions of these bodies are not binding on any church of the Communion.

The churches have similar theologies. We view scripture as the foundation of our faith. We understand the Apostles' and Nicene Creeds as primary statements of our faith, and we do not have a confession of faith beyond those creeds. Our churches maintain the threefold orders of bishop, priest, and deacon, and we understand our bishops to be part of the historic succession of bishops. We find our unity in common worship, particularly the celebration of baptism and eucharist. Our worship practices are included in a Book of Common Prayer (BCP). While at their origins most churches of the communion used the 1662 BCP from the Church of England, most churches today have developed their own Prayer Book. These Prayer Books have a family resemblance but also reflect their local context.

In 2021, the Episcopal Church counted 1.7 million members in about 6800 congregations. In addition to the US, we have congregations in Taiwan, Haiti, Colombia, Dominican Republic, Ecuador, Honduras, Puerto Rico, Venezuela, and several countries in Europe. We are governed by a General Convention of bishops and elected lay and clergy deputies, which meets every three years. Our seminaries include: Berkeley Divinity School at Yale; Bexley-Seabury; Church Divinity School of the Pacific; General Theological Seminary; Nashotah House; School of Theology at the University of the South (Sewanee); Seminary of the Southwest; Virginia Theological Seminary.

2. I remember that you wrote an article about eucharistic inclusion for children. What is the official position of the Episcopal Church on the matter of infant communion? Is it the same as the Church of England? What are the grounds for your agreement or disagreement on this matter?

With the Book of Common Prayer adopted in 1979, The Episcopal Church welcomes all the baptized, including infants, to receive communion. The Church of England officially continues to follow the confirmation rubric, which requires confirmation before admission to communion, although individual dioceses can allow children to receive prior to confirmation. Our differences stem from different approaches to receiving and interpreting Christian tradition. Prior to 1979, the Episcopal Church Book of Common Prayer also included the confirmation rubric. Study of the historical development of Christian initiation led the Episcopal Church to an understanding of baptism as full initiation, including admission to communion. In England, while also recognizing these ancient roots, the church has decided to continue the reformation practice of requiring catechesis and confirmation before admission to communion.

3. When I think of Anglican churches and Episcopal churches, the Book of Common Prayer comes to mind. When I was doing my doctoral coursework, I read about the historical change of the Book of Common Prayer from Gordon P. Jeans' *Signs of God's Promise: Thomas Cranmer's*

Sacramental Theology and the Book of Common Prayer. I found it to be a very interesting but also quite complex history. I would appreciate it if you could explain a bit about the Book of Common Prayer for Korean readers. What are the strengths of the Book of Common Prayer? What does the Book of Common Prayer mean for the members of the Anglican Church living in the twenty-first century? Are there any downsides to the Book of Common Prayer?

The Book of Common Prayer (BCP) is a source of unity for churches of the Anglican Communion. In the twentieth century, more and more member churches developed their own prayer book, so we don't have a single BCP for the entire Anglican Communion. The prayer book provides texts that all churches in each province or member church agree to use, and we understand our worship practices to be our primary statement of belief. Thus, it is fundamental to our identity.

One downside is that the BCP can be restrictive, not easily allowing adaptation to the local context.

4. Is the 1979 edition the most recently revised version of the Book of Common Prayer? If so, what is the significance of the 1979 edition? I would appreciate it if you could be specific as to the sacraments and rites.

Yes, the 1979 BCP is the most recent revision. Prior revisions were very similar to the 1662 Church of England BCP. The 1979 book was influenced by liturgical scholarship and the liturgical renewal movement in the twentieth century.

One significant change is the centrality of baptism. In previous books, the rite of baptism was at the beginning of a section of life-cycle rites, which also included marriage, visitation of the sick, and burial. The 1979 book puts it earlier in the book, before the eucharist, and baptism is now defined as full initiation by water and the Holy Spirit, not requiring confirmation to complete initiation into the church.

The overall shape of the eucharist is similar to that of the Roman Catholic Church and other North American mainline Protestant churches: gather, proclaim and respond to the word, intercessory prayer for the world and the church, celebrate the meal, dismissal. The liturgy of the table for the eucharist follows the structure that Gregory Dix identified: take, bless, break, and give, and the eucharistic prayers all include an epiclesis over both the gifts and the people.

5. I know that there are pros and cons about the need to revise the Book of Common Prayer due to current issues, such as same-sex marriage and funerals for suicides. I'm aware that Dr. Louis Weil, who passed away recently, mentioned that it would be better to hold off the revision for the time being. If a denomination has a liturgical book, could you tell us when should the liturgical book be revised and how much do individual Episcopal churches follow it? Also, do the individual churches have or maintain liturgical freedom and creativity, even when they have the liturgical book?

The 1979 BCP includes many options. For example, a church can write its own form of intercessory prayer, as long as it includes prayer in specific categories: the church and its mission, the welfare of the world, the nation and all in authority, the concerns of the local community, those who suffer or are in any trouble, and those who have died. The book also includes an outline of the eucharist and allows a congregation to develop the service as it chooses, although that is not intended for use as a principal Sunday service.

Some congregations hold closely to the Prayer Book, while others exercise liturgical freedom and creativity. Some bishops insist on close conformity, others encourage some creativity. Since the late 1980s, the church has developed supplemental texts ("Enriching Our Worship") that use inclusive language for humanity and expansive God-language; while authorized for use throughout the Episcopal Church, actual use varies widely. Some congregations occasionally use prayers, especially a eucharistic prayer, from other churches of the Anglican Communion.

Louis Weil and I had different views on the timing of Prayer Book revision, which sparked further reflection in our conversations.

6. In the late twentieth century, I am aware that the baptismal renewal ceremony was held in the Anglican Church. Besides the Anglican Church, several denominations are conducting baptismal renewal ceremonies. Why is this ceremony necessary? Since this ceremony is disparate from Korean church practice, could you explain what this ceremony is about?

Baptismal renewal happens in different ways. When we developed the 1979 baptismal rite, we included a "baptismal covenant" that consists of an interrogatory Apostles' Creed followed by five questions eliciting commitment to Christian life (continuing in the apostles' teaching and fellowship; resisting evil; proclaiming the Good News; seeking and serving Christ; striving for justice). The 1979 baptismal rite calls for the entire congregation to respond to these questions; the candidates (or their parents and godparents) respond to questions of renunciation and adherence to Christ. So, baptism is a renewal of the congregation's baptismal commitment.

The Easter Vigil includes a renewal of the baptismal covenant if there are no candidates for baptism, and it can also take the place of the Nicene Creed on other baptismal feasts when there are no candidates for baptism (Pentecost, All Saints' Day, and the First Sunday after Epiphany, which is the feast of Jesus's baptism). I suppose this need for an explicit baptismal renewal reflects our post-Christendom context, where we need to remind ourselves whose we are and who we are, claiming our identity because we can't take it for granted.

Another form of baptismal renewal is confirmation, which used to be done once in a Christian's life, serving as a completion of baptism and admission to communion. Having come to understand baptism as full initiation, the church came to see that this individual renewal of baptism could be repeatable, used, for example, as a rite of membership in the Episcopal Church or as a reaffirmation after a lengthy period of time away from the church.

Of course, the eucharist itself is a regular renewal of our baptismal commitment, though that is not explicitly stated in the rite.

7. I believe that the book *Censura* by Martin Bucer is an evaluation and critique of Cranmer's Book of Common Prayer. What was the relationship between Cranmer and Bucer and how did Bucer's *Censura* affect the Anglican's Book of Common Prayer?

Bucer's *Censura* was one important influence on the 1552 BCP (the second BCP). Bucer was already in residence in England when the first (1549) BCP was published. One influence was the encouragement for weekly catechesis, rather than every six weeks. Learning the catechism as well as the Apostles' Creed, Ten Commandments, and Lord's Prayer was required prior to confirmation.

8. James F. White said that the reason behind the survival of the Anglican worship tradition, which has lasted for over five centuries, is its inner strength. Also, he said that the tradition of Anglican worship is the most easily identifiable, even after five centuries. He evaluated that

this strength came from the Book of Common Prayer. What were the characteristics of the Anglican liturgy (or liturgical practice)? And what does White mean by inner strength? Is the tradition still convincing for young believers in twenty-first century Anglican and Episcopal churches?

I think White means that the Book of Common Prayer provides a recognizable marker that not only prescribes the forms of worship but also serves as a primary focus of identity. Last summer, the Episcopal Church's General Convention adopted a set of principles to guide the development of liturgical texts, which provides a good overview of characteristics of Anglican liturgy, as understood in the Episcopal Church.

I think the tradition is still convincing for young believers, many of whom are attracted by the beauty of Anglican worship and the sense that they are connecting with a tradition of worship.

9. What are the differences between Anglican worship in the sixteenth century when Cranmer was active and Anglican worship in the twenty-first century? What are the issues on worship for the Anglican Church of the twenty-first century? Could you tell us about some of the discussions? What kind of stance does the Anglican Church take in relation to worship traditions and current culture? Currently, the Anglican Church is known as one of the most liturgical denominations among Protestants. Please tell us what tasks and efforts are being made to renew worship in recent days.

In the twentieth and twenty-first centuries, Anglicans are more open to ritual symbols and action. The sixteenth century Prayer Books were heavily centered on the word and often very didactic. We are increasingly attuned to the need to adapt liturgy to context, seeking forms of worship that relate to local culture.

The International Anglican Liturgical Consultation, a network in the Anglican Communion, has met approximately every two years to confer about principles that guide liturgical development. You can find more information on the Anglican Communion webpage. In the Episcopal Church, the Standing Commission on Liturgy and Music is the body that oversees ongoing liturgical development.

10. **Christianity is declining around the world, and the number of believers is plunging. The number of people wanting to become pastors is also falling. Is there a solution to this problem in the Episcopal Church of the United States?**

Unfortunately, we do not have a solution. Our bishops are very concerned about a shortage of clergy, and seminaries are seeing significant declines in enrollment.

11. **I would like to talk about your book, *Missional Worship, Worshipful Mission*. Please introduce the book briefly for the readers.**

My book explores the relationship between worship in the assembly and Christian mission in the world. I understand worship as one of the ways in which an assembly participates in the mission of God, that is, in God's work through Christ and the Spirit to reconcile all people and all creation with one another and with God. And I understand our missional actions in the world (for example, work for justice and peace; evangelism; interfaith dialogue; service to those in need) to be a means of offering worship to God.

The book is structured according to a Sunday liturgy. An introductory chapter explains the terms worship, liturgy, and mission and introduces two models for the interrelationship of worship and mission: a Möbius strip and a spinning top. Subsequent chapters discuss elements of a Sunday liturgy: gather, proclaim and respond to the word, pray for the world and the church, enact reconciliation, celebrate the communion meal, and go forth. A final chapter suggests ways to plan and prepare for missional worship.

12. **This book is very interesting in terms of the consolidation of liturgy and missiology. Although worship itself is not a tool of evangelism, the interest in the relationship between worship and mission is increasing amid the interest in missional church in recent years. How can our worship be missional? Are there any concerns that it may damage the essence of our worship? Is there any possibility that being interested in contemporary culture and people in contemporary society could flow into liturgical syncretism or consumer-centered worship?**

Worship is missional when the worshipers are drawn into concern for the entire world and find themselves propelled from worship into active Christian engagement in the world, participating in the reconciling mission of Jesus, empowered by the Holy Spirit. Missional worship helps worshipers attend to ways in which the God of Jesus Christ is already at work in the world and enables worshipers to engage in respectful dialogue with those who do not follow Christ. Missional worship invites believers to bring their hopes and concerns that arise in their daily lives and offer them to God, seeking transformation and wisdom to respond.

Yes, there's a danger of developing syncretic or consumer-centered worship, especially as we attend to the local culture. Discernment is always necessary. We have to consider whether our worship is in harmony with God as we have come to know God through Jesus Christ, and whether our practices enable us to turn our attention to God and deepen our relationship with God.

13. How can worship be missional and mission be worshipful as the title of your book suggests? It would be great if you could explain about the Möbius strip (p. 35) and the spinning top (p. 41) in your book.

Both images are ways to think about the continuous flow between worship and mission. A Möbius strip has only one side, so you move from worship to mission to worship again and again. In a spinning top, worship in the assembly (baptism and eucharist) is the core. Action in the world flows out of that core, and then one is drawn back into the core again. Both images suggest a dynamic interplay and rhythm for Christian life.

14. Please tell us what things you pursue in worship. Among the traditional Anglican-Episcopal worship and the recent missional church movement, what is your direction for worship?

My overall goal in planning and presiding at worship is to enable the symbols to speak evocatively and vividly, drawing people ever more deeply into the mystery of God. It involves a dynamic interplay of symbol and action along with text, music, and silence.

15. As a digression, there are research studies regarding missional church being poured out by pastors and scholars, but it seems that there is not enough research on missional worship. What is the North American scholastic trend on missional worship?

I refer to a few books about missional worship in my book (Thomas Schattauer, editor, *Worship in an Age of Mission*; Alan Kreider and Eleanor Kreider, *Worship and Mission after Christendom*; Clayton Schmit,

Sent and Gathered; Ion Bria, *The Liturgy after the Liturgy*), but among liturgical scholars, there have not been significant developments in recent years. A lot of writing about missional church comes from pastors and scholars in evangelical traditions rather than those in more liturgical churches.

16. The on-site worship service has been greatly reduced due to the COVID-19 pandemic. There were debates about online worship, online communion, and online baptism. What was the position of the Episcopal Church regarding on-site worship during this period? Were there any official policies or guidelines from the denomination? I would be grateful if you could share your personal thoughts on online worship, sacrament, and baptism.

The denomination did not develop official policies, but encouraged each diocese to do so, attentive to conditions in their local context. I think that online worship was an effective way to enable communities to gather, to hear the word, and to offer prayer (both intercession and thanksgiving) as a body. Because the sacraments of baptism and eucharist are embodied, involving tangible symbols and actions, they are not readily translatable to an online context; they require a community to gather in proximity to the symbols over which prayers are offered, so that members of the assembly can engage the symbols.

17. One of the features of the Anglican worship service is that it has morning and evening prayer meetings. In Korea, many believers often participate in early morning prayer meetings. In the case of the Episcopal Church, how active are the morning and evening prayer meetings among pastors and laity? How can the prayer meetings be spread to the lay people?

In the Episcopal Church, very few congregations gather for morning and evening prayer. In a few places, particularly those with a significant choir program, evening prayer is sung weekly or perhaps monthly. In some places, clergy will open the church for morning and/or evening prayer, but very few people join the clergy for this.

The pandemic brought new attention to the daily offices, and many online celebrations began. I don't know how many have continued.

In the last decade or so, a number of apps have emerged, enabling people to pray the daily office individually in any setting.

Selected Bibliography

Meyers, Ruth. *Continuing the Reformation: Re-Visioning Baptism in the Episcopal Church*. New York: Church Publishing, 1997.

Meyers, Ruth. "Diversity and Common Worship." In *In Spirit and Truth: A Vision of Episcopal Worship*, edited by Stephanie Budwey, Kevin Moroney, Sylvia Sweeney, and Samuel Torvend, 47–57. New York: Church Publishing, 2020.

Meyers, Ruth. "'I Will Bless You, and You Will Be a Blessing': New Marriage Rites for the Episcopal Church." *Liturgy* 34, no 3 (2019): 42–51.

Meyers, Ruth. *Missional Worship, Worshipful Mission: Gathering as God's People, Going Out in God's Name*. Grand Rapids: Eerdmans, 2014.

Meyers, Ruth. "Re-Imagining Confirmation." In *Signed, Sealed, Delivered: Theologies of Confirmation for the 21st Century*, compiled by Sharon Ely Pearson, 33–52. New York: Church Publishing, 2014.

Meyers, Ruth. "Spiritual Communion as a Response to Hunger for Christ." *Anglican Theological Review* 104, no. 1 (2022): 83–91.

Meyers, Ruth, and Paul Gibson, eds. *Worship-Shaped Life: Liturgical Formation and the People of God*. Harrisburg, PA: Canterbury Press/Morehouse Publishing, 2010.

Meyers, Ruth, and Katherine Sonderegger. "Jubilate: A Conversation about Prayer Book Revision and the Language of Our Prayer." *Anglican Theological Review* 103, no. 1 (2021): 6–26.

Mitchell, Leonel L. *Praying Shapes Believing: A Theological Commentary on the Book of Common Prayer*. Rev. ed. Updated by Ruth Meyers. New York: Church Publishing, 2016.

13
STEFANOS ALEXOPOULOS

Stefanos Alexopoulos was born in Zimbabwe and grew up in South Africa and Greece. He earned his bachelor's degree from Hellenic College in Brookline, Massachusetts, and a Master of Divinity degree from Holy Cross Greek Orthodox School of Theology. He then pursued studies at the University of Notre Dame in Indiana, under the guidance of the renowned liturgical historian Maxwell E. Johnson. His primary focus was liturgical studies, with a minor in Byzantine art and patrology.

Alexopoulos's graduate thesis, titled *The Presanctified Liturgy in the Byzantine Rite: A Comparative Analysis of its Origins, Evolution, and Structural Components*, was published by Peeters Publishers in 2009. Among his recent works is the coauthored book with Maxwell E. Johnson, *Introduction to Eastern Christian Liturgies*. Alexopoulos has also published over forty articles on Orthodox worship and actively contributed to collaborative projects and encyclopedias, establishing himself as a prominent liturgical theologian in the Orthodox church.

In 2003, Alexopoulos returned to Greece and continued his teaching career while serving as a diocesan priest. In 2009, he was appointed Assistant Professor in the field of liturgical studies at the Ecclesiastical Academy in Athens. Later in 2012, he was invited as a visiting professor at Yale University's Institute of Sacred Music. Since 2013, he has been serving as a Professor of Liturgical Studies at the Catholic University of America.

Interview with Stefanos Alexopoulos

I am delighted to have the honor of meeting with you, Fr. Stefanos Alexopoulos. As you are an esteemed liturgical theologian in the Orthodox Church, you also have established yourself as an exceptional scholar of your time. I appreciate your generosity in agreeing to this interview and dedicating your precious time to this undertaking.

1. To begin, may I request that you share with us your academic journey and the factors that have influenced your development as a scholar? Could you also elaborate on the institutions you attended, and explain what motivated you to pursue liturgical theology as your field of study?

I studied at Hellenic College/Holy Cross Greek Orthodox School of Theology in Boston (BA, MDiv) and the University of Notre Dame (PhD in liturgical studies). I initially never thought I would have an academic career. I thought that as a priest I should study in depth what I would be doing, leading in worship the community entrusted to me by the Church. I was blessed to have priest-mentors that transmitted to me their love for the liturgy. I also come from a priestly family, as both my father and my grandfather are priests (my grandfather has passed away), so growing up I was immersed in the liturgical experience.

2. You published an audiobook titled *Orthodox Christian Spirituality 101*. What is the nature of Orthodox Christian spirituality? How does worship relate to spirituality in the Orthodox Church?

I define liturgy/worship as the ritual celebration of salvation in Christ, the ritual celebration of the Gospel. As such, it has a direct and intimate relationship with spirituality. As a liturgical church, the Orthodox Church's liturgy/worship and spirituality are, for me, two very much interconnected and interrelated realities/conditions, and I would not separate the two. The experience of worship ideally leads us in a closer relationship with God, which transforms us, which in turn changes how we live. The experience of worship ideally radiates in all aspects of life, leading us in what Paul says, "It is not I but Christ who lives in me." I would argue that Orthodox Christian spirituality is a liturgical spirituality.

3. In relation to other theological fields, how does the Orthodox Church position and value liturgical theology?

Liturgical theology and, more generally, liturgy is, I believe, at the heart of all theological studies. Orthodox liturgy expresses in a highly worked theological language (see, for example, the Eucharistic prayers of Basil the Great and John Chrysostom) who the Christian God is, how we understand Him, what our relationship with Him is, what the Eucharist is, and what it does. Liturgical texts are highly biblical, filled with direct or indirect references to the Scriptures, and formed in the historical experience of the Church. In other words, in the field of liturgical studies, the other fields of theological inquiry meet and interact: biblical studies, patristics, church history, pastoral theology, etc. I would argue that liturgy is the axis around which all the other fields of theology revolve. How one worships reflects the worshiping community's belief, theological heritage, history, and pastoral outlook.

4. Prior to discussing liturgy, I would like to inquire about the Orthodox perspective on cosmology as a sacramental entity. In *For the Life of the World* by Alexander Schmemann, a sacramental outlook on cosmology is presented, and John Calvin also references sacramental cosmology in his *Institutes of the Christian Religion*. I would be greatly appreciative if you could elaborate on Orthodox sacramental cosmology and the significance of sacramentality, as it is fundamental to grasping the essence of the sacraments.

The notion of sacramentality is founded upon two important events in human history: creation and incarnation. In the former, materiality is created by God and deemed "good"; in the latter, the Word enters into history and assumes matter—he assumes human nature—to save it and to deify it, offering us salvation. The sacraments, then (and I understand sacraments not in the scholastic medieval notion limiting them to seven), and all sacramental acts of the Church point to the fact that salvation is something that affects the whole creation, not just humanity. In sacraments, simple and humble created elements (water, wine, bread, oil) themselves are sanctified, they become vehicles for God's grace and allow us to get a glimpse into the mystery of God. The properties of these elements (water = life, cleansing; bread and wine = nutrition; oil = healing) allow us to understand the effects of sacramental life in the spiritual/faith journey of a Christian. This notion of sacramentality is also behind the understanding that the Orthodox have about the environment and our role as stewards of the environment.

5. In your opinion, what distinguishes Orthodox worship from that of Western churches, and what are the respective strengths and weaknesses of each? I am also reminded of Robert Taft's works, in which he compares the liturgies of the East and the West.

I can only describe my tradition. It is not fair to express an opinion about "Western churches," especially when this umbrella term encompasses a very wide spectrum of traditions from very liturgical to almost nonliturgical.

My definition of liturgy as the ritual celebration of salvation in Christ has emerged from my observance and study of Orthodox liturgy. Liturgy is the communal and personal experience of that reality of Christ's salvation, a continuous reaching of God towards humanity, and our response to God's invitation to partake of that salvation. In liturgy I see, hear, feel, and experience Christ preaching and reaching out, and we, through our participation in the sacraments, experience Christ here and now, being touched and healed, as was the woman with the issue of blood. This fullness of the liturgical experience as God's presence in the worshiping community is what I most appreciate in my own tradition.

The danger in the Orthodox liturgical tradition arises when the ritual is experienced as ritualism, that is, going through the motions without understanding the meaning of what is done.

6. It is my understanding that the Orthodox liturgy is regarded as the closest to the historical tradition of the early church in comparison to other traditions. What factors have contributed to this, and how has the Orthodox Church been able to preserve this tradition over time? Furthermore, is it feasible for the Orthodox Church to pursue creative development of the liturgy while remaining true to its historical roots?

Tradition, and in our own topic liturgical tradition, is dynamic, not static. The study of liturgy demonstrates that, indeed, it is the product of creative development influenced by historical events, doctrinal controversies, and cultural contexts, and this development continues even today but always rooted in the apostolic experience. What I would consider a strength of the Orthodox Church is the sense and reality of continuity, from the apostolic times to today. For example, the celebration of the Eucharist in the

Orthodox Church is highly ritualized, reflecting the historical path of the Orthodox Church through twenty-one centuries of life, but, in its essence, it is still connected to the upper room and the table fellowship that Christ had with his disciples. Bread and wine are offered on a plate (paten) and in a cup (chalice) on a table (altar), and the words "Take, eat, drink" are central to what we do with these. The consecrated bread and wine, the Body and Blood of Christ, are experienced in the way the disciples realized their cotraveler to Emmaus was Christ when he broke bread with them—then their eyes were opened, and they realized that that person was Christ. This is what happens in the Eucharist. In the anaphora, we remember the divine economy (salvation history) as Christ on the way to Emmaus talked to them about what the Scriptures foretold about him, and we see Christ in the broken bread and shared cup, as the disciples recognized Christ at the breaking of the bread.

Having grown up in Athens, where Paul preached, and the uninterrupted presence of Christianity in Athens since then up to today, is just one example of this continuity that is the experience and precious heritage of the Orthodox Church.

7. Would you elaborate on the theological significance of the sacraments in the Orthodox Church? How does this understanding differ from that of Catholicism and Protestantism?

Again, I will limit myself to describing the Orthodox understanding.

The sacramental life in the Orthodox Church denotes and points to the fact that God's grace encompasses *all* aspects of life, from birth to death, with three sacraments having a central role: Baptism, Chrismation, Eucharist. It is through the sacramental life that we are called to grow into Christ. It is through sacraments that we realize Christ's presence among us. I would suggest a reading of Nicholas Kabasilas's *The Life in Christ* for a good presentation of how we understand the theological significance of sacraments. He says: "We depart from this water [Baptism] without sin. Because of the chrism [Chrismation] we partake of His graces, and because of the banquet [Eucharist] we live with the same life as He does. In the world to come, we shall be gods with God." But sacraments are not magic; they are a relationship. They reflect the synergy between God and humanity in that they necessitate a human response: "This is the life in Christ which the Mysteries confer, but to which, apparently, human effort also has a contribution to make."

8. In his work *La Théologie de l'icône dans l' Église orthodoxe*, Leonid Ouspensky provided valuable insights into the history and theology of the icon. However, it seems that the Western tradition, particularly Protestants, has a limited understanding of the icon. While a comprehensive historical and theological discussion would require several books, I would appreciate it if you could shed some light on the icon for those in the Western tradition, especially Protestants, and its relationship with contemplative (θεωρία) methodology.

The theological articulation of how we understand icons took place in the context of the Seventh Ecumenical Council (787)—Christ (and the saints) can be depicted in icons, as he is a historical entity. The reality of the incarnation allows for the depiction of Christ and events in his life and ministry. If there were cameras back then, we would have snapshots of him. The icons offer that. We venerate icons. What does that mean? According to Nicaea, only God is worshiped. When we venerate icons, we offer honor to the persons depicted. How do we understand that? It's like kissing a picture of a loved one. What we do is express our love, and the picture is the medium that allows us to express that love. We do not worship the person, nor the paper and the ink. In a similar way, we venerate (=bestow honor) to the images of the saints, as they are our heroes and our examples of what it means to live a Christian life.

9. Could you describe the way in which personal prayer is practiced by Christians in the Orthodox tradition? How does the Church provide guidance for personal prayer? Furthermore, how does the practice of contemplation relate to Orthodox prayer methodology?

Prayer is central to Orthodox life and spirituality, and I would say that personal prayer flows out of its public prayer and leads to public prayer. In other words, it's the extension, if you will, of public prayer in one's own personal life. For an excellent presentation of personal prayer in the Orthodox Church and the practice of contemplation, I would suggest that one watch the YouTube video of the late Kallistos Ware on "What Is Prayer?"[*]

10. Could you also discuss the Orthodox tradition's perspective on the apophatic methodology (*Via negativa*) in theology? How has this

---

[*] Kallistos Ware, "What Is Prayer?" YouTube, https://www.youtube.com/watch?v=AqTLTUxMGbQ.

approach influenced worship and liturgy within the tradition? And how do Orthodox Christians understand the concept of worship?

Theology, in general, reflects our effort to understand God, but God is beyond human understanding. For if we fully understood God, either we are gods, or God is not god. We reflect about God, and we study God based on God's revelation. We can describe God in a positive way when based on God's way of revealing Himself. For example, when we say "God is love," a positive statement, we are able to say that and reflect upon that because God revealed Himself as such. Another way to "explore" God is to exclude erroneous understandings of God. This does not define what God is, but it defines what God is not. So, when we say that God is "without beginning, without end," these are apophatic/negative statements, excluding the facts that God has a beginning and an end.

This approach has influenced worship in that we view our God in terms of relationship. Both personal prayer and public worship are a dialogue and expression of this relationship between the person, the community, and God. This relationship is defined in terms of living in, experiencing, and growing in salvation in Christ, because liturgy is the ritual celebration of salvation in Christ, as noted in a previous answer.

11. In the Eastern Orthodox Church, it seems the concept of deification holds significant importance. Could you explain the connection between deification, the public liturgy, and the sacraments?

Deification is central in Orthodox theology and spirituality, as it explains what salvation is all about. Deification is founded upon the experience of the incarnation. The Word, the second person of the Holy Trinity, assumed humanity, human nature, in order to restore it and redeem it. The fact that, with the Ascension, Christ ascends into the heavens with his human nature points to the understanding and destination of human nature: unity with God. Deification is nothing else but unity with God, achieving the "likeness." In the patristic literature when discussing the incarnation, the phrase that "God became man so that man can become god" (Athanasius, Irenaeus, and others) points to the understanding of deification. Becoming what we are destined to be.

We live and experience and grow into that reality in the sacramental life of the Church, where unity with Christ is at the center of every liturgical celebration. Liturgy is not just worship, it's a movement, an approach to God and one context in which God approaches us (not the only one, but I would say a privileged one). Central is the participation in the Holy Eucharist, whose purpose is our sanctification and our unity with Christ, so that "it is not I but Christ who lives in me."

12. I think your coauthored book *Introduction to Eastern Christian Liturgies* is a great book. I am grateful that this valuable primer on Orthodox liturgy was able to be published worldwide through the collaboration of Professor Maxwell Johnson, a renowned liturgical historian. I would appreciate it if you could explain the features and strengths of this book for the readers.

Thank you for your kind words. The book is unique in that it is the first effort, after many decades, to offer a comprehensive introduction to the liturgies of all Eastern Christian Traditions, not just the Byzantine. After the introduction that identifies the various Eastern Christian traditions and their liturgical heritage, the chapters that follow are thematic (Christian Initiation and Reconciliation, the Eucharistic Liturgies, the Liturgical Year and the Liturgy of the Hours, Marriage and Holy Orders, Anointing of the Sick and Christian Burial), enabling a comparative study of the various Eastern Christian liturgical traditions. The last chapter discusses the ethos of Eastern Christian worship and liturgical spirituality.

It contains a good topical bibliography by tradition that covers all Eastern Christian traditions, that can serve as a good starting point for anyone willing to explore the topic further.

13. What is the Orthodox Church's stance on the use of hymns and the development of contemporary music in other denominations? Additionally, what standards must worship music meet to be considered proper by the Orthodox Church?

New hymnographic compositions do take place today and are quite prevalent in the Orthodox Church at the local church level, but this new hymnography (in the Greek-speaking world) conforms to the norms of Byzantine music and its system of eight tones. Western contemporary music has not entered Orthodox services (although you have examples of four-part choirs singing in staff notation). Byzantine music relates to Greek demotic music, so in a sense church music was contemporary music in the Greek world up to maybe a century ago. In Orthodox churches in Africa, local music is used in worship; in other words, in the context of inculturation, local music can be used. If by contemporary one means

Western contemporary music, I am not familiar with examples of the use of such music in Orthodox worship.

Music in worship is there to serve the word, the message, and its role is to highlight and bring forth the message. So, the priority is the word/message.

14. Amidst the pandemic, how has the Orthodox Church adapted? With the necessity of online worship, the issue of conducting sacraments such as communion and baptism online has arisen. I would appreciate your views on this matter, and how have the Orthodox approached it?

The pandemic was indeed a very challenging period and experience for the Orthodox Church. The primary way that the Church adapted was the broadcasting of the services via YouTube, Facebook, and other means. The inability to participate in the sacramental life of the Church was indeed a challenge, and we are only now reflecting upon the experience in the Orthodox Church and discussing these issues. For example, there was a 2023 conference in Athens on "Orthodox Theology *in via* in the 'Dematerialized Reality of Late Modernity.'"[*]

Online celebration of sacraments is problematic in my view. Central to my objections is the notion of community and communion "online," the real "materiality" of worship (the use of water, bread, wine, oil) in the communal context, and the necessity of being together. While online contexts may offer us a sense of community, it does not replace and cannot be equated with the in-person experience of community.

15. The decline of the younger generation in Western churches has become a concern, resulting in a shortage of both members and candidates for ministry. How does the Orthodox Church in the United States approach this issue? I would be grateful to hear how the faith is being passed down and how the church is attracting individuals interested in becoming seminarians.

This is a big issue and a big challenge everywhere, and all Churches, more or less, face this challenge. I believe this issue has to be addressed at the local level—in the local worshiping community—by creating vital and

---

[*] Holy Synod of the Church of Greece, "Orthodox Theology *in via* in the 'Dematerialized Reality' of Late Modernity," International Conference on the Centenary of the Journal Θεολογία, Athens, Greece, October 11–14, 2023, https://www.ecclesiagreece.gr/English/theologia100/.

vibrant communities and inspiring the younger generation. The younger generation (and all people in fact) are looking for an authentic and honest witness to the Gospel of Christ, and they are very allergic to hypocrisy. The drop in vocations is partly due to the dramatic secularization of our cultures, but also partly to the failures of our Churches to inspire and communicate the vibrancy of the Gospel and how relevant the Gospel is to the world and today's challenges.

16. Among the Orthodox liturgical theologians, I think Alexander Schmemann is the most famous to non-Orthodox readers. What was Schmemann's contribution to the development of the liturgical theology of the Orthodox Church?

I would say that Fr. Alexander Schmemann has played a pivotal role in the field of liturgical theology, not only in the Orthodox Church, but also in the Christian world. His influence can be seen in the works of current liturgical theologians such as Kevin Irwin, David Fagerberg (Roman Catholic), and Gordon Lathrop (Lutheran), just to mention some well-known names in the field. Schmemann spoke of the liturgy not just as ritual or rubric but as a theological event in which the faith of the Church is presented in its celebration. I believe that the rediscovery of liturgy as a theological event is the most important contribution of Fr. Schmemann to liturgical theology. He also highlighted the relationship between the liturgical experience and life. I would suggest his short but powerful book *For the Life of the World*, a popular book that has been very influential and wide-reaching.

Selected Bibliography

Alexopoulos, Stefanos. "Anamnesis, Epiclesis and Mimesis in the Minor Hours of the Byzantine Rite." *Worship* 94 (2020): 228–45.

Alexopoulos, Stefanos. "The Gospel Narrative in Byzantine Liturgy." In *History and Theology in the Gospel Narratives*, edited by T. Nicklas, K. W. Niebuhr, M. Seleznev, 235–46. Tübingen: Mohr Siebeck, 2020.

Alexopoulos, Stefanos. "'ΦΩΣ ΧΡΙΣΤΟΥ ΦΑΙΝΕΙ ΠΑΣΙ': Evidence from Inscriptions." In *Studies in Oriental Liturgy: Proceedings of the Fifth International Congress of the Society of Oriental Liturgy, New York, 10–15 June 2014*, edited by Bert Groen, Daniel Galadza, Nina Glibetic, and Gabriel Radle, 157–166. Eastern Christian Studies 28. Leuven: Peeters, 2019.

Alexopoulos, Stefanos. *The Presanctified Liturgy in the Byzantine Rite: A Comparative Analysis of its Origins, Evolution, and Structural Components*. Leuven: Peeters, 2009.

Alexopoulos, Stefanos. "Puccio Capanna's Madonna and Child (ca. 1330) through Byzantine Eyes." *Orthodoxes Forum: Zeitschrift des Instituts für Orthodoxe Theologie der Universität München* 30, no. 2 (2017): 181–92.

Alexopoulos, Stefanos. "'The Savior Accomplished the Sacraments in Himself': Symeon of Thessalonike's Christological Approach to the Seven Sacraments." In *Let Us Be Attentive!: Proceedings of the Seventh International Congress of the Society of Oriental Liturgy*, edited by Martin Lüstraeten, Brian Butcher, and Steven Hawkes-Teeples, 11–21. Studies in Eastern Christian Liturgies 1. Münster: Aschendorff, 2020.

Alexopoulos, Stefanos. "The Use of the Bible in Byzantine Liturgical Texts and Services." In *The Oxford Handbook of the Bible in Orthodox Christianity*, edited by Eugen Pentiuc, 243–60. Oxford: Oxford University Press, 2022.

Alexopoulos, Stefanos. "When a Column Speaks: The Liturgy of the Christian Parthenon." *Dumbarton Oaks Papers* 69 (2015): 159–78.

Alexopoulos, Stefanos, and Dionysios Bilalis Anatolikiotes. "Towards a History of Printed Liturgical Books in the Modern Greek State: An Initial Survey." *Ecclesia Orans* 34 (2017): 421–60.

Alexopoulos, Stefanos, and Maxwell Johnson. *Introduction to Eastern Christian Liturgies*. Collegeville, MN: Liturgical Press, 2022.

14
DAVID GAMBRELL

David Gambrell is a liturgical theologian and hymn lyricist. He is currently a Research Fellow at the Institute of Theology and Worship at the Presbyterian Church (U.S.A.). He studied anthropology at Louisiana State University. Then, at Austin Presbyterian Theological Seminary, he earned a Master of Divinity. He earned a PhD in liturgical studies at Garrett-Evangelical Theological Seminary under Ruth Duck, a prominent worship scholar of the time and winner of the Berakah Award. He is an editor of *Call to Worship*, a quarterly journal published by the Presbyterian Church (U.S.A.). In revising *The Book of Common Worship* for the Presbyterian Church (U.S.A.), Gambrell played a leading role, along with Kimberly Long of Columbia Theological Seminary.

Interview with David Gambrell

Thank you for taking time out of your busy schedule and accepting the interview request. Personally, it's a great pleasure to interview a fellow alumnus of Garrett Seminary. I am aware that you have edited *The Book of Common Worship* of the Presbyterian Church (U.S.A.) with Professor Kimberly Long. This interview will explore the necessity and significance of a worship book for churches, as well as the process involved in preparing one.

1. I believe your official title is Associate for Worship in the Office of Theology and Worship of the Presbyterian Church (U.S.A.), meaning your main role is dealing with worship for your denomination. Could you describe a little bit more about your ministry for the readers, please?

I have served as Associate for Worship in the Office of Theology and Worship of the Presbyterian Church (U.S.A.) for fifteen years, since 2007. I have come to think of my vocation as "helping Presbyterians think theologically about worship." In my work I encourage members and leaders of our denomination to think critically and creatively about the relationship between Christian faith, Christian life, and Christian worship—connecting theology and ethics with liturgical practice. In doing so, I seek to rely on primary documents of the Presbyterian tradition: Scripture, the Confessions, and the *Book of Order* of the Presbyterian Church (U.S.A.), particularly its Directory for Worship.

In the course of my work for the Office of Theology and Worship, I have had the honor and joy of contributing to a number of important liturgical projects, including the PC(U.S.A.) Daily Prayer app (2012), *Glory to God: The Presbyterian Hymnal* (Westminster John Knox, 2013), a 2017 revision to the denomination's Directory for Worship, and the latest edition of the *Book of Common Worship* (Westminster John Knox, 2018). I have also taken part in ecumenical work as a Presbyterian member of the eighth round of Roman Catholic/Reformed dialogue in the United States and a representative to the Consultation on Common Texts, responsible for the Revised Common Lectionary.

2. I know that you are not only a liturgical theologian but also actively working as a lyricist. How many songs have you written so far? And how many of those songs were listed in the hymn book of your denomination (or other denominations)? I'd appreciate it if you could also tell me what you think is important when writing hymn lyrics.

I consider myself to be a lifelong church musician, singing in church choirs since my childhood. As such I have a deep love and appreciation for the music of the church, especially congregational song. Like many hymn writers, I started writing hymns as a pastor when I couldn't find a hymn that fit a particular occasion, service, or biblical text. Soon hymn writing became a personal spiritual discipline for me. For many years, I wrote a new hymn each week, often based on one of the Sunday lectionary texts.

When the *Glory to God* hymnal committee called for submissions of new hymns, I was hesitant to offer my own hymn texts, but friends finally persuaded me to do so. All hymns were submitted and reviewed anonymously. As a theological advisor to the hymnal committee, I had a voice in the selection process but no vote. I chose not to speak when the committee was reviewing hymns that I had written. It was humbling to listen in silence while people gave their honest critique, not knowing that the author was in the room! In the end, I was greatly honored when the committee selected fourteen of my hymn texts for inclusion in *Glory to God*.

I think I have written around two hundred hymns. In recent years I am often commissioned to write hymns for church anniversaries, retirements, or other events. Two years after the *Glory to God* hymnal was released, I published a collection of fifty hymn texts, titled *Breathing Spirit into Dust* (GIA, 2015). Five of my hymn texts have been published in collections by other denominations.

3. When I look at your work, I notice similarities to the work of Professor Ruth Duck, who was your advisor. Professor Duck also had a great influence on the study of worship words and the lyrics for hymns. Many Koreans know Professor Duck, and her book has been introduced to Korean readers. Can you tell us about Professor Duck's current endeavors? I would be grateful if you could tell me what influence Professor Duck has made on you as a scholar and as the head of the church's worship service.

Professor Ruth Duck has indeed had a profound and long-lasting influence on the church's worship in general, and on my personal sense of calling as a liturgical scholar and hymn writer. It was a great honor and joy to study with her in the PhD program at Garrett-Evangelical Theological Seminary. My own life and ministry have been shaped by her deep faith, her sincere love and care for people, her passion for justice and equality, and her abiding concern for the church's worship and song. Specifically, as a student of liturgy, I am grateful for Professor Duck's broad knowledge, intellectual curiosity, and wise teaching. As a hymn writer, I have been awed by her prolific creativity and commitment to the craft of hymnology. As one who seeks to guide and teach others in the theology and practice of worship, I have tried to remember and imitate her generosity of spirit, great humility, and patient mentorship.

Professor Duck retired from Garrett-Evangelical Theological Seminary in 2017 and now lives in California. Last year she published a second edition of *Worship for the Whole People of God* (Westminster John Knox, 2021).

4. Could you introduce the *Book of Common Worship* in the PC(U.S.A.) that was revised in 2018? What are the differences from the previous edition? I believe, in the case of the previous edition, it was translated into Korean, and frequently used in many Korean churches in both Korea and the United States. The new worship book seems to be quite bulky and contains a lot of content.

The 2018 edition of the *Book of Common Worship* is part of a long tradition of service books for Presbyterians in the United States. Previous editions of the *Book of Common Worship* were published in 1906, 1932, 1946, and 1993. In 1970, *The Worship Book* was published in combination with a hymnal. Considering these liturgical resources together, one can see that Presbyterians in the United States have published a new service book approximately every twenty to twenty-five years. The 2018 *Book of Common Worship* continues this tradition, carrying forward the values and principles of previous service books, as well as certain orders of worship and prayers from precursor resources.

At the same time, the 2018 *Book of Common Worship* represents the first Presbyterian service book in the twenty-first century. As such, it includes a great deal of new content for new situations in Reformed worship. Notable additions include: sections on the church's ministry (including ordination, installation, and commissioning services previously found in our *Book of Occasional Services*); the church's mission (including urgent concerns of ecology, justice and reconciliation, and interreligious relations); dedication liturgies (also previously found in the *Book of Occasional Services*), new eucharistic prayers and thanksgivings for baptism reflecting a season of sacramental renewal; and selected materials in Spanish and Korean, the two languages other than English primarily spoken in the PC(U.S.A.). Along with these major additions, the editorial team examined each section of the previous service book to determine where prayers and liturgies should be added, changed, or removed. This additional content did result in a somewhat bulkier book—1,214 pages (2018 BCW) instead of 1,002 (1993 BCW). However, smaller and more portable editions were published for pastoral ministry and daily prayer.

David Gambrell | 193

5. Could you tell us how long you spent on the new worship book? Also, how many scholars and practitioners were involved in the project? And the project's approximate budget? It will be of great help to various denominations who want to make a worship book.

From the conception of the project in 2014 to its publication in 2018, the development of this edition of *Book of Common Worship* was an intensive four-year process. The core editorial team consisted of David Gambrell (coeditor), Office of Theology and Worship; Kimberly Bracken Long (coeditor), Columbia Theological Seminary; William McConnell, Presbyterian Association of Musicians; and David Maxwell, Presbyterian Publishing Corporation. Approximately one hundred editorial advisors (pastors, elders, musicians, scholars, and other church leaders) were also engaged in the process of revision. These advisors were sought out with special attention to the diversity of the church, emerging patterns of worship, and new contexts for ministry.

Since the project was undertaken through the efforts of existing staff in the national offices of the church (along with Kimberly Bracken Long at Columbia Seminary) the primary expenses were related to travel and lodging for meetings; these costs were shared by the Presbyterian Publishing Corporation and the budgets of other denominational agencies.

6. I also bought the PC(U.S.A.) *Book of Common Worship* and was able to see and learn many things. However, as I read it, questions arose. For example, a prayer of blessings for pets, a prayer for the case of suicide, and "promises to have children" in weddings seemed radical from the point of view of orthodox Presbyterians. Although these are realistic challenges we face living as Christians today, they must have been very controversial when people first read the book. Did you have interesting discussions or episodes related to these matters when your committee decided the contents of this book?

I am glad to say that the 2018 *Book of Common Worship* has been very well received in the Presbyterian Church (U.S.A.), with little, if any, controversy. I believe this can be attributed to the careful research and extensive consultation that went into the preparation of the revision. As an editorial team, we had a strong sense of consensus about what the PC(U.S.A.) needed in this latest edition of the denomination's service book. In fact, we have heard many appreciative comments about the examples you mention. The liturgy for the blessing of animals is welcomed in connection with increasing ecological concerns. Prayers acknowledging and grieving death by suicide have been (sadly) needed in light of ongoing mental health crises in the United States, including military personnel suffering from post-traumatic stress. Consideration for existing children in the marriage service is a relatively common situation for families in our context.

We wondered if there might be controversy around another aspect of the wedding liturgy—the decision to arrange the marriage vows in such a way that the gender of participants is not specified, rather than indicating "bride" and "groom." This change was needed in light of the movement for marriage equality in the United States, including decisions of the PC(U.S.A.) General Assembly in 2014 and the U.S. Supreme Court in 2015. However, this change has also been largely welcomed and celebrated in the denomination. In fact, for many PC(U.S.A.) members and leaders, this was one of the compelling reasons to publish a revised service book.

7. In the case of Korean Presbyterian churches, most denominations have a worship directory but not a worship book. Even the larger denominations lack the capacity to make a worship book for themselves. I don't have experience in making a worship book yet, but in order to make a worship book, I believe a team of professional worship scholars, competent theologians, experienced pastors, well-versed musicians, and linguists who can accurately and beautifully express the words is needed. Of course, this will require significant financial aid, making it difficult for Korean denominations to make a worship book. Do you think it is essential for denominations in Korea to make and use a worship book despite these circumstances? If so, could you explain why each denomination in Korea should have a book of worship and its importance or significance? Furthermore, if you could give advice to Korean denominations planning to make a worship book, what would you like to say?

I am reluctant to offer advice on the publication of a new service book for denominations in a cultural context other than my own, even for other beloved members of the Presbyterian/Reformed tradition. Therefore, I cannot answer the question of whether Korean Presbyterian denominations should have books of worship. I would not presume to understand all the theological, ecclesiological, liturgical, cultural, political, and practical considerations necessary for such an undertaking, and would defer to you and other leaders in your setting. Any insights I may offer should be regarded with healthy skepticism, knowing that they are steeped in my own contexts and biases. Having offered that disclaimer, I will attempt to respond to these other good questions.

As for the relationship between a directory for worship and a book of worship, I believe these two different kinds of documents can work effectively together. I often use the analogy of a compass and a map. Like a compass, a directory for worship orients us to primary things in the theology of Reformed worship. Like a map, a book of worship illustrates the geographies of particular services, providing well-marked paths of prayer. While Presbyterians in the United States have had books of worship since the early twentieth century, we have been careful to say they are "for voluntary use," not required. Indeed, many PC(U.S.A.) leaders prefer to plan their own Sunday services and pray extemporaneously. However, when it comes to less common events—such as ordinations, church dedications, and funerals—even these leaders tend to rely heavily on published liturgical resources such as the *Book of Common Worship*. When you are traveling in unfamiliar terrain it is helpful to have a map as well as a compass.

Given that, as you point out, most Presbyterian Korean denominations do not currently have books of worship, I believe it would be especially important to engage in an extensive process of collaboration and consultation with all of the constituencies you have named: scholars, theologians, pastors, musicians, and linguists or poets—perhaps with the addition of educators, ruling elders, council staff, and other leaders. The participation of a wide range of well-respected leaders would seem to me to be essential for the development of such a project, particularly when it would be the first service book of its kind.

If Presbyterians in Korea should discern that it would be helpful to have a book of worship, I would hope that it might be a collaborative project among multiple denominations. This was the case for several of the past editions of the *Book of Common Worship*, where mutual efforts toward a common service book anticipated a reunion among divided branches of the church. I understand that this is not always possible; indeed, when pain still lingers from recent divisions, it may be easier to collaborate with ecumenical partners than with our Presbyterian family. However, it is important to remember that the publication of a new service book may be an opportunity for renewed relationship and closer connection in the body of Christ. Even small steps, such as shared texts for familiar prayers or a common baptismal liturgy, can lay the foundation for future reconciliation.

8. **What are some important steps in making a worship book? Could you provide some details of processes, such as forming a committee, selecting a research team, and gathering opinions from the pastors of the denomination?**

The work on a new edition of the *Book of Common Worship* began in 2014 with an agreement between the PC(U.S.A.) Office of Theology and Worship and the Presbyterian Publishing Corporation, in partnership with the Presbyterian Association of Musicians. These three organizations were the same partners responsible for the 2013 hymnal project, *Glory to God*. The fact that our three entities had already established strong and positive working relationships on the hymnal project was critical to the success of the new *Book of Common Worship*.

Here is a rough outline of the process to develop the 2018 *Book of Common Worship*. In 2014 we conducted initial research, established parameters for the project, and developed some specific proposals for revision. From May of 2015 to February of 2016, we held six national consultations at PC(U.S.A.) seminaries—Columbia (in Atlanta), San Francisco, McCormick (in Chicago), Austin, Princeton, and Louisville—inviting pastors, scholars, and other church leaders to offer ideas and feedback on the project. In the midst of these in-person consultations, we also reached out through phone calls and emails to other liturgical scholars, ecumenical and international partners, mission personnel, mid-council leaders, and colleagues throughout the denomination. Where we identified the need for new liturgies or prayers, we searched other PC(U.S.A.) publications (such as *Call to Worship* and *Feasting on the Word*), turned to ecumenical and international resources, and sought new works from contemporary liturgical writers and scholars. Throughout the rest of 2016 we engaged in editorial work reflecting the guidance and contributions we had received, sharing drafts of the revision with reviewers. The manuscript was submitted in the spring of 2017, beginning the process of copyediting, design, proofreading, and publication in 2018.

9. **When selecting hymns for the *Book of Common Worship*, what criteria did you look at? Were there any notable moments in the team discussion of the project?**

With a few exceptions, such as responses in the Service for the Lord's Day and psalm refrains, there is no music provided in the 2018 *Book of Common Worship*. However, the *Book of Common Worship* does provide lists of hymn recommendations for particular services (wedding, funeral, etc.), themes (ecology, justice, etc.), and acts of worship (proclamation, sacrament, etc.). The recommended hymns all come from the previous two PC(U.S.A.) hymnals: *Glory to God* (Westminster John Knox, 2013) and *The Presbyterian Hymnal* (Westminster John Knox, 1990). Many of the suggestions are drawn from the corresponding sections of those hymn books or were listed in the indexes of those publications. Additional suggestions came from the editorial team and editorial advisors, particularly through our collaboration with the Presbyterian Association of Musicians.

10. It stood out to me that all 150 Psalms were in the *Book of Common Worship*. Actually, I expected to see the whole music score for each psalm. However, there is no sheet music in the worship book, only some explanations and psalm tones. Could you explain for Korean readers how it is used in actual worship? Most Korean Christians do not know how to sing psalms. Although there are differences among churches, please tell us about how psalms are used in the Sunday service of the PC(U.S.A.).

The editorial team believed it was important for the 2018 *Book of Common Worship* to include all 150 psalms, as the psalms are our "school of prayer" and an important emphasis of the Reformed tradition. Furthermore, given recent scholarship on the value of lament in Christian worship, we wanted to be sure the full range of the book of Psalms was represented. We were grateful to receive permission from the Evangelical Lutheran Church of America to reprint a fresh translation of all 150 psalms, with accompanying psalm prayers, developed for *Evangelical Lutheran Worship* (Augsburg, 2006). This translation of the psalms was also published in *Psalms for All Seasons* (Brazos, 2012), used by the Christian Reformed Church, the Reformed Church in America, and other Reformed congregations. We celebrate that this translation of the psalms has become, at least for several denominations, a common English version of the Psalter.

Many, but not all, of the 150 psalms are included in full musical versions in *Glory to God* (Westminster John Knox, 2013) and *The Presbyterian Hymnal* (Westminster John Knox, 1990)—in metrical, responsorial, and other formats. Multiple settings of all 150 psalms are also available through *Psalms for All Seasons*, noted above. Since these publications are already available and in widespread use, the *Book of Common Worship* did not seek to duplicate these resources. Instead, the editorial team decided to provide a version of all 150 psalms that could be used in a variety of ways: chanted, spoken responsively (with alternating unbolded and bold print), or read in personal prayer.

While chanting the psalms is not a common practice in contemporary Presbyterian worship, this way of singing is still sometimes taught in seminary settings, presented by cantors in Sunday worship, or used in liturgies of daily prayer. For those unfamiliar with the practice, it involves singing lines of text in the rhythm of speech, with occasional musical elaborations at the beginnings and ends of phrases; these musical variations are signaled with "pointed" texts: small marks indicating where the melody changes. The value of this practice is that it can be used to turn any text into music without changing or adapting the words.

Presbyterian congregations in the United States use the psalms in a great variety of ways in worship. Psalms are often used as opening sentences or calls to worship. Metrical paraphrases of the psalms, such as "My Shepherd Will Supply My Need" (Psalm 23), "Our God, Our Help in Ages Past" (Psalm 90), and "Joy to the World" (Psalm 98), are frequently sung as hymns. Psalms may be sung or prayed in response to the reading of the Hebrew Scriptures, as indicated by the Revised Common Lectionary. Familiar phrases from psalms often find their way into prayers, whether written out or prayed extemporaneously. And Presbyterians sometimes use psalms as preaching texts.

11. In the sacrament section at the beginning of the *Book of Common Worship*, there is an illustration that shows the gestures and actions of the presider of the Lord's Supper. Many pastors have questions about the correct postures and gestures while executing the sacrament, but there seems to be no clear answer to this, except for the *The Lord Be with You: A Visual Handbook for Presiding in Christian Worship* by Don Saliers and Charles Hackett. What are the thoughts and opinions of the PC(U.S.A.) pastors about the matter of gesture or action or the work of proper presiding? Do you have any books on the topic to recommend?

One of the strong convictions of the editorial team was that the 2018 *Book of Common Worship* might encourage fully embodied practices of worship, involving the whole person in prayer. We sought to accomplish this in a variety of ways: through theological and pastoral commentary preceding the orders of worship, through expanded rubrics describing liturgical action, and through illustrations of common postures and gestures in Christian worship, as you have noted. Our intent was not to depict these gestures as required actions, but to offer them as suggestions for leading prayer in a more physical and active way, consistent with historical liturgical use and contemporary ecumenical practice. We believe that such practices—when used with the word and in the Spirit—are a faithful and effective way of proclaiming the good news and engaging the whole body of Christ in worship. As for books on the subject, I would highly recommend *The Worshiping Body: The Art of Leading Worship* (Westminster John Knox, 2009) by my colleague and coeditor Kimberly Bracken Long.

12. Many denominations in the United States have their own worship books. They include the United Methodist Church, the Evangelical Lutheran Church in America (ELCA), and the Christian Reformed Church. What strengths are there in the *Book of Common Worship* of the Presbyterian Church of the United States of America compared to the denominations previously mentioned?

In the last decades of the twentieth century there was a great flourishing in the publication of worship books among Protestant denominations in the United States, including The *Lutheran Book of Worship* (1978), the Episcopal *Book of Common Prayer* (1979), the United Church of Christ *Book of Worship* (1986), the United Methodist *Book of Worship* (1992), and the Presbyterian *Book of Common Worship* (1993). The editors of these liturgies were in close conversation with one another through organizations such as the Consultation on Common Texts and the North American Academy of Liturgy. They sought to learn from one another, to challenge one another, to receive the gifts of each tradition, and to work toward the reconciliation of Christ's church for the sake of a common witness in the world. This resulted in a remarkable ecumenical convergence in liturgical life—through the use of a common lectionary, common patterns for worship, common texts for prayers and creeds, and common celebrations through the Christian year. In many ways, we are still harvesting and feasting on the fruits of those efforts.

In the first decades of the twenty-first century, new seeds are taking root. We are witnessing the fragmentation and polarization of social groups into multiple microcosms; for this reason, the 2018 *Book of Common Worship* speaks in a range of styles and voices. We are wrestling with the legacies of imperialism and racism; for this reason, the 2018 *Book of Common Worship* seeks to account for diverse experiences and includes prayers and liturgies in three languages. We are confronted with the global realities of poverty, violence, and climate change; for this reason, the 2018

Book of Common Worship provides new resources for justice, peacemaking, and care of creation. Nevertheless, we know the world keeps turning, old atrocities are being unearthed, and new worship resources are already overdue. We trust that future generations will correct and improve on our work.

13. The Presbyterian Church (U.S.A.) seems to have a lot of interest in worship. Every quarter, a magazine called *Call to Worship* is published by the denomination, and it contains many ideas about worship and guides for worship planning. Could you introduce the magazine and tell us about how this magazine actually affects the pastors and worship planners of the denomination?

Call to Worship: Liturgy, Music, Preaching, and the Arts is a quarterly journal of the PC(U.S.A.) Office of Theology and Worship, published in partnership with the Presbyterian Association of Musicians. The current editor of the journal is the Rev. Sally Ann McKinsey, who follows the second term of the Rev. Dr. Kimberly Bracken Long as editor. (I served briefly as editor between Dr. Long's first and second terms.) Building on Dr. Long's outstanding work in developing the scholarly voice and prophetic vision of the journal, Rev. McKinsey brings great pastoral wisdom and artistic imagination to her role as editor.

Call to Worship provides theological insight and practical guidance for pastors, musicians, artists, and other church leaders. The annual Lectionary Companion offers liturgical texts and musical suggestions (hymns, psalms, anthems, and instrumental music) for every Sunday and festival in the Christian year. Three thematic issues each year engage current topics and emerging concerns in liturgical theology and practice. Recent thematic issues include: Invitation to Christ, Poverty and Liturgy, Worship in the Time of Covid, Dismantling Racism in Worship, New Topics in Music, Reconciliation, Baptism, Eucharist, and Ministry.

14. Lastly, I wonder if there were any debates or guidelines on worship in the Presbyterian Church (U.S.A.) during the past two years of the COVID-19 crisis. For example, online worship, online communion, online baptism, etc. In the past two years, was there any change in church attendance or any decline in church membership?

As with other denominations, the past few years have been a time of great challenge and change for the Presbyterian Church (U.S.A.). Especially in the first few months of the pandemic, the Office of Theology and Worship was constantly at work in partnership with the Office of the General Assembly, offering guidance for online worship, sacramental practices, and pastoral services such as ordinations, weddings, and funerals.

As we are still in the midst of this time of transition, it is hard to judge the extent of the changes. In-person church attendance has certainly declined, but some churches have reported growth in online participation in worship. Traditional measures of new membership (professions and reaffirmations of faith) took a dramatic dip during the pandemic, but the suspension of in-person worship was surely a contributing factor, and new (or nontraditional) worshiping communities are still growing steadily. It remains to be seen what God is doing in these difficult times, but we trust that the Lord is with us.

Selected Bibliography

Gambrell, David. *Breathing Spirit into Dust: Fifty Hymn Texts.* Chicago: GIA, 2015.

Gambrell, David. *Connections Worship Companion, Year A: Advent Through Pentecost.* Louisville, KY: Westminster John Knox, 2022.

Gambrell, David. *Connections Worship Companion, Year C: Season After Pentecost.* Louisville, KY: Westminster John Knox, 2023.

Gambrell, David. *Presbyterian Worship: Questions and Answers.* Louisville, KY: Westminster John Knox, 2019.

Gambrell, David, and Kimberly Bracken Long. *Book of Common Worship.* Louisville, KY: Westminster John Knox, 2018.

CONCLUSION
ENRICHING WORSHIP
Illuminating the Perspective of Worship through its Deeper Understanding

Twenty years ago, I went to the United States from Korea to study the topic of worship. At that time, I believed that the knowledge I had about worship and the worship I had experienced were perfectly aligned with a biblical understanding of worship.

Looking back now on my days as a young theology student, I not only lacked interest in how other denominations worshiped but also held a narrow and combative attitude toward theological perspectives that were different from mine and toward other worship traditions. My mindset was that only the worship tradition I belonged to was scriptural and correct. As I was exposed to worship from other traditions, I became critical and judgmental of approaches to worship that were unfamiliar to me. Consequently, even though I participated in worship, I could not experience the grace of worship or appreciate the rich heritage and breadth of Christian tradition. In hindsight, I better appreciate the ways in which my arrogance prevented me from fully engaging in worship.

The object of our worship is God, yet I often fell into the folly of imagining God's preferences based on my theological standards. I thought, "God will dislike this;" "God won't accept that;" "This worship style is too casual;" or "This is unscriptural." With such thoughts dominating my mind, I could not receive God's grace in worship.

My attitude toward worship traditions different from my own shifted when I met Professor John Witvliet on the campus of Calvin Theological Seminary. It was enlightening to witness members of the Dutch Reformed Church in a worship setting. I was stunned that a church, highly venerated by the pastors of my denomination, could not only remain within the worship heritage of the sixteenth century Reformers but could also integrate elements of worship drawing on the strengths of worship traditions different from their own. They were aiming to create worship accessible to people living in the present day. In particular, the Worship Symposium organized by the Calvin Institute of Christian Worship opened my eyes to the richness of worship. The jazz vespers I first experienced at the Worship Symposium in January 2008 were particularly striking. As someone familiar with the atmosphere of evening prayer services in more traditional denominations like the Anglican Church, being able to sing praises, pray, and worship together in a jazz style shattered the framework of my previous thinking.

Furthermore, the lectures of Professor Byron Anderson at Garrett-Evangelical Theological Seminary opened my eyes to the formative power of liturgy and ritual, which I had previously only associated with Roman Catholicism due to my limited understanding. Through his teachings, I gained insight into how our worship shapes the faith and identity of individuals and communities, how liturgy and ritual can possess formative power in faith formation, and how the study of liturgy intersects with other disciplines. Above all, I learned that worship should not be confined to religious acts within the church but should be connected to worship in life. I also discovered the close relationship between worship and Christian ethics, realizing that this is a significant challenge facing the church in the twenty-first century.

As a result of their teachings and guidance, I was able to identify scholars who currently have the greatest influence on the theology and practice of worship within several major denominations in North America. Through participation in the North American Academy of Liturgy and the World Congress of the International Association of Liturgy, I had the privilege of meeting and interacting directly with these scholars, akin to meeting stars in the field of liturgical studies whom I had only encountered through books until then, and even had the opportunity to conduct interviews with them.

As I prepared for the interviews, I first examined the biographies and lists of publications of the interviewees. Simply reviewing where they studied and the process they went through to become worship scholars provided me with valuable insights. Among their lists of publications, I found books that I had already read during my master's and doctoral studies in worship, as well as recently published works that were new to me. It was particularly impressive to see some of the interviewees, despite their advanced age, continuously engaging in research and publishing books and articles. With deep respect and gratitude, I found myself frequently praying for their health and well-being.

During my time at Garrett-Evangelical Theological Seminary, Frank Senn taught me worship history. I met Paul Westermeyer at the North American Academy of Liturgy, and I had the opportunity to interact with Will Willimon when I visited Duke University Divinity School as a visiting scholar in 2023. I also engaged with Gordon Lathrop and Don Saliers in the hermeneutics seminar group of the North American Academy of Liturgy. All of them are currently in their eighties. However, they are still deeply involved in research and writing at the highest level of liturgical studies. Most importantly, their scholarly depth, cultivated over a lifetime of studying worship, along with their comprehensive liturgical understanding spanning across denominations, provided optimal conditions for me to find answers to my questions about worship.

John Witvliet, the Director of the Calvin Institute of Christian Worship, Byron Anderson, who served as President of the Societas Liturgica, and Lester Ruth, known for his outstanding contributions to contemporary worship research at Duke University, represent the next generation of these scholarly groups. They are already at the forefront of academia as active professors of liturgical studies. Their eloquent and appropriate responses to questions about theology of worship, liturgical hermeneutics, and contemporary worship demonstrate their excellence in the field.

Interviews with scholars representing various denominations were also highly beneficial. Conversations with Ruth Meyers, representing the Episcopal Church in the United States, Stefanos Alexopoulos, an emerging worship scholar from the Eastern Orthodox tradition, and Melanie Ross, a prominent researcher in evangelical worship, provided opportunities to expand the breadth of understanding of denominational theology and mutual understanding through comparison.

Discussions with David Hogue on the importance of ritual studies for liturgical studies and conversations with David Gambrell on why worship books are important not only provided opportunities to correct misconceptions about the liturgy and ritual that Protestant believers may have but also demonstrated that worship books can be tools to enrich worship rather than exclusive possessions of liturgical denominations.

The essence of my learning through conversations with these great liturgical theologians can be summarized in these eight points.

(1) It is essential to understand liturgical cosmology and sacramentality before discussing worship, liturgy, and sacraments. My conversation with Stefanos Alexopoulos highlighted the importance of this awareness. As seen in Alexander Schmemann's book, *For the Life of the World*, God, who created the entire universe, can sacramentally use anything if He so desires. This perspective is not exclusive to the Orthodox Church. John Calvin also made mention of a sacramental universe.* Recognizing God's good creation and understanding our priestly role and mission before God and creation—not from the perspective of spirit versus flesh, world versus church, or sacred versus profane, but acknowledging God's goodness—changes how we view our bodies and the world. It prompts us to consider the connection between worship and ethics and shifts the focus from narrow debates about sacraments to considering the sacramentality of the entire universe. Such an Eastern theological perspective transcends the limitations of Western epistemology, which often focuses solely on the intellect, leading to a shift toward a more contemplative approach that seeks to apprehend the mystery of God and pursue God Himself.

The concept of sacramentality like this can shed light on the functions and roles of liturgy and ritual. For example, in Protestantism, marriage is not considered a sacrament. As a result, among young believers in Korea, there's a growing trend of disliking church weddings or not having Christian-style weddings. Rather than emphasizing the concept of covenant before God and the congregation, there's more emphasis on the social contract dimension and the celebration of the marriage partners. Therefore, there's little significant difference between the marriages of nonbelievers and believers, and likewise, issues like divorce or family problems are not significantly different between nonbelieving and believing

---

* *Institutes*, Book IV, xiv, 18.

households. However, if within Protestantism marriage is not seen as a sacrament but still carries sacramental significance, it may lead the congregation to approach it differently.

Another example is that while Protestant churches oppose the sacrament of confession, if one considers the pastoral function and effect that can be gained through confessing inner sins that trouble oneself, they may realize the sacramentality within that practice. In other words, reconsidering the liturgical cosmology and perception of sacramentality provides momentum for viewing the church's worship and ceremonies in a new light. This shift in perception of sacramentality became possible through the works of Alexander Schmemann. This greatly influenced several liturgical theologians who dominated the twentieth century through conversations with Orthodox liturgical theologians.

(2) Second, Protestant believers need to reassess their understanding of liturgy and rituals. Through conversations with William Willimon, it was made clear that liturgy and rituals are not merely the heritage of the Roman Catholic Church but are the core of worship found in all worship traditions. Furthermore, their practices hold formative power, indicating that not only public worship but also various ceremonies serve a pastoral role. David Hogue's research, above all, demonstrates that the study of Christian rituals can be performed via anthropology and understood from a neuroscience perspective. In other words, rituals are not merely repetitions of meaningless actions but are a means of human communication. Through them, individuals express their inner selves, receive external information, and through practice, can train the inner selves of believers. It is essential to remember that in the process of engaging in liturgy and rituals, imitation and learning occur, constantly conveying messages to the inner selves of believers through repetition.

At the same time, there is a need to pay attention to the scholarly value of evangelical worship even within liturgical churches. Melanie Ross's research argues that evangelical worship and liturgical worship have a mutually illuminating relationship, sharpening each other like iron sharpens iron.

Her assertion aligns with the arguments of James White, Todd Johnson, Lester Ruth, and John Witvliet.

In fact, I had a preconceived notion that liturgical worship feels more solemn and static, while evangelical worship is more enthusiastic and dynamic but perhaps superficial. However, Ross presents a deeper meaning beyond such schematic and binary relationships. She suggests that these two should be seen as correcting and encouraging each other, much like the relationship between the Synoptic Gospels and the Gospel of John.

Ross demonstrates that worship incorporating prayer books can also be warm and passionate. Furthermore, she emphasizes that evangelical churches can remind liturgical churches that the role of the church extends beyond pastoral care, tradition, and sacraments to also facilitating personal encounters with Jesus Christ, allowing people to experience Him personally and follow Him. In essence, Melanie Ross argues that it is important for churches on this earth to maintain a balance within the diverse spectrum of worship.

(3) It is not an exaggeration to say that in contemporary times, the significance of music is second only to preaching and sacraments within the church. Paul Westermeyer, in his book, *Te Deum*, reminds us of the crucial role music has played in shaping faith throughout the history of the church. When considering the formative power of music, we must examine what constitutes good music and what is suitable for worship. As Don Saliers argues, "Worship music should express reverence towards God" and "worldly culture should be rejected, and a desire for holiness should be infused into music." Above all, it is essential to critically examine the lyrics of hymns from a theological perspective. Since lyrics accompanied by melody possess formative capabilities, they must embody biblical depth and existential significance for the congregation, as well as a depth capable of containing God's word and Christian theology.

As Westermeyer points out, congregational music should be congregational. While there has been an increase in the church's interest and investment in music in recent years, we must not make the mistake of elevating music to the same level as preaching and sacraments. Additionally, as Lester Ruth observes, there is a tendency in contemporary worship for popular songs to come from a small number of lyricists or composers, often associated with specific large churches: it's important to note the centralization and industrialization of songwriting in contemporary worship.

(4) During the COVID-19 pandemic, the question of online communion became a hot topic, and nearly all interviewees expressed opposition to it. While Ed Foley did not explicitly endorse online communion, his reflections on digital engagement suggest a more open stance toward the possibilities of online participation in worship. Summarizing their arguments, while online communion was seen as an unavoidable alternative during emergencies like the pandemic, it should not become a standard practice in normal circumstances. This is because communion is a communal act within the public context of worship, embodying physicality and corporeality, whereas online communion, within the technological context of our times, inevitably leads to fragmented individualism. Particularly, as Byron Anderson states, we must heed the claim that online communion fails to realize the sacred fellowship of the church and undermines the incarnational nature of Christian faith. Considering the communal nature of the church and its unity, emphasis should be placed on the immediacy of the sacrament. Additionally, as Don Saliers points out, it's essential to remember that relying solely on online worship may lead to the loss of sacramentality.

I recall a scene from the movie, *Kingsman*, where they use wearable technology to conduct video conferences. Through advanced technology, the movie depicts characters drinking together and conducting meetings as if they were physically present. In light of this portrayal, I pondered the concept of participation. Should the absence of the body be unequivocally viewed as absence? Aren't there various levels and modes of participation? Even if people are in the same physical space, true interaction may not occur if there is no genuine interest. Conversely, even if people are spatially distant, if there is heartfelt communication, could it be seen as a form of communion or participation? In this regard, I wonder if the research of liturgical theologians might still be necessary in the future amidst technological advancements. (Additional note: While Ed Foley did not explicitly advocate for online communion, his insights on digital worship raise important questions about how Catholic tradition—especially with its medieval precedents—might allow believers to experience communion meaningfully even in physically distanced contexts.)

(5) The fifth point is around how churches define "contemporary worship." I have come to realize that there is no worship tradition without liturgy—even the most nonliturgical traditions like Quaker worship have a form. I have also come to understand that informality is also a form of its own. Therefore, I believe it is essential to reassess our understanding of liturgy, specifically understanding the meaning of each element of worship and how their arrangement and structure can play a role. In particular, with the argument of Gordon Lathrop that regards the word and the sacrament as central elements of worship and suggests that the elements of worship are juxtaposed to form and convey meaning, there is a need for deeper research into liturgical worship centered around the word and the sacrament.

This does not imply that contemporary worship styles or blended worship are inherently wrong or unnecessary. Research by Professor Lester Ruth enhances our understanding of the debate between traditional and contemporary worship. In fact, there is a problem with our perception of the terms "traditional worship" and "contemporary worship." Contemporary worship does not necessarily refer to the present time in 2024, but rather to movements that emerged alongside the praise and worship movement beginning in the late 1970s and gaining momentum in the 1980s through the Vineyard Movement and the megachurch movement in the Western United States. On the other hand, what we now label as traditional worship is closely associated with worship traditions of the eighteenth and nineteenth centuries in the Western world. Therefore, arguments criticizing contemporary worship from a perspective that emphasizes traditional worship, and vice versa, may not accurately reflect the current situation in 2024. Instead, they often stem from individuals' preferences and theological convictions based on past traditions.

Above all, as Lester Ruth points out, the fact that worship in the early church was more vibrant, embodied, and alive, rather than what we now perceive as traditional worship, challenges the binary view of tradition and modernity. This insight opens up possibilities for new worship theology and practice, transcending dichotomous perspectives and paving the way for a more vibrant worship experience.

All the interviewees, representing various denominations, expressed concern about the rapid decline of Christianity and the diminishing number of future generations to inherit our faith. Moreover, amidst the dwindling numbers of prospective pastors to lead and shepherd worship, there seems to be deep contemplation on how to navigate through this crisis. It appears there is no single secret to win over young people; however, it is crucial for the church to regain trust through authentic interest and compassion for the concerns and ideas of the next generations. As Ed Foley emphasizes, listen to the voices of the younger generation and strive to meet their needs. Foley utilizes a Christian humanistic approach, and scientific insights in preaching could be one way forward. The results of neuroscientific research funded by the Lilly Foundation—particularly as it relates to how worship and preaching engage the human brain—are eagerly anticipated, as they may offer new insights into how liturgical practices can be more effective in forming faith and engaging the next generation.

(6) We need to enhance our understanding of the close relationship and complementarity between worship and systematic theology and other disciplines. This is because liturgical study is a kind of comprehensive art: doctrine emerged from the context of worship. However, that doctrine also influences worship. While doctrine plays a role in safeguarding the theology of worship, there is a need to recognize that it can sometimes suppress worship.

In particular, Byron Anderson's research demonstrates the necessity for a philosophical and hermeneutical approach in liturgical studies. Liturgical studies deal not only with texts but with events. By studying how the context in which texts are performed shapes our perspectives and interpretations, we may gain a different insight and depth into the way we perceive the site.

At the same time, we must not limit ourselves to liturgy research alone. Mainly, research by liturgical theologians has primarily focused on historical and sociological studies. However, Gordon Lathrop argues that thoughtful and critical biblical studies can enhance understanding of congregations in worship and deepen participation levels.

While some extremely conservative denominations advocate that they worship solely based on what is stated in the Bible, it is important to remember that worship has evolved within the context of history and culture. Therefore, we need to increase our understanding of liturgy. Additionally, churches classified as liturgical denominations should also enhance their awareness of biblical metaphors and intertextuality in the liturgy.

There is a need for deeper research and discussion on the relationship between church worship and mission. Marva Dawn, in her book, *A Royal Waste of Time*, criticizes consumer-driven worship and argues that worship should not be seen as a tool for evangelism. This criticism is valid in pointing out that modern megachurch worship or churches focusing solely on evangelism may fail to provide worship that nurtures existing believers and sometimes dilutes the essence of worship.

(7) Through my conversation with Ruth Meyers, I have reconsidered the close relationship between worship and mission. It is evident that authentic worship, faithful to its essence, can not only mature existing believers but also be sufficiently missional. In the space of worship, the Triune God is present. This presence is not contingent upon our requests or efforts but on God's promise. The place where God is present is sacred and a space of grace. Through each element of worship conducted in this space, God acts, and these elements convey messages to the participants. Through worship centered around the word and sacraments, participants experience reconciliation with

God and turn their gaze toward the world. As worship transitions into engagement in the world as Christians, worship becomes missional.

The simultaneous and mutually complementary tension between worship and mission must always be maintained. Ruth Meyers puts it as follows: "When we receive the power of the Holy Spirit in worship and move forward in active Christian participation in the world, worship becomes missional. However, at the same time, we need to exercise discernment to ensure that worship is directing our attention to God and deepening our relationship with Him." Her mention brings to mind the Möbius strip or spinning top model. Worship and mission cannot be separated, and good worship encourages us to be missional while also reminding us to continually verify whether our activities in the world are centered around our relationship with God. Worship and mission flow in and out from one another.

(8) Don Saliers argues that the law of prayer should move beyond the law of faith to the law of action. Worship studies and Christian ethics are closely related. Byron Anderson asserts, through the argument of Louis-Marie Chauvet, that right confession should lead to right living. Liturgy and scripture should be validated by ethics. Not only in the United States but also globally, the inconsistency between the words and actions of churches and church leaders has led to a loss of trust in the church. This is true in Korea as well. It becomes a cause for the departure of younger generations and is connected to issues of evangelism and the survival of the church. It even contributes to the decline in the number of people aspiring to become pastors. The book, *Liturgy and the Moral Self*, published by prominent worship scholars in the United States twenty years ago provides valuable information on this matter.

In conclusion, my conversations with these liturgical theologians produce hope for the Spirit-led worship practices of the future. Historically, diverse worship traditions have existed, and while there are differences in worship practices among denominations, it has become evident that the commonalities are greater than the differences. While there may be variations in rituals, forms of worship, and emphases, the central focus on the word and the Eucharist, the understanding of God's coming to us and our approaching God, leading to encounters, communion, and ongoing dialogue, is a common denominator shared by all traditions. Recognizing this provides the possibility of lowering barriers between denominations and facilitating dialogue among them.

There is a common interest in movements such as the worship renewal of the 1960s, the rise of praise and worship movements, the emergence of contemporary worship, the revival of interest in ancient church worship, and the integration of ancient practices with modern ones. This interest transcends denominational boundaries and is characterized by a shift away from denominational distinctions towards a consideration of the history of individual churches, their current circumstances, and the preferences of pastors and congregants in shaping worship. In this context, some churches may offer diverse styles of worship to accommodate generational gaps among congregants, while others may experience division over worship preferences, leading to efforts to integrate generations through unified worship services.

Amid the COVID-19 pandemic, many churches and congregants have experienced online worship services and communion. Through this, congregants who have experienced various worship services from numerous churches besides their own have become aware of better music offerings, found churches that align with their theological beliefs and preferences, and have begun making demands of their pastors. Ultimately, it can be seen that a consumer-centric mindset is increasingly prevalent.

While some conservative denominations seek to enforce uniform worship standards at the denominational level in an attempt to regulate worship practices, such an approach is considered outdated and lacking in appreciation for the diversity within worship theology. The response Martin Luther famously gave when friends approached him about the differences in worship among religious Reformers and demanded a unified worship is noteworthy in this regard. Luther stated, "Please do not turn these into rigid laws that bind people's consciences. Instead, let them be practiced and utilized within the freedom of Christians, in a practical and beneficial manner."*

The current state of worship in 2024 cannot be summed up in one word. There are churches entrenched in what Thomas Long called the "worship wars" twenty years ago, and there are churches caught in confusion over

---

* Martin Luther, "The German Mass and Order of Service," in *Luther's Works*, vol. 53 (Minneapolis: Fortress, 1965), 61.

doing "what is right in their own eyes," as often depicted in the book of Judges (Judges 21:25). However, the phrase that characterizes this era might be "religious decline." Churches are dwindling in what was once called the "age of Christendom"—a time when Christianity held a dominant cultural, political, and social influence in the Western world—but now face a crisis where the next generation of Christian worshipers might cease to exist. In such dark times, what is truly needed is to receive God's grace through worship and confidence in the Spirit to create a new thing even should the old thing pass away.

If the saints gathered in one place to offer worship could feel the presence of the Triune God, if God became the infinite center of worship, and if worship became a place where "there is no place for the world and me, only the Lord who redeemed me," if worship could be an experience where my heart ascends to heaven while praising and praying, shouting out the *Sursum corda*, if communion could signify reconciliation with God and with neighbors, and if worship could prompt thoughts of healing and structural change in the world . . . such worship would transcend theological debates and styles, becoming a precious moment where heavenly worship is experienced right here, right now.

My prayer is that the readers of this book join me in hope for the restoration of such worship in their respective churches. Let us strive not to lose the joy of worship amid theological debates. Instead of being evaluators of worship, let us all become true worshipers, just as depicted in the book of Revelation, joyfully offering worship and praise around the throne of God. Let us earnestly hope to be included in that holy multitude. Amen.

www.ingramcontent.com/pod-product-compliance
Lightning Source LLC
Chambersburg PA
CBHW031604100126
38018CB00001B/3